The Pentecostal Hypothesis

The Pentecostal Hypothesis

Christ Talks, They Decide

NIMI WARIBOKO

CASCADE *Books* · Eugene, Oregon

THE PENTECOSTAL HYPOTHESIS
Christ Talks, They Decide

Copyright © 2020 Nimi Wariboko. All rights reserved. Except for brief quotations in critical publications or reviews, no part of this book may be reproduced in any manner without prior written permission from the publisher. Write: Permissions, Wipf and Stock Publishers, 199 W. 8th Ave., Suite 3, Eugene, OR 97401.

Cascade Books
An Imprint of Wipf and Stock Publishers
199 W. 8th Ave., Suite 3
Eugene, OR 97401

www.wipfandstock.com

PAPERBACK ISBN: 978-1-7252-5451-0
HARDCOVER ISBN: 978-1-7252-5452-7
EBOOK ISBN: 978-1-7252-5453-4

Cataloguing-in-Publication data:

Names: Wariboko, Nimi, author.

Title: The pentecostal hypothesis : Christ talks, they decide / Nimi Wariboko.

Description: Eugene, OR : Cascade Books, 2020 | Includes bibliographical references and index.

Identifiers: ISBN 978-1-7252-5451-0 (paperback) | ISBN 978-1-7252-5452-7 (hardcover) | ISBN 978-1-7252-5453-4 (ebook)

Subjects: LCSH: Pentecostalism. | Philosophical theology.

Classification: BR1644 .W37 2020 (paperback) | BR1644 .W37 (ebook)

Manufactured in the U.S.A.   10/08/20

Scripture taken from the New King James Version®. Copyright © 1982 by Thomas Nelson. Used by permission. All rights reserved.

New Revised Standard Version Bible, copyright © 1989 the Division of Christian Education of the National Council of the Churches of Christ in the United States of America. Used by permission. All rights reserved.

Dedicated to
Elsie Nene Obed

Contents

Preface | ix
Acknowledgments | xxi

Introduction: Logics of Pentecostal Worlds | 1

Interlude: Continental Thought and Pentecostal Theology | 25

1. Who Christ Is:
   Sermon on Encountering Christ as an *Event* of Knowledge | 46

2. Exegeting the Sermon:
   Exploring the Depths of Pentecostal Thinking | 63

3. This Is Not a Christology:
   Writing Epistemology as the Christological Turn | 88

4. Sense and Spirit:
   The Dialogical Imagination in Pentecostal Thought | 115

Conclusion: Unconcluding Provocations | 155

Bibliography | 163
Index | 171

Preface

THE PENTECOSTAL HYPOTHESIS IS the capacity to resist conventional wisdom in personal decision-making. The book is about how Pentecostals use the paradigm of the Spirit in the form of the formula: "It does not make sense, but it makes spirit" in their decision-making processes.¹ This paradigm is in/formed by an alternate way of knowing that is keyed to a particular *theorization* (that is, a way of seeing, thinking about, and experiencing) of Jesus Christ as constitutive of and normative for the good decisions relevant to human flourishing. The book also offers a critical-philosophical analysis of the social-ethical implications of this hypothesis intended for private decisions and social actions. It provides an explanation of the formula that allows Pentecostals to understand their own behaviors not only in terms of their common-sense categories or social meanings connected with the social practices of the hypothesis, but also in terms of continental thought or a system of relevances of philosophical theologians.

This book explains what this hypothesis entails for understanding Pentecostal epistemology, how it challenges the modernist imagination, where it leads to profound theological and philosophical insights (contradictions), and why it is politically and ethically significant to study it. Pentecostal epistemology is a mode of knowing that creates and sustains a space, a horizon for human flourishing. The epistemological is also where the sensation of being truly committed to Jesus Christ, as Pentecostals understand it, is at stake. Pentecostal epistemology is ultimately about living well, Pentecostals living well in the *common*. The epistemological, like the political, is "the site where being in common is at stake," and "having access to what is *proper* to

---

1. This formula is ambiguous, that is, it is both constructive and destructive in its operation as an epistemological guide to everyday life. In this book, I am largely focused on its constructive effect on Pentecostal spirituality, decision-making, and social ethics. In a later work, which I will title *The Pentecostal Incredible*, I will more closely examine its deformative effect on Pentecostal Christians' ways of thinking, explaining, and talking about the world, common life, and human flourishing.

existence, and therefore, of course, to the proper of *one's own* existence."[2] There is the epistemological so long as there is the political, being-together. The epistemological happens because the political happens. The political is where the epistemological, the truth breaks out. The happening of the epistemological, that is, the uncovering of the phenomenological veil over reality, the deliberate movement from sense data to *spiritual data*, standing against conventional wisdom, is the condition under which Pentecostals believe they can really ask what is at stake in being-together and in their own human flourishing in the *common*. The understanding of the political and human flourishing always already belongs to the space, the horizon opened by the epistemological. This unconventional epistemology has found its way into some segments of mainstream politics in many countries.[3]

Conservative Pentecostal Christians have recently generated extensive political and media attention as leading pastors in their circles play prominent roles in presidential campaigns and inaugurations in the United States. Their critics have questioned—or even maligned—their moral-political rationality with its accompanying theological model of the state. But both critics and scholars have left unexplored their pattern of thinking and the justification behind their reasoning. Understanding Pentecostals' epistemology is important for deciphering their pattern of thought and the moral-political rationality it contours and injects into the public square. Such an effort to be germane and fair must begin by understanding conservative Pentecostals on their own terms. "On their own terms" here means offering a thick description of what Pentecostals take themselves to be saying, doing, and purposing in their epistemic practices when they engage in spiritual examination or decision-making. Put differently, it is to enter the inner world, logic, and truth of the Pentecostal particular mode of thought and unconceal it without disparaging it at first impression. By the phrase "on their own terms" I also mean offering an adequate account (keyed to their own way of seeing the world in awe and mystery) of the Pentecostal sense of imagining and feeling that is enacted in the "ability to imagine non-existent possibilities, to see one thing as another, and one thing in another, to endow a perceived form with a complex life."[4] This book is an attempt to understand the epistemology of Pentecostals on their own terms.

This book frames the basic problem of Pentecostal thinking or everyday decision-making as a twin demand for justification—the justification

---

2. Nancy, *Inoperative Community*, x, xxxvii. Italics in the original.
3. See, for instance, Obadare, *Pentecostal Republic*.
4. Nussbaum, *Poetic Justice*, 4.

of "revelational" reason and the justification of religious discourse in the Pentecostal public. The key insight from the analysis of this problem is that revelational reason is not self-sufficient or self-referential, but always points beyond itself or redirects spiritual understanding back to the empirical use of the senses. Centering on a radical yet faithfully Pentecostal reading of the tension between immanentist sense and transcendent spirit, and drawing on the fluid intersectionality of disciplines, this writer argues that Pentecostal epistemology must be located within Christology. In other words, the epistemological disposition of Pentecostals shown in this book is responsive to the promptings of Christology. Before now, scholars have not explored (or have left uncritically undeveloped) the depth and brilliance of the convergence of epistemology and Christology in Pentecostal practices. This book's focus on epistemology surely runs toward a new way forward for Christology, but *this is not a Christology* (*ceci n'est pas une christologie*). On the contrary, I provide a significant, philosophically informed alternative to perpetuating the trend toward anti-modernity, dogmatism, and anti-reason in many recent studies on Pentecostal epistemology, without downplaying the hazards of religious obscurantism. In the book's core, critical theory, dialogism, and theology converge around problems of the void (gap) between sense and spirit, and the notion of *split Christ* that sutures the gap. I intend to approach this with an originality, depth, and clarity that students of religious studies, social ethics, and theology, at all levels of training in philosophy of religion, will find illuminating.

If, indeed, these students find something worthy and respectable in the thinking of ordinary Pentecostals, then this book will have accomplished one of its goals. Furthermore, another purpose is to help arrest the growing trends of knee-jerk shaming and aggressive humiliation of ordinary Pentecostals and their ideas by both liberal and conservative scholars. In America, everyday Pentecostal theology has generally been marginalized or summarily rejected as incoherent, unintelligible, foolish, or even poisonous. This reasoning is pervasive and persistent.

Being Pentecostal in America means that your very rationality is a problem. You cannot escape the gaze, the stereotype, the awareness that others view you as an epistemological throwback to a bygone world. Your worldview is a problem that must be observed and caricatured, analyzed and degraded, solved and dissolved in the acid of modernity. Between you and the other Christians or "scientific America," there is always a question hanging over your head: How does it feel to be primal, primitive, and a problem in twenty-first-century modernity?

In the fall of 2003, I went for a pre-application visit to Princeton Theological Seminary as I investigated schools for doctoral programs in theology.

A female professor told me, "You went to Oral Roberts University for your MDiv—you must be a fundamentalist."

I politely asked, "What does it mean to be a fundamentalist?"

"Fundamentalists are like Osama bin Laden; they are terrorists," she replied.

I was highly offended, but in control of my emotions; after all, I was a tall and big black male. I replied, "I am not a fundamentalist."

Her next question was this: "In your opinion, how old is the earth?"

"At Oral Roberts I was taught the historical-critical method of biblical interpretation," I replied. The meeting did not go any further but quickly ended. I had spent more time waiting for her than having a discussion with her. She was over an hour late to our appointment.

How does it feel to be a problem?, W. E. B. Du Bois might have asked me and other Pentecostals. How does it feel that your (presumed) epistemology is a contagion to which the good students of an Ivy League institution should not be *forcibly* exposed? What was it about my Columbia University MBA background and Wall Street experience as an investment banker and management consultant that did not speak to this scholar about my fitness to engage in critical intellectual discourse? Why is it that my first-class (summa cum laude) degree in economics did not inoculate me against this powerful woman's prejudice about my charismatically inflected stupidity? How does it feel to be told by a male, world-renowned senior professor—on the day you defend your dissertation in record time and earn summa cum laude honors—that "we nearly did not admit you because you were a Pentecostal. I am happy that we did not make the mistake."

I ask you again, How does it feel to be a problem? How does it feel to have four strikes against you even before you walk into your first doctoral seminar? I am a black man, Pentecostal, African, with a heavy Nigerian accent. How does it feel to be a problem? How does it feel to carry the excessive weight of racial inequality, denigrated geographical identity, religious-sectarian prejudice, and stigmatizing-tongued inequality? To borrow the language of Melissa Harris-Perry, how does it feel to be a black male carrying excess weight and living in a crooked room of modernity/postmodernity/structural racism?[5] How does a Pentecostal begin to define himself or engage in epistemological discourse, let alone orient himself in the academy, when he is already defined by stereotypes?

Many Pentecostals feel that that they live in a crooked world and they do not want to align with the images, social imaginary, and expectations of the distorted world. Unwilling to bend precipitously, they take chances

---

5. Harris-Perry, *Sister Citizen*, 28–50.

at shifting or "bending" modernist epistemology to fit their straightened backs. So, they have come up with the distinctions of justification, such as *it-makes-spirit* and *it-makes-sense*.[6] An action or decision does *not make sense*, but it *makes spirit* because the decision or action does not "match" or accurately "correspond" to "some picked-out feature of reality or the world," though "it 'fits' or 'coheres' within [their] given system of established beliefs or within [their] given cognitive picture."[7]

"It-makes-sense" refers to an action or behavior that "corresponds" with "facts" out there in the world or "fits" with the conceptual schemes defined by worldly standards that do not genuinely and meaningfully speak about God or permit reference to the transcendent. "It-makes-spirit" does not deny the importance or authenticity of sense data. In fact, Pentecostals make use of them. The restriction they impose upon them is that they can only serve as *experiential inputs* to spiritual knowledge, which must eventually be intentionally translated into practical reason (empirical sense) so that it can be utilized at the nitty-gritty levels of common-sense experience. Such transmuted reason or sense must always remain "in reference to transcendence."[8] There is a two-sided character to the "rationale" of it-makes-spirit. Pentecostals claim to "find" or "discover" information from the nonphysical realm, but they must "make" sense of it to challenge all who undermine their flourishing, mock their life-view, and despise their God.

In this perspective on life, an action, behavior, or decision is commendable or good when it-makes-spirit; otherwise it is bad. A decision is bad, primarily, insofar as it does not involve the carryover of values from Christology to (transform) epistemological practices and effect transformations in the believer's devotional life. The question of truth, as Robert Cummings Neville taught us, is "the carryover of value from the object into the interpreters' experience by means of signs, as qualified by the biological, cultural, semiotic, and purposive contexts of the interpreters."[9]

The meanings of good, bad, and truth within this life-view are always imbricated in the purposive connection between epistemology and Christology that Pentecostals have forged in the last hundred years. Pentecostal epistemology, as we shall amply demonstrate later, is not as a disciplined investigation or interrogation of knowledge but a response to the voice of Christ rising from the deep of the self. It is a response to a *talking* Christ:

6. The names for these may differ from one Pentecostal congregation to another.

7. Janz, *God, the Mind's Desire*, 59. I came across Janz's excellent book when I had basically finished the writing of this book. Thus, references to it are limited to this preface, which is the last part of the book that I wrote.

8. Janz, *God, the Mind's Desire*, 112.

9. Neville, *Truth of Broken Symbols*, 240.

a call and response that is weaving the fabric of knowledge that empowers born-again believers' existence. Epistemology is a matter of interpreting the master's voice (its own semiotic reality) and applying its import to ordinary life. The Christ that talks here is the Jesus as a personal savior that intimates the believer about things-in-themselves, objects and situations stripped of their empirical appearances, and enables her to grasp such "abstracted" things that "transcend" human *sensory* capacity. He communicates in this "superior" way with the Pentecostal Christian because she believes that she has *crafted* herself by the *techniques of the self on the self* such that her born-again subjectivity "transcends" not only the reality that it ineluctably inhabits but also the intentional referential purview of her human (sinful) thoughts. Here her "holy" subjectivity (in sweet dogmatic dream) entertains the presumption that it can give itself its own sense and declares itself "lord" over empirical reality. These two transcendental loci are always involved in Christ *talk* and its reception. Here we see that it-makes-spirit starts off its life as suspended between transcendence, and its journey into sense or practical reason must also remain in reference to transcendence.[10]

The statement (formula), indeed, speaks to Pentecostals' conception of knowledge. In their reckoning, true knowledge does not exist independent of the experience (or subjectivity, interiority) of the knower. Knowledge is not an external, objective substance independent of the knower's individual consciousness, and in theory is not available to everyone. It-makes-sense in this context refers to the secular conception and practices of knowledge that hold that knowledge is generally available and accessible to all, whereas it-makes-spirit refers to an alternate conception and practices of knowledge that are embodied and generally not available to everyone. The enunciation of "it makes spirit" is a valued marker of the rhythm of a person's closeness to God. Knowledge here is considered to be (or is a reaching-out to) a refined, pure essence of godliness, intimate experience of God. Knowledge is a spirit as it floats above dense materiality, all that easily ensnares humanistic epistemology. It is a manifestation of the spirit of knowledge, if not the spirit of knowledge himself (Isa 11:2). Knowledge is a kind of distilled essence, changeless core, irreducible substrate, a dynamic perfection of a Pentecostal's walk with Jesus Christ. Knowledge is metaphysics of the presence of God; the supreme being is present without mediation, a secure ground of thought that is proper to knowledge and meaning, is good and self-identical, correct and pure, and not secondary, derivative, or complicated. Thus, "to make spirit" is to say that one has made it or is making it to the rarefied, warm level of intimacy with God the Holy Spirit. "To make spirit" is to

---

10. Janz, *God, the Mind's Desire*, 112; see also 107–11.

strategically or ideally turn to this proper, original ground of knowledge and existence in order to make everyday decisions as a born-again believer.

What kind of normative sway does this orientation to decision-making, life-view, or intrinsic obligation to a religious life have over Pentecostals' patterns of thought? This book configures the response to this question with profound insights into the convergence of epistemology and Christology within the impelling matrix of a provocative social ethics. In the process of rigorously analyzing the patterns of thought, this writer tracks and clarifies the seemingly intractable and enigmatic language of spirit in everyday practices and neatly sorts out the confusing interpretations of the dialectics of sense and spirit—indeed, their overlap—in the Pentecostal linguistic frame of reference. The book demonstrates that Pentecostal patterns of thought and language practices are rooted in the abyss of divine freedom or voluntarism.

The belief and practices concerning the "axiomatic" statement of decision-making are also linked to their comparison of God's promises with those of human beings. In this case, sense implies human word/promise and spirit connotes God's word/promise. It-does-not-make-sense means the particular action (decision) the believer is taking is not premised on human promise, which is usually plagued by uncertainty, slipperiness, and ambiguity. It-makes-spirit signifies the yea-and-amen certainty, unambiguity, and the unshakable promise of God (2 Cor 1:20). It-does-not-make-sense-but-it-makes-spirit is, indeed, a liturgical language, a ritualized use of words to suspend legitimate doubts about the meanings of human intentions or actions. It is a liturgical expression of speech that defers questioning and scrutiny of their (believers') words—hoping to lodge them in a safe realm where words have the force of deeds. Pentecostals believe that it is not through their own power or might that their utterances can reach this realm, but the immanent Spirit of God. The whole axiom or aphorism is geared to circumvent the logic of Babel, the preeminent display of human sense lifting itself to reach God. The liturgical expression of it-does-not-make-sense-but-it-makes-spirit "is the opposite of the Tower of Babel. Babel, which means the 'the gate of God,' is man's attempt to open the gate of the place where truer words were never spoken."[11] Pentecostals do not want to reach God, enter into the gate of the place above where the truest words are spoken, or to open the windows of heaven for themselves here on earth below by building or standing on the concrete towers of human sense, but on their intangible words offered to God in faith, in spirit and truth.

11. Fenn, *Liturgies and Trials*, xvi.

Do words spoken in faith remove all ambiguities of human utterances? The axiom may be a nice way to deal with the ambiguity of human sense, but it also introduces its own version of ambiguity. While it reinforces the spirituality of the speaker—and, perhaps, enhances her authority—it simultaneously places her action under God's judgment or in the shadow of false claim. All this begs for a full study of liturgical and sociological implications of Pentecostal religious language. We will not yield to this temptation in this book, as I have determined to limit our study to the theological and social-ethical issues of the formulaic statement.

The theological intensity or boldness of the Pentecostal aphorism invites a meditation on the ultimate goal of Pentecostal decision-making. What are Pentecostals up to when they espouse or avow the statement "It-does-not-make-sense-but-it-makes-spirit"? It seems to me that the ultimate goal of this epistemological frame is twofold: (*a*) uninterrupted unity with Jesus Christ as the ground of their decision-making, decision as *complete transparency* to Christ as the ground of their being, and (*b*) the *continuous self-surrender*, sacrifice of the "who" of autonomously free deciders to themselves as theonomous deciders. In this way decisions are directed to the infinite God and toward the finite believer—whose life has been grasped, shaken, and transformed by the Holy Spirit—regarded as a *symbol* of God (John 5:19). Decisions that meet the criterion of it-does-not-make-sense-but it-makes-spirit bring down (or re-cognize) the infinite God to (as in) the finite concrete realm of everyday activities and the finite up to (into) him. All these comprise the meaning of the symbol "it makes spirit."[12]

The philosophical density of the Pentecostal "axiomatic" statement invites some comparison with Alain Badiou's notion of event and its site.[13] There is something *evental* about the way spirit and sense are juxtaposed in the statement. The decision, the act that is regarded as making spirit or as spirit-informed that does not fit within or could not have arisen from the circumstances, is the "event" that seems to appear from nowhere. The event does not make sense given the site of its appearance. It shouldn't have happened, but it did. The event ruptured normality and demonstrated that what was considered reality, the order of the situation, was grounded on a "void," a cracked arrangement, an "inconsistent multiple." If we do not want to go this far into philosophy, we can say that in the eyes of Pentecostals the event seems to have dissolved the circumstances that birthed it, so "it does not make sense" ultimately means it was impossible for the event to have

---

12. Here I have borrowed Paul Tillich's language to capture what I consider to be the ultimate goal of the Pentecostal axiomatic statement under examination in this book.

13. Badiou, *Saint Paul*.

arisen from its site, from the now retroactively disarranged arrangement of circumstances. All this reminds me of what the philosopher of science Paul Feyerabend once said in his 1975 book *Against Method*: "My trick is to present events which dissolve the circumstances that made them happen. Given the circumstances the events are absurd, unheard of . . . they simply do not make sense."[14]

The philosophical sugestiveness of *It does not make sense, but it makes spirit* demands some methodogical clarification about how we are going to handle the claim it makes. While one is not looking forward to its philosophical testability, it behooves this writer to offer a word or two about the method he would deploy to elicit its truth-value, epistemic status, and ethical significance. The values (truth, epistemic, and ethical) of the claim must be examined or determined neither in isolation from other descriptions, sentences, or constructs of which it is a part nor by a particular set of observations. This book studies the claim within the broad description, version and theory of the self, world and God as put forward by Pentecostals. We must acknowledge that the truth, epistemic, and ethical values of the claim, as Cornel West might put it,

> pertain to bodies of knowledge, descriptions, versions or theories of self, world and God, not to atomic sentences, autonomous statements or isolated claims. . . . When one puts forward knowledge claims from the vantage point of a religious description, version or theory about the self, world and God, one is attempting to support or defend a particular description, version or theory that tries to promote the valuing of certain insights, illuminations, capacities and abilities in order honestly to confront and effectively to cope with the inevitable vicissitudes and unavoidable limit situations in life.[15]

Now a word or two about the origins of this text. I was provoked to undertake the work of this book by a Pentecostal minister on Long Island, New York: Pastor Elsie Obed. She had invited me to speak at her church annual conference on November 25 and 26, 2017. She assigned me the topic of *Who Christ is*. I could not decide on how to approach the topic until the night of November 24, less than twelve hours before I was scheduled to speak. Just before midnight, the idea came to me of interpreting Christ as the one who enables his followers to inhabit the crack between sense and foolishness, meaning and meaninglessness, by configuring their ways of knowing. I delivered the lecture-sermon (which is now chapter 1 of this

---

14. Feyerabend, *Against Method*, xv.
15. West, "A Philosophical View of Easter," 415–20; quotation on 417.

book) without notes in the morning. Moments after I delivered the lecture, the idea came to me at 12:14 p.m. to deeply interrogate all that I had just said. The sermon-lecture was a meditation on the connection between epistemology and Christology as driven by the question, Who is Christ to the world today and what does it mean for a Pentecostal Christian to claim that she knows him? The delivery of the lecture, which lasted for forty-eight minutes, was structured by an aphorism that, to the best of my knowledge, Pastor Elsie Obed formulated and popularized: *It does not make sense, but it makes spirit*. These are provocative words.

This statement is pregnant with meaning and begs multiple interpretations. In it I hear the echoes of what jazz legend Miles Davis said about music: "When you play music, don't play the idea that's there, play the next idea. Don't play what's there. Play what's not there."[16] The Pentecostal believer in the thrust and thrownness of *It-does-not-make-sense-but-it-makes-spirit* must "play" the next fact, the next situation, the next "sense," the reality that's not there. To *play* the next fact is to dwell in the margin, split, in the space, in the void between what's there and what's not there, to mind the gap between sense and spirit.

The nine-word statement is fecund. Its truth is not an argued or reasoned truth but an *experienced* one; its truth is not in reference to facticity but to the guts, inner spirit, inner conviction or God's voice. The truth here seems to irrupt as an *event*, which does not make sense according to the order or rules of normality and opens a space to reimagine reality. The truth of the statement contains an implicit command or reprimand. It urges (asks) the hearer to live life by its wisdom or scolds that faith-sagging Pentecostal for falling under the domination of worldly ways of being, knowing, and doing.[17]

The statement not only declares the speaker's everyday religious orientation and invokes her concept of the person as a "decider" but also exudes the power of performative speech.[18] To use the words of political theorist Wendy Brown, the statement is "tethered to a declarative model of truth ... [the] recognition that a saying can be a doing and a making, that an utterance can bring its own truth into being and thus literally make or re-make reality."[19]

---

16. Quoted in Crawley, "Black. Queer. Born Again," 8.

17. Brown, "American Nightmare," 707, 709.

18. To further explore the political implications of this concept of person, see Habermas, "Learning from Catastrophe?," 703.

19. Brown, "American Nightmare," 707.

The statement is, indeed, bulging with excess meanings. Most importantly, it signifies a concrete way of engaging the world. It is in this sense an *hypothesis* (as per Charles Sanders Peirce), meaning it is a leading principle for Pentecostal thought and action. It functions "as an actual or potential habit for thought and action." As such, it is "assumed, not questioned, and simply acted upon."[20] The main objective of this book is to deeply explore, perceptively interrogate, and succinctly define this habit for thought and action.[21]

What are the implications of all these for moral claims in the public square where democratic citizens generate and address reasons to themselves for the sake of organized collective life and human flourishing? This book's six chapters constitute a series of seminars on the nine-word statement, geared toward precisely defining and conveying their overall meaning for social ethics. The book is dedicated to Pastor Elsie Obed.

---

20. Neville, *Eternity and Time's Flow*, 10.

21. In this habit of thought, spirit underlies the movement and process of sense, constituting the togetherness of all senses. But the modern world makes the false assumption that these are two different topics and has forgotten spirit or deracinated sense from spirit. To-make-spirit, therefore, is not only to re-make the connection but also to grasp the underlying condition within which a sense or the flow of senses takes place.

To-make-spirit is to connect sense in (of) the *being* of the present to the senses in (of) the nonbeing of its (sense's) past and future in their real togetherness. In Pentecostal thinking, the spirit is the context in which a sense is together in all its three temporal modes. Spirit is the togetherness of the temporal modes of any sense. The art of decision-making enables the decision-maker to "see" (to be interpretatively present with) the realities of past, present, and future nestled in a processual moment of sense, sense-data. Decision-making, which ultimately defines the moral identity of the Pentecostal believer, involves grasping for the "moral identity" of (or that is discernible in) sense, sense-certainty. The moral identity of a sense in the present moment as observed by all persons whose insights are limited to Enlightenment rationalism and secular humanism is different from that of the Pentecostal observer. Her perspective is not limited to the mere present of the sense, but also involves the spiritual togetherness of all its moments in all the temporal modes.

The "make" in the it-makes-spirit speaks to ways of putting together (forming) the three modes in decision-making, speaks to crafting Pentecostals' diverse ways of putting together the modes and achieving a certain value in the way they are put together, and even speaks to how they treat the subjunctive character of the forms as if they are real. For this perspective, one may interpret it-does-not-makes-sense to refer to a situation at hand that does not conform to pure subjunctivity of form(s) some Pentecostal has imposed upon it. This way of putting the matter was inspired by Neville, *Eternity and Time's Flow*, 19–28; 89–90; 102–3; 168–70; 186–87.

Acknowledgments

WRITING A BOOK, BUILDING thought, is a process that impels me into concentric circles. Once I get into the circle of manipulating ideas, I quickly realize that I am already standing in the circumference of debt, credits of encouragement, insights, and wisdom of past teachers, and advices given to me through time. No sooner have I grasped this revelation than I discover that all along I was standing in a wider circle of editors, producers, and marketers of books, and funders of research. Circle upon circle! There is also the infinite circle of the Spirit of God that grounds all the circles. Each of these circles demands its recognition. Where do I start?

Definitely, I cannot start from myself, though writing forces me to dwell at the center of my thought and spirituality. This center that I claim was given to me as a gift. It is a gift of God, human beings, and nature. For by grace I write through gift. Writing is not only of works lest any writer should boast. For we are the workmanship of our God, cultural time and space, and unmerited genes, crafted in tears and sweat, dollars and blood for good books, which our families and communities prepared beforehand that we should bring forth. Once again, where do I start?

From the depths of my heart flow gratitude, admiration, and love to the following friends who assisted me in the birth of this book: Babatunde Obadare, Amos Yong, Robert Neville, Kwabena Asamoah-Gyadu, Esther Acolatse, Bill Oliverio, and Abimbola Adelakun. Their comments on an early draft of the text constitute an invaluable help in shaping the book. Immense gratitude to Anwuli Ojogwu, who also shaped the text with her copy-editing skills. Thanks to my daughter Bele Wariboko for producing the figure in chapter 3.

I would also like to thank the following people with Cascade Books: Robin Parry, Matthew Wimer, Charlie Collier, and Jacob Martin for their professionalism in shepherding the manuscript through to its end form as a beautiful book.

Introduction
Logics of Pentecostal Worlds

OPENING WORDS

I STATED IN THE preface that there is a Pentecostal hypothesis about decision-making, about how sense interacts with spirit or humanity interacts with divinity to forge a path toward human flourishing. This hypothesis to a large extent guides Pentecostals' everyday practices, and its fundamental tenets also explain the world or human existence to them. What do we mean by hypothesis? It means a guiding principle for belief and action that is vulnerable to correction. Let me unpack this in two ways. First, I will explain or describe the assumptions that could possibly be behind a principle that makes it an "assumable [truth] for belief and action"; a principle that is temporarily unquestionable in a spiritual community until new experiences and contexts make it obsolete and call for further clarification or expose it as a fallible starting point for everyday decision.[1] Then, I will explain that the principle (truth, judgment) is not intuitively related to the world of the community members, believers and actors, but rather is embedded in a fallible interpretative (semiotic) system that is (periodically) reformulated as habits of the mind interacting with the world. Hypothesis, therefore, is a community's assumable truth for mental habits and personal and social actions (as per Charles Peirce). Hypothesis, as conveyed in these two modes, is part of a believer's or community's habitus.

Let us turn to the first mode. A hypothesis is the set of assumptions upon which the life-view of a community operates and shapes its ethos, dictates its shared decision-making framework, and, most importantly, defines what the members consider meaningful decisions or results.[2] The

1. Neville, *Highroad around Modernism*, 26–29, inspired this definition and the discussions in this paragraph and the following four.
2. Drucker, "The Theory of the Business," 95–104.

community or group has (*a*) specific assumptions about the environment or world it lives in; (*b*) assumptions about its mission (destiny), that is, the difference it wants to make in the world; and (*c*) assumptions about its core gifts (endowments) needed to accomplish its mission and thus transform its world. These three constitute a set of guidelines and guardrails to direct the community's decisions and inform its everyday being and doing, which are never static. A hypothesis is a *theory* about spirituality and the things of life that are dynamic. It is to be constantly tested and refined where the teachings of the Bible (or faith tradition) interact with everyday human activities.

Hypothesis is here not used in the modernist scientific sense. It is inclined to the philosophic usage elaborated by Charles Sanders Peirce and Robert Cummings Neville.[3] In this specific sense as an interpretative sign, hypothesis is a principle for thought and action that enables a group of people to grasp and engage their worlds. Though the principle is assumed and acted upon, and often not questioned, it is still vulnerable to correction. While the formal character of the principle may not be explicitly questioned, its application to realities or the extent of its reach in everyday practices is always changing gradually.

What, then, is the Pentecostal hypothesis? The Pentecostal hypothesis is the capacity to constitute alternate ways of knowing. Broadly conceived, it is the way by which Pentecostals engage the world (their social realities) and the depths of their religious existence.[4] It is a form of interpretation that enables Pentecostals, amid multiple options, to know what is the most fitting decision (action) relative to their interest and commitment to Christ. This interpretation is put into play every day and it is either confirmed or disconfirmed, reinforced or corrected. The beliefs Pentecostals hold about the world are tested daily, and they are always making adjustments to how to pragmatically apply them to the worlds they inhabit. Through experience, they have evolved certain principles, aphorisms, or generic statements to serve as guardrails as they navigate their worlds. In this book, we are examining just one such statement that relates to decision-making. A decision or an action is the fitting thing to do if it conforms to a body of principles and experiences categorized as "spirit" (spiritual); hence, it is not fitting if it merely conforms to sense (Enlightenment rationalism and secular humanism). The statement or summarizing principle under investigation here is "It does not make sense, but it makes spirit." This is tested (contested, attested) almost every day as either true or false when it is put into play.

3. Neville, *Highroad around Modernism*, 25–52.
4. Neville, *Defining Religion*, 78–84, inspired this definition.

A hypothesis is an interpretative engagement with social realities as shaped by *symbols* and it is vulnerable to correction.[5] When Pentecostals speak of people realizing the truth of a statement encapsulating their social imaginary it is about believers becoming true to the intent of the statement. The statement or principle itself is a hypothesis that tests their faithfulness to life-in-spirit, and their spiritualities would be deemed true or false according to its standards. To become a faithful Pentecostal, a believer anointed by the Holy Ghost and *hot* for Christ, is to develop a "hearing ear," that is, to hear Jesus's voice and then make one's life decisions based on its interpretation. The reliance on divine word or fidelity to the divine whispers of practical wisdom does not necessarily mean that the Pentecostal decision model is preoccupied with certainty. The model is also not foundationalist.[6] Given its hypothetical character, the model is always subject to revision. Let me quickly add that the kind of evidence that is required to revise the model is often created or authenticated by the model itself. Tanya M. Luhrmann mentions this in her book on the spirituality of American evangelicals, a group in which she puts Pentecostals. She writes in *When God Talks Back* (2012),

> Knowing God involves training, and it involves interpretation. Each faith—to some extent, each church—forms its own culture, its own way of seeing the world, and as people acquire the knowledge and the practices through which they come to know God, the most intimate aspects of the way they experience their everyday world change. Those who learn to take God seriously do not simply interpret the world differently from those who have not done so. They have different evidence for what is true. In some deep and fundamental way, as a result of their practices, they live in different worlds.[7]

Let us further advance the meaning of hypothesis as used in this book through another angle of inquiry. Here I am reminded of Neville's position

---

5. For an excellent discussion on the use of symbols in theology and spiritual practices, see Neville, *The Truth of Broken Symbols*.

6. Some of my readers may argue—and rightly so—that the turn to spirit from sense is often also a search for a first and indubitable principle of decision-making, a desperate search for an "unshakable" foundation for the coordinates of existence, and a bald claim that one has a unique or privileged insight into the structure of reality. In this sense, it is inherently violent—more so as "a belief that one has access to 'objective reality,' to a reality as it eternally is in itself." Depoortere, *Christ in Postmodern Philosophy*,

7. This a tension in Pentecostalism insofar as there are many Pentecostals who want to convert the hypothetical inquiry about social reality into transcendental illusion.

7. Luhrmann, *When God Talks Back*, 226.

on style as it relates to philosophical arguments. He writes, "Good style is sometimes thought to consist in a clear statement of one topic that leads to the treatment of the adjacent topic and so on to build an edifice with blocks of analysis. . . . But better style has to acknowledge that, because of the plurality of approaches and angles of inquiry, no consistently written chapter [or paragraph] can be more than a partial statement."[8]

To return to our topic, hypothesis is a generic statement about the depths of religious existence that engages decision-making with deliberation, and it is considered to be either true or false. The Pentecostal hypothesis of *it-makes-spirit* is deemed generic because it is not precise and it is meant to be universally applied to all decisions that Pentecostals face in their everyday life, ramifying in many directions. It is also deemed generic because it is a process of correcting or improving a thinking that began with sense data or sensation, which is basically where all thinking starts.

To conclude this prologue, let me state that in this book we shall interrogate the hypothesis that guides the everyday decisions that are made in response to specific divine speeches (words) addressed to Pentecostals, who are attuned to hear them and committed to acting upon them. The Father, Christ, or the Holy Spirit talks and they decide on what to do or how to live and to live well in the phenomenal realm. Pentecostals posit their "fidelity" to the irrupting of divine words as opposed, if not infinitely superior, to any habit of mind, meaning, or *sense* that relies only on Enlightenment rationalism and secular humanism. Hence, they proudly say, "It does not make sense, but it makes spirit." I want to explicate this hypothesis, investigate whether it makes a pragmatic difference in the way Pentecostals experience the world, or contributes something worthy to our understanding of the roles senses or intuition play as guide to decision-making.

Preview of Arguments and Directions

The Pentecostal hypothesis as a guide to decision-making or deliberation functions as an integral part of Pentecostal phronesis, that is, practical wisdom. Pentecostal phronesis is a synthesis of two ways of knowing—two sources of knowledge. Let us call them sense and spirit, or sensibility and understanding, or sensation and concept. Pentecostals make judgments, engage in thinking by bringing these two sources or forms of knowledge either simultaneously or sequentially. The "spirit" is a set of concepts, ways of proceeding, logics of discernment, or creative self-interpretations of themselves that is used to organize their worldly sensations or information

---

8. Neville, *Eternity and Time's Flow*, xv.

about the world. Thinking or discernment is a process of give and take from the two sources of knowledge. This immediately raises at least two questions. Is there a gap between sense and spirit or a necessary interdependence between them in Pentecostal decision-making? If it is the responsibility of it-makes-spirit to transform the present, given empirical fact, sense, then it means the present is always already past and it is leaning forward to the future, to initiating something new.[9] The task of this book is to explore how these two interact to produce practical wisdom. Along the way, it will also explore the gap between the two as a space where creative dialogue at its deepest level is always becoming and unfinishable. This is a gap that both connects and disconnects sense and spirit—a gap that creates interdependence between them

The thesis of this book takes as its point of departure the split between sense and spirit in Pentecostal epistemology. From this point of departure, I will gradually determine the two terms in relation as that dimension of epistemology that transmutes into social ethics. Epistemology is a matter of the ethos of both the ways of knowing and the seekers engaged in the search. We will discover how sense is structured as spirit and, reciprocally, spirit is structured as sense. The interdependence of the two leads us to consider something like "sense of the spirit" and Pentecostal active reflection and self-awareness of how the correlation of sense and spirit advances our analysis of the Hegelian ethical issues of "shape of the spirit" and "absolute spirit."[10]

In the movement from epistemology to social ethics, we make some daring effort to locate the social dimensions of Pentecostal Christology in the twilight border between sense and spirit. Christ is the sense of the spirit and the spirit of the sense. Christ is the referential ideality of Pentecostal sense of existence, the ultimate goal of the praxis of the spirit, and the model of the finite human being living into the infinite. Christology is here framed as an epistemological concern. It-makes-spirit is the revelation (pneumatological imagination) of the Holy Spirit in the inner life, the self-disclosure of the infinite Christ, the spirit of Christ, God as realized in Pentecostals through faith within a given historical situation. This faith is a "personal act of commitment, of confidence and trust, not a belief about the nature of things. . . . Now when [they] fail in faith, [they] fail in this faith; and when [they] transgress, it is this [Christ they] transgress against; when [they] reason falsely it is in violation of the first principle

---

9. This way of putting across my idea was inspired by Clark and Holquist, *Mikhail Bakhtin*, 75. I wish to thank my friends Drs. Erica Ramirez and Ekaputra Tupamahu for revitalizing my interest in Mikhail Bakhtin.

10. Nancy, *Sense of the World*, 8, inspired this sentence.

given in this [conviction]."¹¹ In this context, to order knowledge is to make a christological gesture; to explain Christ is also an epistemological gesture. And to explain reality or order the coordinates of one's existence by christologically inflected epistemology is indeed a religious gesture.

In this sense, Christology is not about interpreting Christ but about entering this sense/spirit that Christ himself is, and then using it as an explanatory framework of life. Christology is a praxis, not a poiesis. The Pentecostal believer in deploying it as a way of knowing and knowability is changed, transformed, and what Christology is *is* only discernible from its praxis. As a matter of praxis, Christology is also a matter of the ethos of knowing, seeking, and doing. This book opens the praxis of Christology as a movement of being-toward truth, the work of uncovering (or adequately placing) the spirit behind (or within) pragmatic everyday decisions.[12]

Our task is to examine what *it-makes-spirit* is and offer insights into what Pentecostal knowing is. How do Pentecostals move from *it-makes-sense* (or nonspiritual sense, consciousness, "provisional knowledge") to spiritual consciousness, un-sense, "true knowledge"? The project of this book is to examine step by step the movement and to interrogate if it offers insights into a knowing that is fundamentally different from secular knowing.

The common understanding of it-makes-spirit is that it is a Pentecostal shorthand form of fundamentally grounding knowledge in spiritual reflection and consciousness—that is, in religious faith. But our study will demonstrate that this function cannot be divorced from the social grounding of epistemic justification and human rationality.

We will endeavor to grasp and express the truth of it-makes-spirit not only as *intuition* or individual religious conscience, but equally as *normativity*. The issue here is, How does a Pentecostal believer authoritatively represent her intuition (her claim of it-makes-spirit) and indeed herself to other believers? And what could it possibly mean for her to say it-makes-spirit (that is, speaking from, to, and for the whole belief system or the Holy Spirit they share together)? This is a normative issue.[13] The passage from intuition to normativity can also be viewed as a critical passage from "ethical substance" to ethical subjectivity. When the spirit grasps a person, the

---

11. Niebuhr, *Meaning of Revelation*, 154.

12. Nancy, *Sense of the World*, 9, inspired this way of rendering my ideas.

13. Here we are talking not only of sociality of shared norms, customs, and institutions of a form of life, and shared rules of justification, but also ethical action or decision as rooted in the universality of the Holy Spirit, the particularity of a given, contextual ethical tradition, and the individuality of a person's reception of the Holy Spirit or individualizing religious conscience.

person not only locates herself in (or identifies herself with) the thick unity of her community's ethical substance but also grasps herself as subject (a self-conscious person engaged in the self-differentiating process of producing objective knowledge on the basis of a reflective standpoint).

This movement is from the relatedness of mind (embodied rational techniques, procedure) and world (objects, things, facts, actions, events, and so on) to the transformative relationship the mind exercises over the world (as in facts, events, and so on), resulting in spiritual formation. The immediate presence of the world to the Pentecostal mind is transformed into attaining a "higher" knowledge mediated by connections between the world, mind, and Holy Spirit. Such connections live in each believer through her common attunement to the practices and language of a particular Pentecostal form of life ("shape of spirit"). The effect is the creation or sustenance of a "shape of spirit." To appropriate Hegel's term for this: immediate knowledge passes into the "shape of spirit" of a particular Pentecostal community, which conjoins "shape of consciousness" and "shape of world." "Shape of consciousness" is basically about a people's representation of the natural world, their representations of individual perceptible things and the background forces that explain them and their regularities. "Shape of world" refers to the skills, tacit knowledge, practices, and intersubjective agreements that enable persons in a community to negotiate their social world. Terry Pinkard explains how shape of spirit (or a form of life, being-in-the-world) works in this way:

> Any shape of spirit embeds within itself a joint conception both of what the *norms* are within that form of life and what it is about the *world* that makes those norms *realizable*, what in the world *resists* their realization or tends to make their realization *rare*, and what in the world is thus to be *expected*. As embodying a tacit grasp of a unity of the "is" and the "ought" within which agents live, a shape of spirit thus forms the overall contours of the ways in which those people, individually and collectively, *imagine* how their lives, individually and collectively, ought to go and how they reasonably expect them really to go.[14]

The movement from it-makes-sense to it-makes-spirit is in a certain perspective the transformation of reason into spirit. This transformation rides on an understanding that "it is a fundamental misjudgment to take reason as the highest human faculty, the fundament of moral and legal action, and goal of history."[15]

14. Pinkard, "What Is a 'Shape of Spirit'?," 144.
15. Hegel, *Phenomenology of Spirit*, 173.

We will demonstrate that the turn from it-makes-sense (the rational) to it-makes-spirit is not a flight into the subjective or the utter rejection of the standards of rationality. While at this, we will investigate and lift the depth of conceptual thought, philosophy being worked out within the context of it-makes-spirit. This philosophy is discerned in the passage between it-makes-sense and it-makes-spirit. We shall engender a new Pentecostal philosophy, initiate something new as we explore the interval that separates it-makes-sense from it-makes-spirit, uncovering a common truth embedded in the encounter between them. The "truth" or rather the high point of Pentecostal epistemology is as much in it-makes-spirit as it must also be in it-makes-sense. That is, it is not completely in one or the other, "but somewhere between the two, in the passage that is effected between one and the other. To put this somewhat differently, philosophy is something that moves, that passes, and that takes place . . . in a place where the connection between thoughts gestates."[16] In this process, in this unscripted common space, we activate a dialectic that is neither it-makes-sense nor it-makes-spirit, but christological. (Let us put the christological dimension of our argument in abeyance for now.)

The split between it-makes-sense and it-makes-spirit is significant because it points us to something that the theologizing and philosophizing of Pentecostal epistemology has not yet achieved. To master the meaning of this split is to follow its dynamic or tendency beyond the limits of extant Pentecostal theology that impede learning—that is, to surpass it by showing fidelity to the split internal to the movement. The split constitutes such a crucial point to rigorous formulation of Pentecostal epistemology that we might say we are faced with a choice between an adequate understanding of the split or no theorizing of Pentecostal epistemology. Pentecostals are never so close to a rigorous everyday epistemology as in the moments when they pose it-makes-sense in contradistinction to it-makes-spirit. In the mirror of this positing or rejection, without doubt, Pentecostal discourse brings into clear relief its own limitations, the power of its unacknowledged internal movements and internal contradictions. In the positing of the contradictions, we discern the failed beginning of a rigorous epistemology, of a system of thought that is open to, speaks to, makes common cause with, and even challenges other philosophical systems of thought. The "embedded truth," the pending meaning of everyday Pentecostal epistemology is simultaneously a justification and refutation of "secular" philosophy. This interplay is enacted in the "passage" between it-makes-sense and it-makes-spirit.

---

16. Macherey, *Hegel or Spinoza*, 3.

What takes place in the frame of this positing of the internal movements and internal contradictions is a promise that is inhibited from being kept—a truth stuck in aborted movement. Thus, the frame is characterized by incompleteness. It is incomplete not because the decision-maker does not at some point cut off deliberation and take an action. It is incomplete because the philosophical tendency or the promise in passing from it-makes-sense (or it-does-not-make-sense) to it-makes-spirit is prevented from running its course. Indeed, Pentecostal discourse (or tradition) is lived contemporaneously but understood theologically backward and must be understood theologically forward. All Pentecostal everyday practice that is observable today is rooted in a certain interpretation and appropriation of a Christian theological tradition, but it gives us glimpses of (or we claim to see) an "indigenous" Pentecostal philosophy forming in the clouds of the horizon. For many years, like the servant of Elijah (1 Kings 18:42–44), I have been running between the church and the academy, looking for the signs of the philosophical downpour, and now I can say, "A philosophy as small as a mustard seed is rising from the horizon." The bearers of this philosophy emerging from the hurly-burly of everyday life, from the partial orderings of practical knowledge, from the womb of unstructured haphazardness of social life, are plain Pentecostals.

This book is a philosophical analysis of ordinary and "holy" Pentecostals' theology in the form of epistemology or their epistemology framed in theological terms.[17] In the pages ahead, I track this double-voicedness with a polyphonic style of unfinalizable discourse, structural paradigms of Christology, and theoretical constructs of continental philosophy tinctured with American pragmatic thought. When all is said and done (though not as a final word) what I present is not a Pentecostal philosophy as an object the ordinary folk possess, but a *feeling* for philosophy. A feeling (sense) for philosophy is "an integral attitude (by means of the whole person) toward a higher and ultimate value,"[18] that is, a whole human being engaging with a personal subject of how to know based on demands of ultimacy encountering an active answerable consciousness. It must be a feeling for philosophy because "divine reality, in its simultaneous transcendence and immanence, is the basic fact of *religious* consciousness and experience, but it cannot be understood in [solely, purely] rational terms."[19] Besides, the basic claim of it-makes-spirit (the claim that the immanent self is in contact with a transcendental being or realm) contradicts rational thought and constitutes a

---

17. Contino and Felch, "A Feeling for Faith," 5, inspired this sentence.
18. Bakhtin, *Problems of Dostoevsky's Poetics*, 294.
19. Poole, "Apophatic Bakhtin," 156.

fundamental antimony in the sight of the fierce guardians of the philosophical academy.[20] Those who regard themselves as holy, ordinary Pentecostals return the "insult" and treat academic, university philosophy as passé and irrelevant to their everyday living. But this book demonstrates that philosophy is the repressed, the shadow side of Pentecostal everyday theology. It uncovers the philosophical premises and dynamics of their theological-epistemological paradigm.[21] In addition, I try to make sense of Pentecostal religious practices or issues as a philosophical problem to be understood within the limits or constructs of (secular) philosophy—perhaps all this is due to personal temperament and interest. The resort to philosophical constructs is not geared toward fitting Pentecostal practices into an external template, but to awaken the philosophical possibilities that lie within them and nudge Pentecostals to write their own academic philosophies on their own terms, on self-sufficient communal standards. As we shall demonstrate later, it-makes-spirit may hold some prospects for the emergence of some self-sufficient communal standards. A close reading of the Pentecostal materials shows that because of either its dynamics or other forces at work the materials are increasingly subjected to the "slow, subtle moulding of the [philosophical] artifacts" of the modernist tradition.[22] With this insight we are able to see how it-makes-spirit somewhat functions as the Hegelian "absolute spirit" (self-sufficient standard[23]) in its social ethical dimension, that is, to see how Pentecostals use it-makes-spirit as a self-sufficient standard to justify or assess their beliefs, norms and practices in their own communities or in personal decision-making.

Hopefully, with this method or approach to Pentecostal studies, that is, bringing latent Pentecostal philosophic ideas into rigorous conversation with continental philosophical constructs, I am pointing the way to an emerging non-isolationist Pentecostal philosophy at the congested intersection of everyday practices and theoretical analysis or inquiry. Thus, this book not only reveals the dialogue that is taking place between everyday Pentecostal faith and academic philosophy but also sets the two on a new vista of dialogical imagination.

---

20. Poole, "Apophatic Bakhtin," 156, inspired this sentence by his discussion of Sergei N. Bulgakov's apophatic theology.

21. Lock, "Bakhtin and the Tropes of Orthodoxy," 100.

22. Neville, *Truth of Broken Symbols*, 263.

23. As Molly Farneth, an astute interpreter of Hegel's *Phenomenology of Spirit*, puts it, "Absolute spirit . . . is the self-sufficient standard generated by a community that is engaged in the process of creating, sustaining, challenging, and transforming its norms and judgments over time." Farneth, "Hegel's Sacramental Politics," 185.

It would be splendid if this new vista turned on the hinges of Pentecostal practice. The axis of Pentecostal practice is the gap between sense and spirit, order of being and irruption in being.[24] *Sense* "stands for the positive ontological order accessible to knowledge, for the infinite multiplicity of what 'presents itself' in our experience, categorized in genuses and species in accordance with its properties."[25] *Spirit*: "what makes spirit," as they say, is the nonbeing, something of a different dimension, from an order inaccessible to extant knowledge and often regarded as something coming from outside or beyond. This naming of a happenstance or event as *making spirit* is not an objective consideration but how Pentecostal believers see, evaluate, and symbolize what has taken place in their lives.

The gap is the difference between sense and spirit. The gap is the fleeting presence of the eternal in the temporal process, the flashes of the absolute in the positivity of being, or the Real shining through hard, concrete reality, and yet it resists, eludes symbolization by "the always-total texture of knowledge."[26] To be faithful to Jesus Christ is not only to dwell in this gap but also to practice fidelity to the irruptions in being that one has experienced; it is to subjectively engage the gap.

The peculiarity of the Pentecostal theology of being and rupture is that both being and rupture coexist in the same person. Christ is the order of being, the one in whom all things, all matter, all creation consist (as they interpret Col 1:17), and is the contingency of rupture, the spirit whose movement is unpredictable and given to breaking the mold. Christ is a kind of *coincidentia oppositorum*. Christ in this hermeneutic sense is the gap that both separates and connects sense and spirit, being and rupture. The split Christ is a hypostatization of the (conceptual) gap, a direct "ontologization" of the (epistemological) gap or a transformation of the gap into a "new positive order of being,"[27] to a new positive order of being that is not necessarily beholden to rationalist logic but "functions as an index of itself and of the falsity of the field [or the story, opinion, *doxa*, "fact," "truth"] subverted by it."[28]

Many people have talked about Pentecostal epistemology; few have grasped the christological energy that drives it. In this book, we shall examine the deeper issue of the fusion of epistemology and Christology, showing how epistemology performs itself inside Christology. To the rest of the

24. This is an allusion to philosopher Alain Badiou's language.
25. Žižek, "Paul and the Truth Event," 74.
26. Žižek, "Paul and the Truth Event," 77.
27. Žižek, "Paul and the Truth Event," 77.
28. Žižek, "Paul and the Truth Event," 77.

world, epistemology may be a disciplined investigation or interrogation of knowledge, but to the Pentecostals it is a response to the voice of Christ rising from the deep of the self. It is a response to a talking Christ: a call and response that is weaving the fabric of knowledge that empowers existence. It is a matter of interpreting the master's voice (its own semiotic reality) and applying its import to ordinary life. Pentecostal epistemology is captured in the narratives of Christology and the processes of *Christformation*.

The christological structures of their thought (everyday practical theology) and understanding of human life create the *habits* of their epistemology. Such structures are not necessarily conceptual schemes or inner representations that mediate Pentecostals' grasp of existence or the world. They are more like "horizons" of understanding that arise from persons being interpellated by the story of Jesus Christ, and which ground their ongoing openness to the "text" of reality and their rejection of any conception of the goal of knowledge that abhors all future surprises.[29]

The name Jesus Christ operates in Pentecostal circles in at least four ways: theological, devotional, ethical, and political.[30] First, it is the personal name of the Son of God, Savior and Lord, the anointed one of God, and so on. The person bearing this name is believed to be God and is worshiped as such. Jesus Christ is the savior, sanctifier, baptizer, healer, and the soon-coming king.

Second, the name relates to ritual and spiritual practices in both communal and personal worship or devotional life. Here the name of Jesus is invoked to aid earthly life in areas such as deliverance, quest for miracles, and accessing spiritual powers.

Third, the name points to a model of political governance that holds the Christian God as the ultimate sovereign ruler of political systems and who does not kowtow to the pluralism of the current liberal elite. It also speaks to the practices that Pentecostals hope will enact the kind of political agency/citizenship that will please their God.

Fourth, the name stands as a model of excellence, a pattern of behavior, a religious symbol that shapes their practical everyday life. Pentecostals aim to shape their lives to conform to the pattern of behavior to which the name of Jesus, as a symbol of excellence, refers. In this study, we will focus on how the symbol is interpreted to serve as the prime shaper of epistemological practices that aim to improve personal decision-making. Pentecostals refer to their epistemological practices or decision-making model like the

---

29. Taylor, *Dilemmas and Connections*, 25, 31–33.

30. These three terms (theological, devotional, and ethical) are exactly carried over from Neville's thought; I have adopted them for heuristic purposes. See the triad of operating patterns in other religions in Neville, *Truth of Broken Symbols*, xviii–xix, 2, 10.

internal structures of a christological doctrine in many respects. They believe (in a mythopoetic way, if you like) that their decision-making process refers to some aspects of Christ's *two-natures-being* as *like how it was*. This is to say their decision-making model not only reveals their faith commitment to Christ, but also in certain respects reveals something about his character of subjecting the flesh (sense, or personal will) to the Spirit (the divine will). Pentecostal epistemology iconically discloses Christology.[31] It is an epistemology that aims at some kind of isomorphic modeling of Christ's nature. When a Pentecostal, on taking a decision, says, "It does not make sense, but it makes spirit," she not only understands her decision as right and that she has done something to change or resist the regnant rationalistic model of decision-making, but also performs the act of honoring Jesus Christ and performatively enacts Christ's two-natures-being.

"Jesus is the Christian symbol of God, and we engage God by means of that symbol. Jesus to be sure is many symbols, and it is through Jesus"[32] as source of truth that Pentecostals engage God as a supreme way of knowing in their quest for knowability. Jesus Christ is the Pentecostal symbol of an epistemology by which the truth of every decision, situation, and encounter is revealed. Here a decision or action is deemed truthful when it embodies or it is shaped by the ethical ideal of Christ's teachings and work that are set in the context of pneumatological understanding of reality.

This book provides the intellectual or philosophical infrastructure behind this epistemological practice. To fully appreciate the connection between Pentecostal epistemology (quest for the thing-itself[33]) and Christology, we need to understand that Pentecostalism is driven by the search for truth. Pentecostal spirituality (in its praxis and reflections) is the fabric into which their knowledges, experiences, fears, and hopes are woven, and it is, at least in relation to their being-in-the-world, the condition and context of philosophizing or theologizing. The issue here is not just about gaining access to revelatory truth but also about having access to knowledge and truth about the world and self, and how they can be known if one is not limited to the phenomenal realm. There is something more. The fundamental premise of Pentecostal spirituality is to contest reality as the conditions and limits to access knowledge and truth, while endowing it with spirit. The spirituality of Pentecostals seeks to raise self-conscious subjects who can do something

31. Neville, *Truth of Broken Symbols*, 40–41.

32. Neville, *Symbols of Jesus*, 217.

33. The "thing-itself" or the "thing-in-itself" is a term made popular by Immanuel Kant. It refers to thing-as-such, the unknowable real of an object, which cannot be known by human senses. Because the nature of thing is beyond the sensory reality, Kant denies that it is possible to know such a thing as such.

to themselves (technology of the self: purifications, ascetic exercises, and so forth) to access the noumenal realm for knowledge. They do not believe that subjects are locked in the phenomenal realm. Spirituality as an ensemble of practices, inquiries, and experiences constitute both for the believers and for knowledge the price to be paid to have access to the truth.[34]

Epistemology is also linked to Christology through aesthetics as the norms to see things properly and in their appropriate worthiness. In the words of my colleague Robert Cummings Neville,

> The aesthetic dimension has to do with the norms for seeing things clearly, with understanding what matters, and what matters for what. The word *aesthetic* goes back to the Greek problematic of transforming the effects of all the things with which we interact into perceptions. Perception is an attainment, not a merely automatic natural condition, and good perception is difficult to attain.[35]

Pentecostals believe that commitment to Christ is sufficient to provide "the imagination for good perception," and to cause them "to perceive better, to make discriminations, to develop taste [sensibility, and style of thought] regarding what matters." Epistemology "is a struggle to come to better perception."[36]

Readers who have been paying close attention to our discussion on the connections between epistemology and Christology that Pentecostals create might be wondering how the nature of Christology (or Christ, for that matter) is carried into epistemology (decision-making or interpretation of reality). This concern or question is, perhaps, linked in the readers' mind to the truth of epistemological appropriation (of the symbols) of Christology (or Christ). What is carried across is not the *form* of Christology but the *value* of it. Pentecostals discern certain values in the life of Christ and its interpretations, and these values are carried over so that their intentional understanding of the decision-making process is "conformed to them, properly qualified."[37] Truth of the connection between epistemology and Christology lies in the carryover of values from Christology to (transform)

---

34. See Wariboko, *Nigerian Pentecostalism*, 42–43.
35. Neville, *Truth of Broken Symbols*, 220.
36. Neville, *Truth of Broken Symbols*, 220–21.
37. "Religious symbols are true if they transform people's practices so as to embody the religious object, properly qualified; they are true if they effect transformations in devotional life so that the soul becomes more and more conformed to the religious object, properly qualified. They are true if they carry over the values in the religious object so that the intentional understanding of the mind is conformed to them, properly qualified." Neville, *Truth of Broken Symbols*, 243.

epistemological practices and effect transformations in the believers' devotional life. The question for truth, Neville argues,

> is not whether a form is repeated but whether what is of worth in the thing is grasped by the interpreter. The form of that grasp in the interpreter's experience might be quite different from its form in the object interpreted. Surely the interpreter's form will be influenced by the purposes and contexts of interpretation, as well as by the forms of the interpreter's body, culture, and semiotic systems. . . . Truth is the carryover of value from the object into the interpreters' experience by means of signs, as qualified by the biological, cultural, semiotic, and purposive contexts of the interpreters.[38]

From the foregoing, readers might have also noticed that this book does not share the philosophical coordinates of the division between rationalist epistemology (sense) and religious epistemology ("spirit"). It is too simplistic and rigid. The book contests the division, showing that reason (sense) is an internal condition of spirit, and rationalism's firm hold on Pentecostals is much discernible when they feel most free and spiritual—feel most autonomous, distant from the grip of reason—in their everyday decisions. To make this point clearer, let me draw from Mladen Dolar's work refuting the false division between laughter and ideology. It is generally believed that ideological issues are serious, fanatical, and comedy is playful, helping citizens to keep a distance from the machinations of the assemblage of ideology. This line of argument goes on to say that through the use of irony and jokes comedy undermines the fanaticism of ideology. Dolar's point in the passage below is that this division is too simplistic and often laughter can serve the purpose of ideology, play the role of its internal condition.

> Laughter is a condition of ideology. It provides us with the distance, the very space in which ideology can take its full swing. It is only with laughter that we become ideological subjects, withdrawn from the immediate pressure of ideological claims to a free enclave. It is only when we laugh and breathe freely that ideology truly has its hold on us—it is only here that it starts functioning fully as ideology, with the specifically ideological means, which are supposed to assure our free consent and the appearance of spontaneity, eliminating the need for the non-ideological means of outside constraint.[39]

38. Neville, *Truth of Broken Symbols*, 240.
39. Dolar, *Voice and Nothing More*, 4.

Now let us replace laughter with spirit (it-makes-spirit) and ideology with sense (it-makes-sense) in the quotation above and you get the point that when Pentecostals think that they are free from sense, it is exactly when they are in its firmest grip. In this book I am tracing the various paths and movements of it-makes-sense to it-makes-spirit. I give voice and body in a variety of ways to the impasses and contradictions in the movement. The Pentecostal journey to it-makes-spirit starts from turning material and physical facts (knowledge) into pure discarnate spiritual knowledge. This book not only shows this movement; it illuminates the internal reverse movement of pure discarnate knowledge to its material, sensuous form. It-makes-sense is not the limit or the opposite of it-makes-spirit but its origin and power of being (sustenance, relevance). The power of it-makes-sense sets it-makes-spirit in motion, to begin with. The Pentecostal-celebrated turning of sense data into spiritual data and the unconscious turning of spiritual information into reason, material communal norms, are one and the same movement, driven by the split character (ontological incompleteness) of reality. Reality always adds up neatly—and always with a remainder. Reality is reality because it has an excess over itself. It is internally unstable.

Outline of Chapters

Chapter 1 ("Who Christ Is: Sermon on Encountering Christ as an *Event* of Knowledge") addresses who Christ is in the life of Pentecostals. Using the mode of sermon, it explores what Christ means for the behavior, comprehension of existence, and prehension of possibilities of human flourishing for persons who have already accepted him as their Lord and Savior. The chapter portrays Christ as the middle term of existence, the in-between space, the body that connects sense and spirit in Pentecostal livingness. Belief in Christ provides the access to or the passageway from the sensible (phenomenal) realm to the noumenal realm. As an in-between he simultaneously connects and disconnects the kingdom of sense from the kingdom of spirit. The importance of this chapter for the overall project of this book is that it demonstrates how Christ, the name Christ, or a group's appropriation of his two natures functions as an episteme, as a principled system of understanding the world, Christian spirituality, and decision-making. In the chapter we get preliminary hints about Christology becoming epistemology, and receive pointers to Pentecostal knowing or knowability as deeply christological. This kind of Christ-obliged epistemology simultaneously connects and disconnects Pentecostals from the general societal knowledge practices and sets up the tension expressed in "It does not make sense, but it makes spirit." Overall, this chapter makes a bold attempt to capture in philosophical language a form of everyday epistemology emanating from a people who know God's grace, embrace the mystery of God's way, and reckon the fear of God as the beginning of wisdom—all in the context of participating in Christ.[40] For Pentecostals, the born-again experience of Christ does not just result in new epistemology; it is new epistemology.

The discussions in chapter 1 are carried out within the Pentecostals' private domain of internal intelligibility within which they use local terms, rhetoric, and style of argument to address shared topics. Chapter 2 ("Exegeting the Sermon: Exploring the Depths of Pentecostal Thinking") takes the ideas of the private domain into the public and shows what they bear publicly on some of the concerns and language of philosophical theology. In this way, the chapter provides us with a perspective for integration with other discourses, and a common space to assess the justifiability or the philosophical density of the assertion "It does not make sense, but it makes spirit." This is an epistemological hypothesis that resonates with Christology as a frame of reference for reading and interpreting human existence or reality.

We can only approach the depths of the richness and fullness of this Christ-obliged epistemology if we take the time to learn the intricate, intimate, and (arguably) intrinsic connections between epistemology and Christology in everyday Pentecostal practices. The importance of Christology is that it reveals the character of Pentecostal mundane epistemology. For such an epistemology, the world comes to it in the light crystal of Christ's life and it is returned as assumable truths to the eager hearts of believers. In very simple terms, chapter 3 ("This Is Not a Christology: Writing Epistemology as the Christological Turn") demonstrates the christological enframing of Pentecostal epistemology. To ordinary Pentecostals, one of the offices of Christ "is to cheer, to raise, and to guide [Christians] by showing them facts [what really counts as knowledge, episteme, wisdom] amidst appearances [and opinions]."[41]

Chapter 4 ("Sense and Spirit: The Dialogical Imagination in Pentecostal Thought") is the heart of this book. It shows how Pentecostals struggle to know what really counts and discern spiritual wisdom amidst appearances of sense. For ordinary Pentecostals, sense (knowledge based on Enlightenment rationalism) is interpreted as *inertia*. Sense (worldly knowledge, merely phenomenal understanding of situation or existence) tends to remain dominant, in force, or in its self-sufficient motion unless deflected by

---

40. Pardon the allusion to Barth, *Church Dogmatics*, 1/1:422.
41. Emerson, "American Scholar," 162.

countervailing spiritual (divine, noumenal) knowledge, wisdom. The degree of power of sense is measured by the spiritual power required to overthrow its control or deflect its self-referential inertial motion. "It does not make sense, but it makes spirit" is a paean to *coup d'état*, to the overthrow of the power of sense, so to speak. But does the (supposedly) powerful blow against the state of worldly knowledge liberate Pentecostals from the "ungodly" grip of sense? Not exactly! Our study reveals that while the primary desires for good decisions are not in the thralldom of Enlightenment rationalism, the secondary desires or the means of actualizing or executing the decisions themselves are. Pentecostals appear to be trapped in a circle: phenomenal (sense) data must be transformed into noumenal data, spiritual insights, and then translated back into improved, enlarged, expanded sense data to work in the material world. More importantly, it seems to me that the whole practice of *it-does-not-make-sense-but-it-makes-spirit* is a form of giving and exchanging of reasons by members of a community. The resort to *it-makes-spirit* happens as a way of justifying an action, offering reasons for decisions made, appealing to communal standards of acceptable behavior. The meaning of *it-does-not-make-sense-but it-makes-spirit* is always negotiated in interactions, rather than settled ahead of its utterance and outside of interaction rituals. In all this, we begin to see an incipient democratic process of Pentecostal citizens in their own communities (polities) generating and addressing reasons to themselves for the sake of the organization of collective life and human flourishing. It-makes-spirit, indeed, brings Pentecostals to the borders of secular justification of arguments. The chapter challenges us to consider that the real animating force of the statement or hypothesis may lie in the inherent exchange of defeasible reasons in a democratic culture. It-makes-spirit, as it will be demonstrated later, is a nascent path to public reason, at least within the Pentecostal community. Will this incipient path ever come to fruition? I cannot tell today but let us keep hope alive.

The concluding chapter is titled "Unconcluding Provocations." The arguments in the previous chapters bring us to the realization that there is a "third term" (precisely, a context of mutual relevance) between sense and spirit, and it is discourse (language).[42] Pentecostals have ignored it as they pitted spirit against sense as if the relationships between the two are immediate. Pentecostals, like all other human beings, can only think and grasp the world through language or discursive practices—whether they are concerned with matter (sense) or with spirit (or inner sphere of consciousness)—and thus it is difficult for them to disentangle the decisions

---

42. See Neville, *Highroad around Modernism*, 266–68. The phrase "context of mutual relevance" is no doubt a crude reference to his insightful "ontological context of mutual relevance."

they make via sense (world) from decisions they believe derive from a realm otherwise than commonly available or accessible sensorium. So, in the end, what makes sense or makes spirit is subject to the interpretation of a community of believers conscious of the Word of God and submissive to the Holy Spirit, as the American theologian Amos Yong taught us.[43]

Yong's triad of Spirit-Word-Community speaks to a deep sense of order that governs Pentecostals' seemingly spontaneous expressions of truths or the variety of their effervescent interpretations. It-makes-spirit as an expression draws its deepest meaning from an underlying biblical worldview. James K. A. Smith lays out this biblical worldview as an ontological claim that informs Pentecostal thinking and counters the "shutdown naturalism of modernity."[44] Esther Acolatse has eminently described this worldview or ontological claim and named it as "biblical realism."[45] The social practice of biblical realism is the grammar that gives coherence and meaning to it-makes-spirit as an expression. Before Yong, Smith, and Acolatse, James Loder hinted about it-makes-spirit with his notions of convictional knowing and logic of the spirit.[46]

All these interpretations do not even address the difficult issue of discernment of spirits. What spirit is the spirit in it-makes-spirit? Are we always certain about who or what it/he/she is?[47] Even if the spirit is the Holy Spirit there would still be some tensions relating to any celebration of it-makes-spirit as the distinguishing mark of authentic decisions by spirit-filled believers. There is always this background question: Are Pentecostals who are (unduly) vested in *it-makes-spirit* not turning the Holy Spirit into a resource for their own use in decision-making or into a magic mirror for reading off best decisions? We should all remind ourselves not to forget that it-makes-spirit is a hypothesis that interprets social reality or senses and is itself subject to correction, requiring the testing of the spirits, and should not be made to technologize God's Spirit. More importantly, we hope that Pentecostals will cognize that the "make" in their *it-makes-spirit* does not refer to any of the three forms of power used to change people's behavior:

---

43. Yong, *Spirit, Word, Community*.

44. Smith, *Thinking in Tongues*. This ontological claim, according to Smith, is the fundamental conviction that the Spirit of God that animated early Christians is still active among Pentecostals, speaking to them, surprising them, healing them, and manifesting God's presence in their midst.

45. Acolatse, *Powers, Principalities and the Spirit*.

46. Loder, *The Transforming Moment*; Loder, *The Logic of the Spirit*.

47. Wariboko, *Split God*, 45–64; Wariboko, *Nigerian Pentecostalism*, 116–41, 262–64.

force (coercion), persuasion, and incentives (bargaining).[48] The "make" means attunement to the Spirit of Christ; it is about *letting* the mind that was in Christ *be* in the believer (Phil 2:5–8). To make spirit is *letting-be*.

A Word on Style of Presentation of Arguments

I have written the chapters in a format and style that situates them between what is accessible to plain nonphilosophic educated laypersons and practitioners of the philosophic discipline. I provide lay readers with conceptual and argumentative resources to better articulate Pentecostal beliefs and practices. For professional philosophers, this work invites them to examine the convictions and assumptions that they bring to the "reading" of Pentecostalism and to redefine their own assessments of the movement in the light of the strength of the arguments that I advance. To this group and other scholars, I also crave their indulgence if they find that I have not referenced all the relevant published writings on the subject. I have limited myself because I do not want to write an impossibly long book and I want to keep the level of discourse accessible to seminarians and graduate students in religious studies, even as I tilt toward some specialized academic inquiry or philosophical theorizing.

"I am all too aware of having attempted both too much and too little."[49] Too little because I have not exhaustively engaged the philosophical literature on epistemology. Too much because some of the depths I have plumbed to elucidate the connections between everyday religious practice and implicit Pentecostal philosophical theorizing might be considered a tad too sophisticated to the workaday Pentecostal. I will adjudge this work to be successful if it enables scholars, lay readers, and Pentecostals to pose heretofore unasked questions about Pentecostalism. I did not set out to produce a "system" or holistic construct of Pentecostal philosophy.

My books—especially this one—are never intended to be well-rounded, systematically staged monologic wholes. They are an ever becoming, developing idea.[50] I try as much as possible not to impose a single authoritative voice on them. They (precisely, my entire body of work and not individual books) are constituted as fundamentally polyphonic, dialogical, and unfinalizable. I have created them as characters independent of myself. They are points of view on the world. Together, they are polyphonically Pentecostal; none coincides with itself, each a play on freedom and unfinalizability of a

---

48. Grant, *Strings Attached*.
49. MacIntyre, *Ethics in the Conflicts of Modernity*, xii.
50. Bakhtin, *Problems of Dostoevsky's Poetics*, xxxiv.

point of view, opinion on the world and self. None of the books should be construed as sacrificing its full and valid open-endedness, dialogical penchant for the sake of monologic philosophic design. Each is best viewed as a participation in an ongoing dialogue. Mikhail Bakhtin's words on how dialogism plays out in Fyodor Dostoevsky's novels will serve to illuminate the point I am trying to make:

> Dostoevsky's novel is dialogic. It is constructed not as the whole of a single consciousness, absorbing other consciousnesses as objects into itself, but as a whole formed by the interaction of several consciousnesses, none of which entirely becomes an object for the other. . . . Not only does the novel give no firm support outside the rupture-prone world of dialogue for a third, monologically all-encompassing consciousness—but on the contrary, everything in the novel is structured to make dialogic opposition inescapable.[51]

While in my previous books the dialogic quality of thought was not always explicit, in this book it is so. In discussing Pentecostal epistemology through the lens of decision-making organized around the tag "it-makes-spirit," I have presented various viewpoints without drawing them into my own conception of the truth or forcing all viewpoints (consciousnesses) into a coherent system of thought. It appears just when I am about to lead the reader to a position that sums up or affirms the Pentecostal worldview, I turn the table against it. And when the reader is about to dismiss the Pentecostal worldview as déclassé, not akin to any respectable academic philosophy, I demonstrate its affinity, kinship, family resemblance with the work of a rigorous philosopher. Readers who are used to systematic, coherently woven presentations of philosophical-theological topics may consider this lean toward heteroglossia and unfinalizability a weakness, a mark of a divided authorial mind. "Instead of imagining a deeply divided authorial mind, half-consciously struggling with contradictory convictions or emotions and betraying this inner division in a confused text, we have a text that *consciously* writes out the to and fro of dialogue, always alerting us to the dangers of staying with or believing what we have just heard."[52]

I would say I have made the presentation of arguments or viewpoints polyphonic. I have made conflicting viewpoints stand on their own, independent, and in opposition to one another, with the hope that this method gives us a fuller revelation of it-makes-spirit as the ground and tool of Pentecostal decision-making. I want the reader, especially those who are not familiar

---

51. Bakhtin, *Problems of Dostoevsky's Poetics*, 18.
52. Williams, *Dostoevsky*, 3.

with Pentecostal style of thought, to know that there is no single consciousness or viewpoint on the meaning, use, and operations of it-makes-spirit; rather, there are multiple, independent consciousnesses. It-makes-spirit is a spiritual capacity, but it appears in plural forms among Pentecostals. A believer does not learn or utter it-makes-spirit, but *a* it-makes-spirit so it becomes an insight for a situation (decision) in a distinctive and particular manner. "That which is common to all is achieved only in ways that are not common to all."[53] Let us put this in more theological language, before turning to Bakhtin and his conception of polyphony as a style of philosophic argumentation. The Spirit is a common blessing to all, for the manifestation of the common good, as Paul reminds us in 1 Corinthians 12:7, but it alights differently, in diverse forms among the believers. No one possesses the Holy Spirit as her own exclusive property, nor does anyone possess all of the Spirit's gifts, potentialities, and actualizations. One possesses a gift or gifts of the Spirit, and so becomes a believer with distinctive and particular gifts. So the manifestation of it-makes-spirit "is achieved in ways that are not common to all." Describing Dostoevsky as the master of dialogism, which Bakhtin considers to be fundamental to the understanding of truth and human relationship, he states that

> *a plurality of independent and unmerged voices and consciousnesses, a genuine polyphony of fully valid voices is in fact the chief characteristic of Dostoevsky's novels*. What unfolds in his works is not a multitude of characters and fates in a single objective world, illuminated by a single authorial consciousness; rather *a plurality of consciousnesses, with equal rights and each with its own world*, combine but are not merged in the unity of the event.[54]

It-makes-sense assimilates the encyclopaedia variety and plenitude of impulses, opposing voices, and forces of decision-making to form a preexisting coherent framework. It-makes-spirit by contrast revels in fluid sociological puddings of everyday life, discursive asymmetries, immediacy of sensorial diversity, and a certain hermeneutic open-endedness in living contact with uncongealed present time-space fabric. Hence it-makes-spirit is a testament of an evolving resistance against the sociohistorical category of Enlightenment rationality, a witness to a transcript that the human cannot be incarnated in any epistemological category. As Mikhail Bakhtin writes,

---

53. Norton, "Pentecost," 397.
54. Bakhtin, *Problems of Dostoevsky's Poetics*, 6 (emphasis in the original).

> An individual cannot be completely incarnated into the flesh of existing sociohistorical categories. There is no mere form that would be able to incarnate once and forever all of his human possibilities and needs, no form in which he could exhaust himself down to the last word . . . no form that he could fill to the very brim, and yet at the same time not splash over the brim. There always remains an unrealized surplus of humanness. . . . All existing clothes are always too tight, and thus comical, on a man. But the surplus of un-fleshed out humanness may be realized not only in the [regnant paradigm, but also in other points of view]. Reality as we have it [in the Enlightenment model of rationality or even in the Pentecostal worldview] is only one of many possible realities. It is not inevitable, not arbitrary, it bears within itself other possibilities.[55]

Bakhtin's statement bespeaks of the *Pentecostal principle*, the human capacity to begin, to resist confinement of actualization of potentialities, or to refuse any fixed destiny for human becoming.[56] The Pentecostal principle is an indispensable component of any effort to decipher or to adequately comprehend it-makes-spirit. The inherent features of the Pentecostal principle that are discernible in it-makes-spirit are heteroglossia, a multiplicity of discernment styles, and a reaching out for the new. It-makes-spirit enacts a dialogical sense (performance, comprehension) of empirical data and its interpretations as a text. By their ethos of it-makes-spirit and by the means of it-makes-spirit, Pentecostals in their behavior and cognition enact the peculiar transformation of the monologism of Enlightenment rationality to produce a polyphony of responses, multiplicity of interpretative styles.

As we now prepare to turn the page to chapter 1 (which is a transcript of an oral sermon on the theme of this book), let me sound a note of warning. Some readers may conclude that in it I departed from scholarly objectivity and detachment when I was speaking to a Pentecostal congregation in a New York church. This conclusion may arise not from the quality of the ideas discussed in the sermon-lecture, but, I suppose, from its rhetorical style. To the academic ear, the conversational style feels a bit "clumsy" in contrast to the sophistication of the rest of the prose in the book. I crave the indulgence of such delicate readers; for I was, indeed, conveying deep philosophical-theological ideas in a typical Pentecostal preacher's language. I was working from the inside resources of Pentecostal tradition, culture, and age-old resistance to orthodox Christianity to configure the meaning of Christ and the usual Pentecostalist claims to *know* him for members of a

55. Bakhtin, *Dialogical Imagination*, 37
56. Wariboko, *The Pentecostal Principle*.

congregation, so that each member can identify themselves in the common construction.

The chapter is "so Pentecostal" in the sense that the version of "Christology" that informs or undergirds Pentecostal epistemology, which it is highlighting, is rooted in experience. Christology is posited as believers' understanding and appropriation of the meaning of Christ's life in the light of their everyday lives. Everyday Pentecostal Christology, among the other million things that it can do, is in the service of epistemology—but it is also its directional principle. Epistemology is *"the power of a historical reality, grasped in"* christological frames.[57] For everyday Pentecostals Christology *"contains the possibility of making understandable"* old and new realizations of potentialities of a person, institution, sociality, event, opportunity or a historical origin.[58] The epistemic frame of Christology when applied to analyze "any historical, social, cultural or political phenomenon" enables Pentecostals to apprehend "its power, inner drive, potentiality, teleology, and the potential for transformation."[59]

Before we actually turn to chapter 1, there is an interlude that explains how continential philosophy is used as a methodological tool in this book and how it is pressed into the service of Pentecostal sensibility and ways of argumentation.

---

57. Tillich, *Socialist Decision*, 10.
58. Tillich, *Socialist Decision*, 9.
59. Meditz, *Dialectic of the Holy*, 79.

Interlude
Continental Thought and Pentecostal Theology

It-does-not-make-sense-but-it-makes-spirit is at once a response to the rationalist spirit and a symptom of its own abjected other.[1]

INTRODUCTION: A CRITIQUE OF PENTECOSTAL REASON

THE SUBJECT OF HOW conservative Christians experience God and how that experience and relationship with God shape their everyday life, precisely their decision-making process, has recently gained momentum in the academy. Tanya M. Luhrmann's *When God Talks Back* is a key book in this regard, to mention only a celebrated example of the genre in the field of anthropology. She investigates how God becomes real for modern people like American evangelicals in the midst of overwhelming modernist skepticism.[2] For evangelicals God is so personal and real that they feel a "foundational certainty" (her own words) about information received from the supernatural realm.

> The technical term for it is *noetic*: a sense of knowing somehow deeper than everyday knowledge, bedrock rather than topsoil. And the story of absolute knowing is often told in this way: I knew it was true, and then I found out it was. For those who tell these stories, the evidential confirmation ... stands as testimony to the real point of the story, which is that the sense of certainty preceded its confirmation.[3]

1. This epigraph is written by the author of this book.
2. Luhrmann, *When God Talks Back*.
3. Luhrmann, *When God Talks Back*, 58.

One of the key questions that guided her research is this: Why would millions of Christians consider the evidence of their senses wrong because of their faith in God, a being they consider real and personal?[4] Her response is that they have or believe to have a personal relationship with God. Luhrmann attends to the question and its attendant response with the methods of psychological anthropology.

I attend to the polarizing question through the lens of philosophical theology and I limit my attention to Pentecostals, who are not necessarily evangelicals. I deploy philosophical methods to one of their faith-affirming statements, "It does not make sense, but it makes spirit," to see whether it makes sense or not, is coherent or not, or, more importantly, to understand and explain it theologically (philosophically). The statement that invites my philosophical attention is not so much a rule (vague or not) to guide discernment as it is a justificatory warrant for the claim that a personal decision is based on faith in Christ, and that the decision is valid in relation to the believer's experience of a real and personal Savior. (The justificatory warrant in this situation should not be mistaken for "public" or "civic" reason.[5])

---

4. Luhrmann, *When God Talks Back*, xii.

5. Pentecostals in this book now have a somewhat passable philosophical analysis of their reasoning process and all others can now evaluate it for all that it is worth. The analysis is made without caricaturing them, without saying they are stupid to think in a particular way, and now the next stage in their history and political process is how to move toward public reason. (I dream!) In my ethical, philosophical scholarship I have emphasized the giving of public reason in the public square. I was doing this before I turned some of my attention to Pentecostal studies. One thing I have always emphasized is that in the public square we must all come to it, not naked but fully clothed—that is, with our own identities and interests, but we must be ready to make our persuasive arguments on the basis of publicly accessible reasons. I have made similar arguments for Pentecostals engaging in the public square in my 2012 book *The Pentecostal Principle: Ethical Methodology in New Spirit* (chapter 3). This book (*The Pentecostal Hyothesis*) is doing a different kind of job: it is only an attempt to demonstrate a path of meaning and reason within the Pentecostal tradition.

Scholars in other traditions, such as Islam, are also grappling with this issue of civic or public reason for certain classes of adherents of their faith traditions. Professor Abdullahi Ahmed An-Na'im makes this point by defining what he means by "civic reason" for Muslims:

> The separation of Islam and the state does not prevent Muslims from proposing policy or legislation stemming from their religious or other beliefs. All citizens have the right to do so, provided they should support such proposals with what I call "civic reason." The word "civic" here refers to the need for policy and legislation to be accepted by the public at large, as well as for the process of reasoning on the matter to remain open and accessible to all citizens. By civic reason, I mean that the rationale and the purpose of public policy or legislation must be based on the sort of reasoning that most citizens can accept or reject. Citizens must be able

The statement does more. The statement is a re-cognition of the fact that the person has taken a risk in faith, consciously violating common sense. The aphorism also enables the person espousing it to *do* something with her words: she attempts to convince whoever is listening to her to live his life in (increased) imitation of Jesus Christ or to invite a person to take his own risk in faith. If the person could learn to pattern his whole life after Christ and to take a risk in faith in Christ, then his way of knowing and being could become the vehicle by which the supernatural wisdom of Christ enters his everyday decision-making process and transfigures facts.

In the contrast between sense and spirit I discern an interpretation of fact as on one hand a fait accompli, the what is, or fulfilled situation, and on the other as the very potentiality-to-be of a situation. Pentecostals discern every situational fact with a "surplus always exterior to [its] totality," as though fact or sense does not fill out the "true measure of [the] being" of a situation.[6] They hold that it-makes-sense pertains to inclining people to accomplished facts. It-makes-spirit orients believers to the transfiguring power of Christ, to the Son of God who is the hope of the world, to the One who will be (Exod 3), and to the possibility of realizing the impossible (Matt 10). Spirit is not the mere contrary of sense but rather the existence and renewal of possibility itself. Owing to these insights, I suggest that we translate the aphorism "It does not make sense, but it makes spirit" into more inclusive language in this manner: Life does not create limits but creates the possibility-to-be.[7]

The aphorism in a way signals the playfulness of Pentecostalism as a religion.[8] The believer's serious imagination of God as master of the universe and her earnest expectation of finding answers to prayers are playfully set in the context of "free activity," layered between the hard reality of ordinary life and a spiritually accessible world of infinite possibilities. This in-between is a space of "epistemological double register: real but not real, not real but more than real, absolutely real for all time but not just real in

---

to make counterproposals through public debate without being open to charges about their religious piety. Civic reason and reasoning, and not personal beliefs and motivations, are necessary whether Muslims constitute the majority or the minority of the population of the state. Even if Muslims are the majority, they will not necessarily agree on what policy and legislation should follow from their Islamic beliefs (*Islam and the Secular State*, 7–8).

6. The two quotations are from Levinas, *Totality and Infinity*, 23.
7. This paragraph was stimulated by Kearney, *The God Who May Be*.
8. For discussions of religion as play, see Wariboko, *Pentecostal Principle*, 72–100.

[this] moment.... [T]his playfulness enhances the complexity of the belief commitment that [Pentecostals] make."[9]

In the light of these multiple layers of the aphorism's meaning, I do not approach it merely as a philosophical specimen of deluded minds, but on Pentecostals' own terms. My analysis is resistant to easy, dismissive attitudes and scornful stereotypes of rationalists without foregoing the necessary scholarly distance that conduces to richly probing analytical discourse.

This text is ultimately a critique of Pentecostal reason. My point of access to this subject is epistemology as it intersects with everyday Pentecostals' belief in who Jesus Christ is. I hope to describe their thinking as clearly and closely as possible as they would like to state it if they had the same tools and philosophical language as I do. I will then offer an internal critique. This criticism comes in many forms, including (a) showing that the Pentecostal form of reasoning is not ready for public policy discourse in a pluralistic society; (b) showing that even as private as they think their reason is it has some elements of the social as it is developing some "public reason character" within the Pentecostal community; (c) suggesting that not everything that "makes no sense" automatically makes spirit—Pentecostalism is, indeed, not a war against the reasoning mind, even as Pentecostals maintain that their full humanity exceeds the so-called "reasoning mind"; (d) maintaining that within a certain interpretative lens the statement could be interpreted as a "spiritualization" of ignorance; and (e) making the argument that the scholars that write Pentecostal theology have been writing in ways that do not really reflect the "wisdom" or otherwise of the folk on the ground. There is a riot out there! But scholars have been writing sanitized versions of the folks' theology and I want to lay bare before them the real "story" with all its shock value. I aspire to do this not because I am a better thinker but because I am not beholden to their standards of scholarship. Everyday Pentecostal theology is shocking to the academic mind and to many other minds, such that even many an uppity Pentecostal theologian struggles to sanitize it for the religious academy. If the typical academic reader is "shocked" by Pentecostal reason as described in this book, then I have succeeded a bit in the sense of capturing some of what is going on among ordinary Pentecostal folk. I believe that it is only when we take them seriously at face value that we can actually reveal their mindset to all of us, scholars and non-scholars, and hope to engage them in the public square of any deliberative democracy.

The preceding paragraph might prompt some worries or fears in some of my readers. Thus, this is the point where this writer must deploy the word "lest" to save his skin, to parry some of the inevitable arrows that are aimed

---

9. Luhrmann, *When God Talks Back*, 100.

at him. I will take refuge in two "lests." Lest any Pentecostal theologian accuse me of being blind to my own sins when I talk about uppity Pentecostal theologians, let me acknowledge who and what I am. Some of them might consider my continental philosophy–laden Pentecostal studies books as evidence of an "uppity Pentecostal philosopher" or "uppity Pentecostal social ethicist." Others might argue that even my claim to write Pentecostal stories (theologies) from the ground up while ensconced in a prestigious academic chair of social ethics in a first-class university is elitist—not to mention my training in Ivy league institutions and the acquired sophisticated style of writing. I am not ignorant of all this. I am a sinner, guilty as charged! But I want you to hear my plea for your merciful judgment. There is a crucial difference between my work and those of the Guild Pentecostal theology—at least, so I hope. Believe me, I am trying to capture the riotous or subversive Pentecostal theology on the ground, warts and all, with the best of my skills. The guild theologians are trying to use the best of the skills they have to write Pentecostal theology as a clone of respectable, establishment, cohesive in-group, mainline denominational theologies, seeking to smoothen the rough edges of the shocking, abrasive, unpalatable Pentecostal theologies at the popular ground level. Do not get me wrong, I love what they do; the only problem is that I do not have the temperament to do what they do. (More on this "lovers' quarrel" about the direction of Pentecostal theology later.)

Lest again I give the impression that this book, as a critique of Pentecostal reason, is overwhelmingly negative or overly concerned with bringing Pentecostals into the rigors of deliberative reason. It is rather a radical affirmation of Pentecostal reason as a mode of discourse, accentuating its distinctive features and contributions to the spirituality of everyday Pentecostal folk. Here the word "critique" is akin to the sense Martin Heidegger has used it, rather to his interpretation of Kant's understanding of critique. In *What Is a Thing*, he writes, "We are accustomed to hearing something overwhelmingly negative whenever this word is mentioned. For us, to criticize means to find fault, to tally mistakes, to point out shortcomings, and to dismiss what is thereby found wanting. We must try to distance ourselves from this customary and misleading meaning when faced with the title *Critique of Reason*."[10] He goes further to state that

> "critique" comes from the Greek *krinein*, which means "to sort," "to sort out," and thus "lift out that special sort" . . . "Critique," far from being something negative, designates the most positive positivity, the positing of what must be put in place before everything else as the determining and decisive agency. Critique

10. Heidegger, *What Is a Thing?*, 118.

is thus decision in this pre-positional sense. Only in consequence of this, because to criticize means to select and to bring out what is special, uncommon, and at the same time measure-giving, is it also to reject what is commonplace and unsuitable.[11]

This affirmation or critique of Pentecostal reason should not be construed for what it is not. This book as a whole does not suggest to the reader to accept Pentecostal reason as equivalent to (Enlightenment) reason qua reason.[12] It is only an attempt to demonstrate a path of meaning and reason within the Pentecostal tradition. Pentecostal reason is highly stylized but it is embraceable, graspable, through the grasping of one of its spiritualities. The epistemology of Pentecostals inclines them to risk sense-knowledge "precisely at moments of unknowingness, when what forms [them rationally] diverges from what lies before [them], when their willingness to become undone in relation to" sense-certainty (or modern imaginary) constitutes their chance of becoming Pentecostal.[13] Here I have adapted or resituated philosopher Judith Butler's description of the ethical task to Pentecostal spiritual (epistemological) imagination. I do this precisely because it appears to me that the spiritual imagination is an important element of the ethical stance of Pentecostals. This is not to suggest that Pentecostal empathetic or spiritual imagining can be substituted for public rationality or be allowed to trump rule-governed moral reasoning in deliberative democracies.

Rightly or wrongly, I have found a lot of good resources in continental philosophy in my endeavors to explore this dialogue (which is at once ethical, epistemological, and theological) between faith and reality at its deepest level in many of my books. Continental philosophy also equips my scholarship to affirm and unsettle Pentecostal epistemology, which in a sense is Will to Spirit as Knowledge. Epistemology takes place in decision. There is, in addition, the decision of epistemology. This twofold positioning of epistemology, the doubling of epistemology, is the presencing and presentation of the Will to Spirit, the power of being. There is another dimension to Pentecostal epistemology: it is a sort of homecoming, interpreted as a dwelling between the Rock of Salvation and the nothing. In the midst of uncertainty, unforgiving modernist rationalism, and confusing postmodern relativism, turning to Christ as the source of stability and ballast of knowability

11. Heidegger, *What Is a Thing?*, 119.

12. Professor Ebenezer Obadare urged me to make this point clearly.

13. Butler, *Giving an Account of Ourselves*, 136. I have crudely adapted Butler's account of what ethics requires of us. She writes, "Ethics requires us to risk ourselves precisely at moments of unknowingness, when what forms us diverges from what lies before us, when our willingness to become undone in relation to others constitutes our chance of becoming human" (136).

is reassuring. Epistemology (that is, the christologically inflected one) is a shelter above the abyss or bewildering confusion. In a sense, Pentecostals think of epistemology spatially.

The spatial mapping of epistemology is a reference not to the structural arrangement of known, unknown, and justification of knowledge, but a gesture of symbolizing or internalizing the fundamental "slash" in Jesus's body, humanity/divinity. As will be explained later, the hybridity of Jesus Christ intervenes in Pentecostals' epistemology through anamorphosis, preventing their way of knowing from stabilizing itself into the symbolic structure of modernist epistemology, destabilizing them from rationalism's stabilizing harmonious whole. The name of Jesus Christ or the disposition toward it represents the traumatic core, the fundamental antagonism, in the social relations between Pentecostals and contemporary regnant forms of rationalism. With me, all this advances the possibilities or my scholarly inclination for a philosophical thinking of Pentecostalism.[14]

Continental Philosophy as a Methodological Assist

The rest of this interlude sketches the arguments for my employment of continental philosophy as the theoretical, polyphonic, transdisciplinary framework that undergirds or funds my reflections, imaginations, and discourses on Pentecostal christologically inflected epistemology. Christologically inflected should not be construed to mean Christology by any stretch of the imagination. I advise the reader to avoid the temptation to read this book as a theological or doctrinal argument about Jesus Christ. Although it appears to link Christology to epistemology, it is not really about Christology. At best, it is Christopraxis of Christopathy and the epistemological in this respect is not about the *that* of knowing, but the *how* (the performative dimension) of knowing which is affective, emotive, and an embodied practice. This book in this way puts Jesus back into the center of Pentecostal imaginary without being a christological text, and thus extending the Pentecostal pneumatological discussion in surprising generative ways.[15] At the

14. Ebenezer Babatunde Obadare read the first draft of the manuscript for this book with utmost care. He pointed to me areas that needed clarification and suggested ways of strengthening my arguments. This section of the interlude called "introduction" was prompted by his questions.

15. I thank Amos Yong for helping me to articulate this important contribution of the book. He read the first draft of the manuscript and urged me to highlight this insight of the book. Yong also pointed me to the language of Christopraxis and Christopathy. I would also like to thank Robert Neville, who likewise read the first draft. Their promptings and queries are the immediate causes for writing this interlude to

heart of this study is the thesis that it is Christ who is informing (who is at the center of) Pentecostal epistemology, like the way the cathedral, usually the tallest building and spiritual center of the town, informed Christians in the medieval period.

The book is not on Jesus Christ *per se*, not about the historicity of Jesus but his present functioning in a particular mode of Pentecostal epistemology. In discussing who Christ is in this book there is a great deal of focus about how he functions in Pentecostal epistemology but not much about who he is or was as a person. Thus, there is no unified "sensed"[16] argument about Christ, as the focus is on how Pentecostal epistemology works through the formula "It does not make sense, but it makes spirit." There is a reason why the presentation of the Pentecostal mode of epistemology and its lapidary formula do not follow the style of a unified "sensed" argument as we usually find in a straightforward academic style. The Pentecostal hypothesis (or Pentecostal hypotenuse?[17]) cannot be stated directly—at least I could not

---

better acquaint readers about the role of continental philosophy in this book.

16. This is a play on the aphorism, it-does-not-make-sense-but-it-makes-spirit.

17. The Pentecostal hypotenuse is an alternative way of expressing the ideas of the Pentecostal hypothesis through some rudimentary mathematical language. What I mean by the Pentecostal hypotenuse comes from the intersection of Christology and hard social reality and in turn it is their conditioning element. When the gears of Christology mesh with social reality together they cast a long shadow on Pentecostal reason (thought, thinking, reasoning). I will name this shadow as hypotenuse.

The word "hypotenuse" as used here comes from the geometry of the right triangle. It is the line that connects the vertical and horizontal lines that meet at the base to form a 90-degree angle. Imagine two poles, one standing straight and the other on the floor; bring them together, and they meet at an angle. Then get a third pole to connect the top of the vertical pole to the other end of the horizontal pole, and voila, you have a right triangle. The third pole is the hypotenuse and it basically means "stretch" or "to stretch below." The hypotenuse is the side of the triangle opposite the right angle. According to the famous Pythagorean theorem, the length of the third pole is calculated as the square root of the sum of the squares of the other two sides, or the square of the hypotenuse is the sum of the squares of the two sides.

The Pentecostal hypothesis is like the hypotenuse that stretches to cover the two ends of Christology and social reality to form a triangular explanatory framework. The hypotenuse is the way of seeing and knowing that reflects the real or expected right practice (orthopraxis and orthopathos of Pentecostal spirituality) that forms at the intersection of faith in Christ and the Pentecostal Christians' responses to hard realities of social existence.

Christ(ology) is imbricated in the hypotenuse in two ways. He is the savior of those who are the creators and bearers of the hypothesis. The hypothesis is an expression of faith in him as Lord and savior. Second, his hybrid nature as God Man, his divine/human body, informs the very character of the hypotenuse as a connector between sense and spirit, noetic knowing and everyday knowledge. Social reality is also present in the hypotenuse in double intensity. First, the hypotenuse is an attempt to explain, predict, and control social reality. Second, the hypothesis is part of the tools that help

discern a better way to state it directly. At a distance the Pentecostal hypothesis offers itself as a glorious, alluring, desirable object of immense beauty, but as you draw closer to touch its voluptuous enspirited self it slips through your fingers. It now offers itself only in shape-shifting, fleeting, transfinite profiles. I have chosen to shed light on this enigmatic mode of epistemology and its semiopaque formula through many discussions, many angles, and many different literatures, working by analogy among them. This way of exposition mirrors what I take to be the Pentecostal way ("how") of knowing. So, I have deliberatively adopted a Bakhtinian, polyphonic style of dialogue to draw explicit attention to the ways pluralistic, multi-voiced forms of arguments (could) exhibit Pentecostal epistemology (sensibility). The mind of the everyday Pentecostal, as Pentecostal qua Pentecostal, in making decisions does not cherish the straightforward academic style of argumentation. For an example, let us bring into focus a Pentecostal preacher delivering a message. The message involves stories of characters and events operating at a high symbolic level. The natural and supernatural forces in the stories are commingled to enable human beings to perform unimaginable feats. Usually such a message carries a high emotive charge, which overflows to the audience. The preacher bears the burden of generating, sustaining, and appropriately controlling the emotional reaction to his narrative, of controlling other disruptions so as not to be diverted from his logic or the development path of his story.

This logic is not always temporal, not that of a sequentially unfolding narrative. It is often a spatial one; the oral narrative is a map in which relations and meanings are tied together by their placement both in the performance and the virtual landscape that the preacher "talks" into being. In this mixing of logics, time and history, space and lateral connections are made to flow together, without any one of them occupying a privileged position. This kind of oral literature resists attempts to classify them according to any

---

to constitute the constructed social reality of Pentecostals. The Pentecostal hypotenuse stands opposite Christology and social reality not as a simple unit but as a complex, "squared" process itself, a kind of constituting and constituted power of imagination. It is product (sum) of Christology and social reality, some interpretative lens generated at the intersection of the two. Or, rather, it is the stretch of imagination that connects the objective (social reality) and subjective (trust in Christ, who Christ is) dimensions of faith. The Pentecostal hypotenuse is not a mere outcome of Christology and social reality. It also frames how Pentecostals understand or interpret Christ(ology) and social reality.

The Pentecostal hypotenuse is in this sense reflexive, recursively reflexive, dialogical, circular, and correlational. I should immediately add that neither the Pentecostal hypothesis nor the Pentecostal hypotenuse is a complete description or explanation of the Pentecostal mindset. Each of them is merely a heuristic device to help us understand a small part of the worldview, pattern of thought, or lived experience of Pentecostals.

schema such as space-time logic, stylistic criteria, or character of speech act as the performance refuses easy conformity to a single type (trope).[18] I am attempting to capture this style in this book by the way I present the arguments and exposition of the discourse. I am deliberately submitting the text to the polyphony (cacophony?) of Pentecostal life to be "haunted" by the spectral weight of linguistic code-switching, or rather tongue-switching. This Pentecostal style could be annoying to those who are used to straightforward academic writing that proceeds in a linear, rigid, logical fashion. It takes some openness to the other to appreciate the truth of Pentecostal epistemology, which is wedded to and made through contradictions, unorthodox theology, dynamic inner tensions of spirituality, and transfer of religious energy to intellectual issues. By adopting the Pentecostal preacherly rhythms and presentations, I transfer the necessary vital tensions between spiritual reality and intellectual (logical, rational) vision to these pages. This book itself is a site of Pentecostal epistemology, a discourse written on (or as) the site of a Pentecostal polyphony. This transference, this manifestation of the sensibility (certain ethos) of the fire-spitting "dotard" of a Pentecostal preacher in your personal reading space, may jar your sensitive intellectual lobes—and I apologize. Too many of their type are gradually making themselves and their unauthorized styles visible in the theological academy that once loathed them and is still loath to accept them fully. Forgive me, I am one of them, sinners in the academy—of whom I am chief.

The mind of this group of sinners, Pentecostal qua Pentecostal, does not cherish the rigid academic style of strictly staying in your lane of argument. They float through boundaries and borrow materials from all relevant sources to drive home their points. Their theologization, sermon, or performance is not linear and always logical in sequence, but it is always becoming, pressing into places of surprise, and modeling the unpredictability of the Spirit. The performer, preacher, or theologian has enough skills to take in as much contingence as possible without dissipating or impairing the logic of his message. He works through analogy, eclecticism, bricolage, emphasizing how Christ (or Holy Spirit) is currently functioning in his life and the lives of his listeners. In this manner the argument of this book is multiphilosophic (for instance, postmodernism with a dash of pragmatism) and adopting scriptural and nonscriptural (not necessarily antagonistic) ways of interpreting Christ. To capture this "functioning" of Christ in the Pentecostal *how* of knowing in theological-philosophical terminology, I have named it the "middle space" in chapter 1.

---

18. Wariboko, *Charismatic City*, 3.

It is important at this juncture to advise the reader that when I extend the notions of epistemology (philosophy) to Jesus Christ or draw attention to Pentecostal "functioning" of Christ as a "middle space," it is only done at the symbolic level. It is at the symbolic level because there are key distinctions between Christ as God and Christ as pressed into concrete, quotidian service of correlating biblical resources to existential questions. The symbol of "middle space" is applied only to indicate that there is an analogy between Christ's body as a hypostatic hybridity and the Pentecostal way of knowing. For them this hybridity is not only soteriologically important but also epistemologically relevant in navigating daily decisions. (More on this later.)

Centuries ago the orthodox Chalcedonian vision of Christ struggled with this hybridity. Anyone familiar with ancient Greek philosophy knows that the doctrinal language of the Chalcedonian Creed is heavily laden with philosophical sensibility or acuity. Today, many Christian theologians still turn to philosophy for some of the language they need to express themselves. Pentecostal theologians in general are relatively slow in appreciating the helpfulness of philosophy when responsibly deployed. But my scholarship on Pentecostalism has deliberately drawn from philosophy. The reader will have already noticed that I have turned to continental philosophy to help us make sense of Pentecostals' pressing of Christology into making personal decisions. For everyday Pentecostal folks Christology has epistemological and existential consequences—not something you hang on a wall and admire. Continental philosophy provides me with the method and approach to produce the kind of phenomenological analyses that take into account the core and rhythms of the consequences. In the course of four books (*The Pentecostal Principle, Nigerian Pentecostalism, The Charismatic City,* and *Split God*) on Pentecostalism, I have come to the understanding that foregrounding the phenomenological analysis of Pentecostalism with continental philosophy is conducive to the philosophical theology of the everyday dimensions of Pentecostal movements. Using continental philosophic interlocutors for my analysis rather than the usual "suspects" (a tiny circle of Pentecostal theologians) has enabled me not only to probe the intellectual aspect of the movement but also to extend the study of Pentecostalism into philosophy. Theologians, social ethicists, religious studies scholars, social scientists, and historians have spent an ocean of ink on Pentecostalism, but philosophers have largely ignored the movement. There are some possible benefits in trying to pry open the philosophical subtleties of Pentecostalism and to invite those who are better or professional philosophers to help us clarify some of the conceptual issues and other neglected matters in the movement.

Now there is always the genuine concern that some of the continental voices I have invited or engaged as interlocutors in the four books might provide (provoke) an alien framing of the issues of the movement that distorts rather than illuminates the Pentecostal sociality. Although the possibility is always there as in any other scholarly effort to invite so-called outsiders to an internal discussion, I guard against it in the following five ways. First, continental philosophy is a methodological tool and not the determinant of the regnant issues of Pentecostalism in my studies. It is not deployed to disparage Pentecostalism or to say its leading interests and concerns are non-kosher, primitive, or lackluster. I *emic-ally* deploy continental philosophy to interrogate, conceptualize, clarify, and rigorously analyze the internal regnant issues, elements, themes, concerns, and practices, and to lift up their assumptions to intellectual scrutiny.

Second, in this task continental philosophy is not only a tool for critical intellectual scrutiny but also a methodology of interpretative understanding that aids this writer to grasp the subjective meaning of Pentecostal practices. This methodology sustains my motivating force to understand Pentecostal social actions and ideas, which are often viewed by other scholars as foolish, irrational, and bizarre, as reasonable, "logical," and plausible once I comprehend their subjective meaningfulness.

Third, continental philosophy is invited to play a role as a third space between the everyday social practices of Pentecostals and the regnant academic theological discourses that I am always contesting. To borrow the language of Reinhold Niebuhr, I use continental philosophy to afflict the comforted and comfort the afflicted among the cohorts of scholars studying Pentecostalism. The goal hopefully is nudge both philosophers and scholars of Pentecostalism to new terrains of knowledge, to a better understanding of Pentecostalism.

Fourth, the knot that holds the texture of my philosophic discourses of Pentecostalism is the Pentecostal worldview, which serves as their hermeneutical root note. Though the language and categories of continental philosophy are deployed to organize the data for analysis, it is the Pentecostal sensibility that provides the tonic key to properly discern the ontological, epistemological, ethical, imaginative, and theological implications and senses of Pentecostal practices.[19]

Finally, continental philosophy, deployed in the ways I have described above, enables me to figure out Pentecostal philosophy from the immanent intelligibility of everyday Pentecostal practices and to reflect on Pentecostal

---

19. This way of articulating my ideas is indebted to Suna-Koro, *In Counterpoint*, 249.

spiritual exercises as a form of philosophy, philosophy put into action, or philosophy as *bios*. This kind of reflection has enabled me in my previous works and in this book to bring to the fore the underlying values, principles, and inner conflicts and contradictions that animate Pentecostal movements. Mining this shaft of Pentecostalism, I have uncovered the ambiguities, ethical tensions, and ethos embedded in Pentecostal life that many scholars of Pentecostalism have ignored, or I have brought into sharp focus issues that have remained beyond their sightline. The neglect or oversight might be attributed to two things. On the one hand, at present, the authorized version of Pentecostal theology has no tools to do this kind of work or to do it effectively. On the other hand, social scientists have yet to invest in studying Pentecostal philosophy as a way of life, a mode of seeing and being in the world. My utilization of Pentecostal philosophy as a third space (between theology and everyday practice, between theology and the social sciences) enables me to bridge or fill this gap. A careful attention to this third space has also informed my socio-ethical studies of Pentecostalism. My social-ethical analyses of Pentecostals avoid spewing out vague moral imperatives or calling for ethical demands that flow from the so-called consistency of systematic theologies. Swerving from these common tendencies, I put the accent of my work on excavating the social ethics of Pentecostals as lived experience, not as argued in theological tomes, not as sermonized in the pulpits, and definitely not as glamorized on the evangelists' trails.

I have stated five *emic* ways I try to guard against continental philosophy, the so-called "illegal aliens" and "caravans of invaders" usurping the internal discussions of Pentecostal theology. The whole discussion above and what comes up later could be construed as a methodological defense of the philosophical approach of this book. It is also to provide some direction to students who are attracted to exploring continental philosophy as a tool for Pentecostal studies. Let me quickly add that they might not immediately receive affirmation for their inclination. They will be (initially) resisted by many senior Pentecostal theologians.

A good number of Pentecostal theologians have accepted without interrogation the image of Pentecostal discourse and continental philosophy existing in stark opposition, as in faith and godlessness, or belief and unbelief in Jesus Christ set in competition. They have fears of conflation. Yet how does such anxiety about drawing the two types of discourse (in its expansive Foucauldian sense) closer actually betray a threatening discursive proximity? In this book and in my previous volumes, I have actually drawn attention to various forms of conceptual proximity, and how certain Pentecostal ideas (practices) fit into the disavowed philosophical framework. Yet I have been careful not to conflate the two forms of discourse even as

I draw on the language of philosophy to articulate ideas and practices of Pentecostals. I have also resisted formulating a middle way, a *compromise* position, between Pentecostal theology and continental philosophy that can be considered a systematically unified account of both disciplines, incorporating the insights of the two areas. Rather, I have sought the *co-promising* option. As the name suggests, this involves adapting and adjusting, finding out what is co-promising between a philosophical(-theological) idea and hard social realities (Pentecostal practices) and then negotiating them in a way that does not sacrifice principles. My books seek to create a *co-promising* position, a space that opens both disciplines of Pentecostal theology and continental philosophy to possible polyphonic dialogues and for mutually beneficial options. With this space of co-promising options, marked by the absence of mediation that comes with "compromise," my *style* of scholarship becomes hard to be neatly categorized. What do you think it is? Scholars who have read my four Pentecostal studies books give multiple answers to this simple question. Some say it is philosophy, others say it is theology, and still others, religious studies. Yet some say it is social ethics.

But why should we unequivocally choose between these four options? Anonymous peer reviewers of my manuscripts on Pentecostalism often vehemently insist that I must choose. Imagine poor me, arguing with faceless all-powerful scholars and hard-driving publishers to let me be what I am. I do not always win this contest of authenticity. All this sounds wrong to me. Pentecostalism is best served when at least some of those who study it are not forced into narrow straits of scholarship, compelled to live in the ghetto of any one academic discipline. Pentecostalism is life—about human lives—and as such, like any aspect of life, it cannot be adequately comprehended by one focal lens but by manipulating a multiplicity of lenses. This is what I try to do in my scholarship in the hope of bringing to light ideas, assumptions, knowledges, "unorthodox" tendencies, and radicality concealed (primarily to academic bigwigs) in everyday practices of Pentecostals. This has always pushed my scholarship beyond some of the arbitrary limits set for "proper theology" of the Pentecostal masses.

I like exploring the *theology unbound* (in all its *enchantic* fury, always interrogative and interruptive) of everyday Pentecostals because they remind me of the unvarnished character of religion—that is, of faith naked and unashamed, faith whose opposite is not unbelief, un-faith, but disaster. In the everyday Pentecostal worldview, this is disaster in the sense of interment of a person's destiny, the ruin of a life cut off from divine purpose, or the loss of an identifiable center of personal existence. Unvarnished religion (Christianity) puts its adherents in the spaces where Christianity might have started its journey into the procrustean, Protestant liberal respectability that is desperately, forlornly ever seeking the hands of modernity in holy matrimony. Everyday Pentecostals in their plugged-in innocence and jouissance do not fail to remind those of us who study religions the character of religious discourse. According to John Caputo, "Religious discourse arises at that precise point when the legs of sense give way beneath us, when we run up against the limits of sense and non-sense, the point that divides sense from non-sense, when we lack the categories we need to make sense. Then we set out in search of a vocabulary of excess, of the limit and the excess of the limit, words to describe the slash between the limit and what lies beyond the limit."[20]

Tracking the slash, the split, discerning the traces of excess, and tracing the vocabularies of the crack do not always make for the kind of theology that the masters of the Pentecostal theological guild celebrate. Oftentimes their language, their language games, and their tools are not suitable for indwelling the split, abiding with the slash, meditating on the excess, or spanning the crack. I have been compelled to pick up their rejected stone of continental philosophy to build the cornerstone of a form of Pentecostal theology as a study of cracks. *Oui, ja,* yes—*crackology* or *splitology*.

This particular, if not peculiar, focus has meant that I start my thinking or study of Pentecostalism from locations or loci different from where the Pentecostal theological guild starts its work; and I also employ a different methodology. My phenomenological descriptions and analyses of Pentecostals always start from the lived messiness of their "theologies," concrete situation, existence, and the liturgy of everyday life. I have never been interested in putting forth well-packaged theological tomes that do not help readers to actually understand what is really going on in the life-worlds of Pentecostals. In my analyses of Pentecostal issues, I draw on whatever resources I deem relevant to the questions at hand—regardless of academic homes: continental philosophy, social ethics, theology, sociology, history, economics, political theory, and so on. The fact that the philosophical (methodological) style and technical vocabularies that come out of this bricolage are different from the language of the "big men and women" of Pentecostal theology should not be construed to mean that the questions I raise and my responses to them are off-kilter.

I do not stand apart from the big names because of hubris or petulance ("Here I stand, I do not care about your concerns"). I understand the weariness, if not trepidation, with which most Pentecostal theologians approach continental philosophy of religion. Continental philosophy has often been used to deny God as a *being* Pentecostals pray to, used to define

20. Caputo, "Is Continental Philosophy of Religion Dead?," 30.

God out of existence, crafted to replace or substitute (the name of) God with features of human experience or structures of human existence, weaponized to denigrate the Bible and caricature faith in transcendence, and has used its so-called rationality to shame, belittle and humiliate Pentecostals (Christians). But this is not all there is to continental philosophy. It can be used, rightly, to illuminate genuine belief, offering succinct phenomenological descriptions and analyses of religious practices, to uncover, interrogate, and elucidate the assumptions behind religious behaviors and actions, to show forth the particular forms that God or doctrines take in religious discourse or practice, and to articulate rather than to deny the everyday theologies of ordinary folk.

Pentecostal scholars in the theological academy who are comfortable with continental philosophy as a methodology and appreciate the scholarly focus on everyday Pentecostalism as a relevant source of theology have a different concern than what I have stated so far. Many in this group interpret my scholarship on Pentecostalism as not "correctly" (orthodoxly, loyally) framing the Pentecostal sociality. They also hold that my work is often not beholden to the pedigree or style of thought of the regnant Pentecostal theologians, that is, my scholarship does not take its lead or bearing from the dominant Pentecostal academy and its forms of theological thought. So ultimately "correctness" here is a measure of dependence on a tradition that a particular set of thinkers or interlocutors affirm. It is indeed not true that my scholarship is not rightly framing the Pentecostal sociality. My scholarship is always at the core of the Pentecostal sociality and ethos, but contrary to regnant guild practices. My style—conceiving itself as an immanent critical theology—is to think what the leading Pentecostal theologians and scholars leave unthought. There are also differences in terms of what I understand by theology or the theological. For me the theological is not about textual analysis, not about debating the fine points of dead thinkers, not about internecine quarrels over acceptable (faithful, authentic) interpretation of an author's thought, or reinventing (updating) the works of key figures of the past. It is never about enunciating an authoritative last word on a thinker and definitely not about disembodied reason seeking its own purity. It is about how to understand the present *situation* (the contemporary world as currently lived/experienced) of the followers of a religion and showing how it can be transformed to improve human flourishing for them. The theological is the open invitation to explore the possibilities (both sensible and uncertain/unforeseeable; with determinate content or with promise-to-come/impossible) for the good, justice, peace, love, and hope in a given situation as it is (or ought to be) nudged, pushed, pulled, and prepared for human flourishing for all persons in it. The theological is a practical subject arced toward interpreting and transforming text-flesh, text-reality, and not textbooks. Pentecostal theology must be attuned to the "from below" dimensions of lived *Pentecostality*. By Pentecostality I mean the conditions of Pentecostals living under oppression and domination, their theorizations of their being, doing, feeling, and knowing, their interpretations of their remembered, lived, and desired temporalities, and their specific deployment of religion (rightly or wrongly) to boost their empowerment, agency, and human flourishing. Pentecostal theologians need the aid of social sciences, continental philosophy, and other disciplines to give us a good understanding of Pentecostality.

Walking the chosen path of continental philosophy (to create the third space) to knowledge production in Pentecostal studies has not been easy for me. One is aware and wary of two ferocious lions that follow one on the sides of the path. The stout lion roars that going too close to continental philosophy will mean Pentecostal philosophy becomes too similar to continental philosophy and effectively disappears, making no distinctive contribution to either continental philosophy or Pentecostal philosophy (theology). The old lion roars that too much of a distance between what Pentecostal philosophy is and what (continental) philosophy is would render Pentecostal philosophy unrecognizable as genuine philosophy. I am ever trying to grasp this middle space, to map it, but it seems to always elude me—teasing me, winking at me, and egging me on like a coquettish lover who eludes me like the *real* itself. After multiple fruitless nights of finding my way in the space I realize that there is really no space between the lions, the imagined lions. The so-called middle space, an in-betweeness, is not an alternative terrain to launch a counter-Pentecostal theology, not an alternative territory to think continental philosophy in the name of Pentecostalism. It is rather a space that cuts across, cuts open, and is a cut within Pentecostal theology and continental philosophy. In a different metaphorical register, the elusive breach, middle space is the "Third Space" of contrapuntality, the staging of intellectual conversation as a counterpoint, yes, a fugue.

Jesus Christ as Hybridity

This talk or methodological sensibility about middle space or third space summons or recalls imagination or conception of Jesus Christ as a kind of spiritual "Third Space," the one who connects divinity and humanity and bridges the gap between God's wisdom and human rationality.[21] Jesus Christ is a divine hybrid. As the postcolonial theologian Kwok Pui-lan puts it,

21. Thanks to Amos Yong for urging me to connect my notion of Jesus Christ the

> The most hybridized concept in the Christian tradition is that of Jesus/Christ. The space between Jesus and Christ is unsettling and fluid, resisting easy categorization and closure. It is the "contact zone" or "borderland" between the human and the divine, the one and the many, the historical and the cosmological, the Jewish and the Hellenistic, the prophetic and the sacramental, the God of conquerors and the God of the meek and the lowly.[22]

How does the Pentecostal way of knowing at once mimic, culturally authenticate, and scandalize this symbol (the Third Space) in problematizing the operative epistemological binaries of reason/irrationality, matter/spirit, immanence/transcendence?[23] This is the task of this book: investigating the connections between the hybridity of Jesus-Christ and the hybridity of sense-spirit of Pentecostals while avoiding the temptation to write another book on Christology, or even on Christology through the lens of "Third Space" or hybridity. As the Latvian-American theologian Kristine Suna-Koro asserts,

> It almost goes without saying that much, much more can be said about Christology through the prism of hybridity [especially juxtaposed with the Chalcedonian vision of Christ].... What exactly does the *dense* postcolonial notion of hybridity, let alone Third Space, have to do with seemingly impenetrably arcane Chalcedonian Christology (except, perhaps, sharing an aura of impenetrability)? Quite a lot, I submit. Let's start with the obvious: both are imaginaries of relationality, indeed asymmetrical relationality. Both are also discourses that highlight the "how" of relationality: particularly, the "how" of boundaries, identities, and relational asymmetries that are contested, destabilized, subverted, and rendered fluid—yet not simply annihilated.[24]

The Pentecostal epistemology explored in this book is rooted in Christology that no less opens into a pneumatological discourse. It accents Christ as the betwixt and between person of the Godhead who undergirds knowledge (decision) that is not purely of one dimension of reality. In chapter 1,

---

middle space of Pentecostal epistemology to the postcolonial theoretic notion of "Third Space."

22. Pui-lan, *Postcolonial Imagination and Feminist Theology*, 171.

23. This way of putting across my thought is indebted to Keller, Nausner, and Rivera, *Postcolonial Theologies*, 13.

24. Suna-Koro, *In Counterpoint*, 241, 244.

we begin to explore the *how* of Pentecostal knowing as a subtle contestation of metaphysical and epistemological binaries, and as a non-hegemonic epistemic praxis. It is a pneumatological praxis that starts with (or reflects) the presupposition that all believers' personal decisions should be grounded in and linked to Jesus Christ, the author and finisher of the faith of the Pentecostal Christian. The chapter presents the polyphonic hybridity of knowledge, knowing, and knowability as a *locus theologicus* and posits the contrapuntal Pentecostal life as *locus epistemologicus*, all under the sign of Jesus Christ as the middle space. Jesus said, "For where two or three are gathered together in my name I am in the midst of them" (Matt 18:20). In Pentecostal epistemology he is not only in the midst of them in their daily struggles, he is also the *mid*, middle. He is not just a co-participant in their company, he is also the participative act itself in which the direction and significance of decision or decision-making are present. Decision (as the *signature* of their faith) is in the form of Christ and Christ is the substance of decision. This is to say, decision is sought in the midst of, in the hybrid space between, sense and non-sense (spirit), and decision's ground of being is Jesus, and decision is a potential vehicle through which his revelation can take place.

As the *participative act* Christ is not merely a being-in-their-epistemology, but a being-in-the-midst-of-their-epistemology. To be in-the-midst-of-their-epistemology is to be one with their epistemology, as in the case of models of knowing and justifying knowledge. In the case of being-in-their-epistemology there is a separation between Christ and their epistemology. Epistemology is conscious of Christ, but it is a consciousness of Christ as not being the model.[25] Put differently, epistemology is not deemed a tool of their God through which the believer seeks his/her dignity and expresses his/her ethos. The form of Pentecostal epistemology that I am characterizing as Christ-in-the-midst-of-their-epistemology is itself a social ethic, an ethic anchored by the narrative of Jesus's life. Pentecostals believe that the narrative of his whole life fundamentally connects social ethic and epistemology to Christology.

In this book I am attempting to explore the epistemological dimensions of everyday Pentecostal Christology, their interpretation of his character and nature as epistemology. For Pentecostals Jesus did not have an epistemology, but the story of his life as a whole is an epistemology. His life is an enfleshment of epistemology. For them the validity of a truth claim

---

25. The distinction I am drawing between being-in-their-epistemology and being-in-the-midst-of-their-epistemology refers in some crude fashion to Sartre's distinction between being-in-the world and being-in-the-midst-of-the-world. See Sartre, *Being and Nothingness*.

is always (in)formed by the story of Jesus that claims them, the story that gives them the meaning and courage to affirm their decisions without fear of being contradicted by Enlightenment rationalism.[26]

In thus relating knowing and not-knowing, sense and non-sense to the very identity of Jesus Christ and to the believer's relation to him, Pentecostals reveal that at the heart of their quest for knowledge, the *how* of knowing is "not so much an epistemological, but rather what can be defined as an *ethical* relation to the real."[27] For them, epistemology is not simply a grasping of reality or the process of knowing, but the ethical imperative of decisions and their consequences that are yet to be actualized and authenticated by faith in Christ.

In this space, as we demonstrate in chapter 1, knowing and not-knowing intersect language and experience of Christ(ology) and are entangled in personal decisions. The reasoning process of Pentecostals operative at this intersection is not (easily) assimilated into the modernist rationalist framework, as it is an attempt to grasp a truth that is otherwise available. Yet the reasoning process is not a quest to return to some lost world of Christian spirituality, not a preservation of the freedom of Spirit in knowledge production as known from (as in) the past, but rather a journey into a possible future—the future of *tacit* knowledge as an *ethical* relation to the Messiah.

We have discussed Pentecostal epistemology as a way of living into the story of Jesus Christ. While this is largely true for Global Pentecostalism, there still remains a question about which of the "Pentecostalisms" constitutes the primary driver for my analysis or provoked my initial thought on the Pentecostal hypothesis. It was my observation of African Pentecostalism(s) and its extension, manifestation, amplification, exemplification, or adaptation in the United States that ignited my preliminary thoughts.[28] This does not mean that the discursive arguments of this book are only valid for African Pentecostals at home or in the diaspora. I might have been sent off on my intellectual journey by an African apple falling on my head, but the gravity of my meditation weighs on Global Pentecostalism as a whole. Yet I am not offering a universally (that is, the Pentecostal universe) valid epistemological model. If we interpret any one model coming from

---

26. This paragraph is indebted to the language and ideas of Hauerwas, *Community of Character*, 3–52.

27. Caruth, *Unclaimed Experience*, 95. I have no doubt crudely pressed Caruth's phrase about traumatic awakening to my purpose because of the clarity it brings to my own ideas.

28. I am grateful to Kwabena Asamoah-Gyadu for urging me to make this fact clear to readers.

anywhere (including Europe and North America) as a universally valid way of Pentecostal epistemological quest, then its meaning is distorted. Nonetheless, there is something valid about it beyond its immediate locale as an expression of faith in Jesus Christ or as an integral part of a pattern of life whose center is Jesus Christ. In this sense, the particularity of the African story (model or practice) might lay claims to universal significance or global relevance.

Yet again, I do not claim to speak for African Pentecostalism or Global Pentecostalism with my theorization of the Pentecostal hypothesis in the pages of this book. I cannot hope to convince the reader of the comprehensive correctness of my philosophical arguments as they relate to either of them, but I do hope at least that the apple that landed on my hoary head displaced me enough into the ever-present crack, split between African Pentecostalism and Global Pentecostalism, to help you situate the Pentecostal hypothesis in the texture of worldwide Pentecostal religiosity. By making this concession or confession to you as a reader, have I not betrayed one of my guiding principles for writing this text? I wanted you to decide for yourself—without any single authorial intention or consciousness—under which geographical rubric of Pentecostalism you want to locate this book. Local or global? By succumbing to the temptation to situate the issues of this book as speaking from African (African Diaspora) Pentecostalism to Global Pentecostalism, are we not assuming there is a single "thing" or "consciousness" called Global Pentecostalism?[29] What if Global Pentecostalism does not exist as a distinctive instantiation or "collective entity" of Pentecostalism, but rather as the cut that traverses, that is within, and that opens each of the *Pentecostalisms* beyond itself?

I must now resist the temptation of fleshing out this argument, as it would take us too far afield from our immediate concern. The job at hand now is to turn to chapter 1 and grapple with the issue of epistemological dimensions of Christology, the centrality of Jesus for Pentecostal epistemic identity. The chapter suggests that any discussion of Pentecostal epistemology is inadequate if it fails to account for how Pentecostal believers in Jesus construct their epistemology, how the meaning and truth of their commitment to him engender their epistemic identity—or if it presupposes a separation of epistemology from Christology. What the chapter does not suggest is the identification of Christology with epistemology.[30]

---

29. This same question applies as well to African Pentecostalism.

30. Hauerwas, *Community of Character*, 36–37, 42. I acknowledge my indebtedness to the ideas and language of Hauerwas in this paragraph.

1

Who Christ Is

Sermon on Encountering Christ as an *Event* of Knowledge

I AM GRATEFUL TO preach from the pulpit of The King's Temple.[1] My assigned topic this morning is *Who Christ is*. We are all Pentecostals here, so let me tell you that I want to do my job in a very simple manner. I do not want to excite you; I only want you to understand who Christ is. My lesson will start in earnest with a summary statement of who Christ is. Next, I will read the story of Abraham and the binding of Isaac and explain what it means in the context of the topic. Finally, we will explore who Christ is as an elucidation of the summary statement. At the end we will understand what our sister, Pastor Elsie Obed, has been saying for years, on a different level. She often says, *It does not make sense, but it makes spirit*. The statement says something profound about who Christ is. It is my hope that the spirit of God will reveal to us the full meaning of the statement in the context of understanding who Christ is.

Let me now give you the summary statement of who Christ is; please write it down, if you can, because it decodes everything that I am going to say today. *Jesus Christ is the space, the split where the world does not make sense. Jesus Christ is the empty space between meaning and no-meaning.* To

---

1. The King's Temple is located at 36 Franklin Avenue, Hewlett, New York. This sermon-lecture was delivered on November 25, 2017, at its annual Word and Wisdom Conference. The leader of this church is Pastor Elsie Nene Obed. She is a Nigerian-American.

know him, you must be willing to step into that space, inhabit it, and be faithful to that space.

I now turn to the story of Abraham. We are talking about Jesus Christ, but we will approach him today through Abraham. Oftentimes, when we talk about Jesus Christ and the story of Abraham and Isaac, people think that Isaac reveals who Jesus Christ is. This is true, but we are going to learn today that if you understand Abraham, you will also understand something very crucial about Jesus Christ, which is "how to know him." We often focus on Isaac because he was about to be sacrificed. But that angle of the story only tells us the function that Jesus Christ did as a savior. Sometimes, we may understand things or people by their functions—other times, by what or who they are. You may understand your mother as somebody who gives you money to pay school fees, but it is different from understanding your mother as who she is. Sometimes, these two dimensions of a person are joined, but they are not the same.

Let me now read the story of Abraham and try to decode it as much as the Holy Spirit will allow us to do today. Genesis 22:1–19 says,

> Now it came to pass after these things that God tested Abraham, and said to him, "Abraham!"
>
> And he said, "Here I am."
>
> Then He said, "Take now your son, your only *son* Isaac, whom you love, and go to the land of Moriah, and offer him there as a burnt offering on one of the mountains of which I shall tell you."
>
> So Abraham rose early in the morning and saddled his donkey, and took two of his young men with him, and Isaac his son; and he split the wood for the burnt offering, and arose and went to the place of which God had told him. Then on the third day Abraham lifted his eyes and saw the place afar off. And Abraham said to his young men, "Stay here with the donkey; the lad and I will go yonder and worship, and we will come back to you."
>
> So Abraham took the wood of the burnt offering and laid *it* on Isaac his son; and he took the fire in his hand, and a knife, and the two of them went together. But Isaac spoke to Abraham his father and said, "My father!"
>
> And he said, "Here I am, my son."
>
> Then he said, "Look, the fire and the wood, but where *is* the lamb for a burnt offering?"
>
> And Abraham said, "My son, God will provide for Himself the lamb for a burnt offering." So the two of them went together.

> Then they came to the place of which God had told him. And Abraham built an altar there and placed the wood in order; and he bound Isaac his son and laid him on the altar, upon the wood. And Abraham stretched out his hand and took the knife to slay his son.
>
> But the Angel of the Lord called to him from heaven and said, "Abraham, Abraham!"
>
> So he said, "Here I am."
>
> And He said, "Do not lay your hand on the lad, or do anything to him; for now, I know that you fear God, since you have not withheld your son, your only *son*, from Me."
>
> Then Abraham lifted his eyes and looked, and there behind *him was* a ram caught in a thicket by its horns. So Abraham went and took the ram, and offered it up for a burnt offering instead of his son. And Abraham called the name of the place, The-Lord-Will-Provide; as it is said *to* this day, "In the Mount of the Lord it shall be provided."
>
> Then the Angel of the Lord called to Abraham a second time out of heaven, and said: "By Myself I have sworn, says the Lord, because you have done this thing, and have not withheld your son, your only *son*—blessing I will bless you, and multiplying I will multiply your descendants as the stars of the heaven and as the sand which *is* on the seashore; and your descendants shall possess the gate of their enemies. In your seed all the nations of the earth shall be blessed, because you have obeyed My voice." So Abraham returned to his young men, and they rose and went together to Beersheba; and Abraham dwelt at Beersheba.

Now think about this important story. To understand what was going on with Abraham is a key to understanding who Jesus Christ is. But this story does not make sense, that is the first thing you have to realize, and no matter how many times you have heard it, you must to come to this realization before you can penetrate the story. Here is a God who never accepts human sacrifice saying to Abraham, "Go and sacrifice somebody to me." It does not make sense. Here is a man who had been waiting for this son that he was promised, and God was telling him, "Go and kill your son." The man agreed. He never told his wife. We are not told Sarah's opinion; he just went along with the divine instruction to kill his son. It does not make sense.

It appears Abraham had come to that point where on one side everything made sense, while on the other side of it, everything was meaningless and foolish. Poor Abraham is split in the middle and he has to make up his mind whether to sacrifice his son. Being put in this situation did not make sense. How could God say to him, "Kill your son"?

What was going on in his mind? Imagine his mental agony in the three days it took him to walk to the designated place of sacrifice. He must have been repeating, "It doesn't make sense." If you over-spiritualize the story or over-rationalize it, then you miss its import. If God were to ask you today to kill your son, you would be in a deep crisis. You would respond, "God, it doesn't make sense." But in the story, we have Abraham, whom God has asked to do something that absolutely does not make sense. There is no record of God giving such an instruction to believers in the Bible before Abraham got his. Abraham had no past story to rely upon. Today, we know from the Bible that God offered God's son for the sins of the world. We can say Isaac represents Jesus Christ, but Abraham did not know this. He was at the point where the divine instruction did not make sense. The God he knew was not that kind of a God who would ask him to kill his son. Even more perplexing to the old man, Isaac was the son God had promised would inherit the father's name. Yet, Abraham obeyed.

Even by the world's standard today, the divine command still does not make sense. God's instruction and Abraham's obedience do not make sense. The normal way that the world derives meaning from its knowledge system does not apply here. Meaning has been suspended, and Abraham was at the point where God's instruction to him sounded foolish. Even his own actions sounded foolish. Alas, he was caught in the middle, like this aisle between the pews. On one side of the aisle it makes sense by the standards of human wisdom, and on the other side, it does not make sense. But God was calling him to be in the middle, and Abraham could not just walk into it; he had to leap into it. His obedience, his faith propelled him into the middle. He still did not know after leaping whether it made sense. Belief is taking a leap into what does not make sense, and it is in that space that God is.

When everything that you are doing in your own Christianity, in your belief, is calculated and goes well, there is no difference between you and the world. For you to know Christ you must come to that space where *it doesn't make sense, but it makes spirit*. It does not make sense means it is foolish to the world. It means obedience or action has no meaning; you cannot calculate or grasp it. Whatever it is, it does not make sense, but you must still come into that middle space of not knowing. Oftentimes, we do not want to stand in that space where it does not make sense, as we think that it is a space of absolute foolishness to the world. For it is in the crack, that space, where Jesus Christ is about to meet us.

When we say it does not make sense, many people in the world assume it means foolishness. But we know that there is a space, a little crack, between absolute sense and absolute foolishness.² That is where belief, your faith and Christ dwells. Until you can be in that space with God, you are never going to know who Christ is. Abraham was in that space.

Let us not forget, it does not make sense to kill Isaac—God does not accept human sacrifices. But this God asked Abraham to do it, and he obeyed. Abraham was not foolish; he knew that there was something wrong because the story did not make sense. How was he going to explain it to his wife? How was he going to explain it to his neighbors? How was he going to explain it to himself? Yet he obeyed, though he knew his obedience did not make sense. He knew it was foolishness. He also knew that the foolishness of God was far superior to the wisdom of human beings. So between the wisdom, sense and foolishness of the world, and the foolishness of God, he knew there was a space where God was beckoning to him to enter and meet with Him. Therefore, until you are ready to enter that space, live and be faithful, you will not know who Jesus Christ is.

So when they say Abraham is the father of faith or belief, it means that he took a leap into that space. Faith is about jumping into what is missing in the world. Amid the fullness of the wisdom of this world, there is always something that is missing. By his actions, his neighbors would have thought too that there was something missing in his world, if not in his head. His action did not make sense given the calculations and permutations of the world. This space of a missing element in the world was where Abraham preferred to abide. This is the space where we also need to be—the site where the world does not make sense, where its calculations do not make sense, where it seems like something has gone missing in the chain of causation that normally makes sense. Until you are ready to be in this space where Christ is, you will not meet him.

The example of Abraham for us is that he showed with his commitment that what was missing in his world was more important to him. He demonstrated that the missing element had greater hold on him than what was in the world. You cannot get the professors of the world to declare that Abraham's actions made sense. Rather, they would say that something is missing in the communication between God and Abraham. They would ask him, "Abraham, are you sure something is not missing in your head?" because his radical obedience cannot fit into their calculations or permutations. Father Abraham must have said, "You know what, ladies and gentlemen, I am going to take everything I need. I am going to move out, and I am going to do it." It is in this display of faith that he will meet

---

2. I need to clarify that I am not suggesting that everything that "makes no sense" automatically makes spirit. Pentecostalism is, indeed, not a war against the reasoning mind.

the God of the middle space, and his faith will be confirmed. He was not hailed as father of faith at places where everything made sense, because the world is made to make sense and exclude the kind of radical obedience he exhibited. Please note that there is nothing wrong with the world. It behaves to type. The world makes sense because everything happening in it must (ultimately) reveal its cause and effect. Everything in the world is linked together. Everything that happens, by definition, has its own cause and effect. The world operates by a tight chain of cause and effect. If you throw up a stone, it will come down. You cannot break the chain.

This is the reason the world will quarrel with you and say there cannot be a miracle, because the world operates in a tight chain of cause and effect. Trouble starts, metaphorically, when someone who believes in God declares that if you throw up a stone it will not come down. The religious point here—and not necessarily the scientific one—is that such a person is believing in something that is missing in the world. Until you are ready by faith to step into that missing link, missing space in the chain, you will not meet God. The Bible informs us that the chain of cause and effect is not a perfect formation, adding that there is a missing link, a space in it where God can step in and do whatever God wants. Are you willing to meet God in that space?

Abraham believed in such a God. Whatever he was asked to do did not make sense, but he knew that somewhere in that space where it does not make sense, God will be there. So belief, for Abraham, is about something asserting itself without asserting its meaning. Being convicted by the existence of the space, the missing link means you are allowing something to come upon your life to assert itself that will not give you any meaning, will not make sense as we generally understand the term. How do we find meaning in the world? Once we know the cause and we know the effect, we say it makes sense; there is meaning in the matter or event. Your mom asks you, "What do you think you are doing? What is the meaning of what you are doing?" You answer, "I am trying to hurry so I can go to the party." Your mom understands that there is meaning in what you are doing, and you are not crazy. This kind of meaning-making, the one that all reasonable people will accept, was not available to or exercised by Abraham. When the divine instruction came to Abraham—or rather "hit" him—it asserted itself in his life but did not assert its own meaning. That was, perhaps, the reason he could not even explain it to his wife; he could not even explain it to his son. There was no way to make sense of God's word.

When something about the word of God hits you, when something about the life of God hits you, the divine asserts itself in your life without giving you a meaning. When this happens, you must be ready to step into that space where there is no sense or immediate meaning. As you step into that space, into that site, God says to you, "I know what I am doing." To meet Christ is to meet Christ in that space. But if you fit him into the chain of signification, the chain of cause and effect in this world, you will never know him. To know Christ, you must be willing to accept that Christ is the missing element in the world.

What does it mean to say Christ, the Spirit of Christ, who is omnipresent, could be missing in the world? As God, Christ *belongs* to the world, but he is not *included* in the things of the world. He belongs to the world situation as a whole in his *generic* omnipresence, but he does not belong to any of the subsets of the dominant ways of doing things or interpreting human existence. He is "present" but not "represented" in the world. He is the *excluded part* of the world's regnant systems of knowledge. He is the missing element in the world situation, he counts for zero, effectively a "void" in our civilization's dominant ways of being, knowing, and doing.[3]

The world is there, but there is something missing in it. There is a crack or split in it. He is the missing element that will not allow the world to come to full self-identity, to coincide with itself. No matter how much the world tries, it cannot come to its own full self-understanding except when Christ comes into it, abides in it. Because Christ is not there in the world, the world cannot come to an understanding of its true identity, come to what it is supposed to be—cannot fully understand why it is here. Never mind that the world's experts will tell you that everything is complete, every cause and effect is in order, and that they know what they are doing. The world's boast and its contents are meaningless, unimportant to Jesus Christ—and it should be so to you as a follower of him. "Do not love the world or the things in the world. If anyone loves the world, the love of the Father is not in him" (1 John 2:15).

To know Christ means that you cannot hold on to the contents of this world. Once you hold on to any content, any institution, any substance, any wealth as if that is *the Christ*, then you have missed him. The creative, irruptive empty space we are talking about is not in the things of the world. In any institution, in any organization, in any factory, in any church, in any government, the people of the world will try to cover that empty space with their own stuff. Human beings do not like to have a space where there is nothing. They will cover it up by saying to you, "We are the big name, we have money,

---

3. This paragraph was added during my transcription of the oral sermon. During the presentation it came to my mind, but I thought the ideas expressed in this paragraph were too abstract. I felt that the Badiousian inflection of my thinking here would not be easily grasped by my audience in the heat of a kinetic Pentecostal sermon. This is the only place in this chapter that I added new material.

power, or class. We are the preferred gender, skin, or race." Churches will claim they have Christ because of the miracles they have performed in his name. This is the reason Christ said even those who believe in him will not be running around looking for miracles, signs and wonders. Our church leaders are like the rest of world; they cannot abide with or in an empty space, so they will fill it with their own contents. The world and its church cannot deal with the fact that they cannot make sense of themselves without Christ, without stepping into that space that does not make sense but makes spirit. They cannot confront the imperative of this space, so they look for things to conceal it. But Christ says to them, "I am not in your contents." For Christ is always the missing element in their chains of claims, in their chain of causes and effects, in whatever the world is doing.

If you hold on to any of their claims, things, or contents you have missed Christ. You must accept Christ in pure belief, without content. Some of us think that we have accepted Christ, but what we have is *belief with content*. We accepted Christ because the Catholic Church is what we know, and it is the content through which we accept him. We accepted Christ because of a Pentecostal church. We accepted Christ because of that preacher, that national church, that ethnic church, and so on. We have not come to Christ because of pure belief. We have not said to Christ, "Yes, I believe in you. There is nothing the world is offering me. I am going to stay in that space where the world is not offering me anything—is not offering me a name, is not offering me wealth, nothing. In that space, I am going to hold on to you as if nothing else matters."

We have not done this, and we cannot do this. We, therefore, do not really know him as if we are always reaching out to him through other people's contents, through the things of the world. We need the grace to be in the space. Abraham was "forced" into the space where nothing made sense. He was where he could not even hold on to traditions. He could not say this was how my fathers in the faith used to sacrifice their sons to God. He could not even tell his wife. He could not even pretend to have a quarrel with his wife, because a quarrel with his wife would not solve his problems. He came to the point where he only had to say, "I wholly accept this God without any sense or anything in the world giving me cause to believe him. I am going to confront that space." Unlike Abraham, we often process Christ through national pride, race arrogance, biographies, family histories, and, as Paul said, through genealogies and everything else. We seem to have cornered the market on Christ. But we have got to accept that when we think we have balanced all our equations and ensured that our chain of cause and effect fits perfectly together, that is when Christ is missing. Christ is that space where everything does not make sense. And until we step into that space we are never going to know him, never going to know his ways.

Since we do not want to step into the space that does not make worldly sense, we are running to places to find Jesus Christ. In Luke 17:23 and Matthew 24:23, he said they will tell you to go here and there to find me, but you will not find me. What is he telling us here? He is never in the *here* and never in the *there*. It means he is somewhere between the *here* and the *there*. Remember, he is everywhere, omnipresent. When they say go here and he is not *here*, and they say go there and he is not *there*, you do not want to forget that he is *in* the world. It means that he is there, in between the *here* and *there*, but they are either telling or selling you something for profit to distract you. But the sellers, traders in the father's house, can never see the in-between and they will never let you see it, because if they let you see it and encounter it, you will never come back to their programs and you will not do what they want.

You can deliver yourself from them. You need to bring yourself to the point where you can declare, "Whatever they have been telling me in the past, whatever they are saying on my left and on my right no longer matters. I am going to meet my God in that in-between where nothing else in the world can make me believe God, and where nothing from the world can support me. I just have to encounter God where it doesn't make sense."

When the world or your friends hear you say, "It does not make sense, but it makes spirit," they will say to you that you are being foolish, irrational, and that you have allowed your religion to make you stupid. But note that they are not correct; their interpretation of your statement is wrong. When a true believer utters this aphorism, this is what he or she is saying: somewhere in between the senses there is the spirit of God. The senses are the things that we know from our human calculations, from our physics, from our own economics, from things we know and how they fit together. But in between all of that there is a space in existence where the world's theory does not fit together, where its wisdom does not fit together, where its knowledge does not fit together, where the system does not fit together. Christ is never where the popular opinion says he is. He is not in what excites the multitude and the leaders alike.

Paul knew this very well. Read all the books of the Bible attributed to Paul and you will not see where he mentions one miracle of Jesus Christ. He said I can do miracles, but I am not really interested in them (1 Cor 12:1–11). He said I can speak in tongues, but I am not really interested. But I am only interested in one thing, the crucified Christ who is resurrected: "I determined not to know anything among you except Jesus Christ and him crucified" (1 Cor 2:2; see also 1 Cor 15:12–19). Paul was only interested in the resurrection. Why was he not interested in miracles? He believed in miracles but was not interested in them because he was more interested in the power of resurrection. The power of resurrection is not the opposite of death. And it is not the opposite of life. It exists in between death and life. It is a crack. Somewhere in between life and death, there is a space called resurrection and human beings cannot walk through this space. Only Jesus Christ has walked through it. Paul in Philippians 3:10 says he wants to know Jesus Christ and the power of resurrection. Paul desired to know that man who walked through that space between death and life, who dominates that intersection where death meets life. He desired to know that power that does not make sense to the world. Death and life make sense. If you are born you will die one day; even if you live for a million years, death will visit you eventually. We know how death and life operate. We may be scared of death—some may even be scared of life—but we know how to explain death and life. How death and life operate is part of the human sense of the world, part of our meaning and signification. What the world does not know is resurrection.

But Christ says, in between life and death there is a little space where there is resurrection, and I passed through it after my crucifixion. The one who created life and death and knew that in between them there is a power bigger than both life and death says, "I am the resurrection and the life. He who believes in me, though he may die, he shall live. . . . Do you believe this?" (John 11:25-26). Paul believed it and was so hungry to enter that in-between space of the power of resurrection. He prayed to know this crack, to know of Christ's resurrection. Note that in the prayer of Philippians 3:10, Paul did not say I want to know the power of life; that would have made complete sense to his hearers in the world. He wanted to know the space that does not make sense to the world. He wanted to enter it like Abraham. Thus, when he came back to confront Abraham's story in Romans 4, he seemed to say Abraham knew that God would raise Isaac even if he were to be sacrificed in order to fulfill his promise to Abraham and Sarah. Though not explicit, Paul hinted that Abraham understood that God had the power to fulfill the promise he made to him, even if he had sacrificed Isaac.

Do you believe Jesus when he says he is the power of resurrection? Jesus Christ wants to meet you in the crack as he met brother Paul and Father Abraham. Once you are in this safe space you transcend both life and death. You may be alive or dead, but you are above their powers. Just as you can be in the world but not of the world. The world cannot give you the Jesus Christ that I have been describing to you today, because they cannot place you in the space that Abraham and Paul inhabited. To know this Christ, to know who he is, you must first come out from the sense system of the world.

You must acknowledge that there is a space between the senses of the world and utter foolishness, and in that crack dwells Jesus Christ. Go there and meet him! He is waiting for you. But if you are willing to dwell in the world, *be of the world*, and unwilling to step into that space, then you will not really know him. You must *subtract* yourself from the world to encounter Jesus.

Paul understood that resurrection was a subtraction from the worldly systems or sites of wisdom. In any system the people in it know how things are given, how things work or happen. But then suddenly something appears in the system that does not belong to it and they cannot explain it. This is what Jesus's resurrection was to the known regimes of death and life. It was a subtraction or extraction from the system of death because it does not annul death. It subtracts from the site or power of death, creating a disjunction within death. The resurrection occurred in a crack that did not belong to both systems of death and life.

Unless you are willing to subtract yourself from the path of the world, willing to say no to it and be carried by God's grace into the crack in the systems of the world where Jesus dwells, you will not really meet him. Christ names this space and its contingent order of grace. All these do not make sense to the world. Christ himself as the one who sutures divinity and humanity does not makes sense to our contemporary world. This is the reason in the beginning of this lecture I called on your most imaginative and creative powers to conceive Jesus Christ for our age as that space, that split where the world does not make sense—the empty space between meaning and no-meaning. To truly know him you must be willing to step into this rejected, despised space. But let me warn you the world will do everything in its power to make sure that you do not get there. The struggle will start from your home. Your husband or wife will tell you not to go there, that living into that space does not make sense. It is all foolishness, she or he will say.

If you want to start a ministry and decide to walk into the space, the "old prophets" will tell you that ministry is no longer done in this way. Deception of young ministers by old prophets is nothing new. In 1 Kings 13 we are told that God gave an instruction to a young man of God to go into a city and execute certain tasks and that he should neither eat nor drink water in the city. This instruction at a certain level does not make sense. Here is a man who is to travel several miles to a city to perform some tasks, and after successfully executing them, he should not eat or drink to refresh himself. The Bible did not even bother to tell us why God gave that instruction, adding to the supposed irrationality of the demand.

An old prophet in the city heard that a young man came into his city and successfully executed God's task. He invited the young man to come into his home and take some refreshment. The man hesitated and repeated the prohibitions of God about eating and drinking in the city. The old prophet convinced him to eat and drink. Perhaps he ate because deep down the prohibition did not make any sense to him; it was not meaningful to a weary man. For his disobedience he died at the outskirts of the city as he was returning home. The old prophet who encouraged him to disobey God said, "Thus says the Lord: 'Because you have disobeyed the word of the Lord, and have not kept the commandment which the Lord your God commanded you ... your corpse shall not come to the tomb of your fathers'" (1 Kgs 13:21-22). Basically, the old prophet was mocking him for disobeying God, calling him a foolish man.

All this is not surprising because the world has always worked hard to ensure that believers do not come to that space we have been discussing. But know that everything profoundly worth knowing about Christ is always found in that space, where things do not make sense. Believers have always missed this space because when God asks them to do something they try to fit it into known patterns of the world. The world has a big appetite to take in everything that you bring and give you an explanation. Its experts may even be wrong today, but tomorrow they will say we were wrong and here is a new explanation. The world will always give you an explanation that will take you away from the space because this site does not make sense to its experts. But God is saying to you, if you care to listen, "My ways do not have to make sense; they only have to make spirit." Here, it-makes-spirit does not mean utter foolishness, but only points you to the little space between sense and foolishness. God wants you to find it and dwell there. And this is where you will encounter and know Christ. It is in the same space that Abraham was able to encounter God. When the Angel of the Lord saw that Abraham was in the space, God said to him, "In blessing I will bless you. Now I know that you fear God." Note that the Angel of the Lord did not say now that I have tested you and known that you are a certified murderer, or now that I know that you are willing to kill your son, I will bless you. This is not the point at all; the lesson is that Abraham had brought himself to that space where everything does not make sense, yet he obeyed God. And it was at this point that he heard the divine blessings.

Are you willing to be in that space where it does not make sense, to own it and be faithful in it? Let me tell you, you cannot just casually walk into this space. You must leap into it; you need to jump into this *eventual site*. You must jump into the part of the worldly situation that does not properly fit into the senses, into a place where nothing of the world appears to belong. It is basically *unrepresentable* when observed from the view of the regnant sense systems of the world. You will be jumping into an abyss—the space that has no foundation. When you leap into the space that has no foundation, you will appear to be endlessly falling, but as you keep falling, the everlasting arm of God will emerge to hold you. God is always already there waiting for you.

But when you do not want to fall, and you are looking for a foundation to stand on, you will miss the space. The space has no foundation; it is an abyss, a bottomless pit between sense and foolishness. If you do not want to fall, you can decide to leap over to one side and the world will say you are either a foolish or a wise person. The space is a terrible thing to waste with your leap because you think it has no foundation and there is nothing in it. But you have forgotten that the world arose from nothing. It came out from completely nothing, from nothingness. It is from that nothing that God began to call things into existence. This is why Paul says, "God calls those things which do not exist as though they did" (Rom 4:17). Paul understood that it is in that space where things do not make sense, where there is nothing, that good things came forth, creation and miracles came out. It is in that empty space between the senses and foolishness that the Spirit of God dwells.

The world came out of nothing, the Bible tells us. While it was coming out, who was framing that nothing? It was the word of God, Jesus Christ. Hebrews 11:3 says, "By faith we understand that the worlds were framed by the word of God, so that the things which are seen were not made of things which are visible."

When you are ready to step into that nothingness where creation started, you are ready to encounter Jesus Christ. Today, Jesus is asking you to *manifest your who* in that empty space. He is in it already, waiting for you, because he is always framing the nothingness. The world will always give you something to prevent you from stepping into the empty space. But Jesus gives you the "nothing." The world will always give you what it has, and that is something. For you to meet Jesus Christ you must be willing to accept what is not in the world—something the world looks upon as nothing. The world tells us all the time that there is nothing in Jesus, so why are you going to him? It says to us, What is that prayer that you are praying? It is for nothing. What is that faith that you have? It is nothing. But know that it is in that nothing that is between the something of the world that God dwells in our midst. Praise the Lord!

Are you willing to encounter Christ in this way? To know Christ demands that you first know the space where the world does not make sense. You must know him as the nothing of this world, the missing element of the chain of meaning, senses, and signification. When you pass through that zone of nothingness, you will realize that he is everything in the world.

It is only when you are ready to step into what the world says counts as nothing that you realize that he is everything in the world. This is so because it is from this space of nothing that he controls the world. It is from this space that creation came and is continually renewed. "In him," the Bible says, "all things consist" (Col 1:17); so between every space of everything he is there. This means, for instance, that the power of God is even in the spaces that hold the cells of your body together. By the way, *in him all things consist* does not refer to human beings alone, but to everything in world. It means that in between everything, in between anything that holds anything together, he is there in that space. He holds the consistency of everything together. He holds the space between foolishness and sense. If you are ready to go the way of arrogant worldly sense, you can go. But if you can say, "I want to be in that space where he holds everything together," then you will find out that he really holds everything together for you. Praise the Lord!

As we wrap up, let us return to our earlier discussion on belief. Belief is what enables a person to prepare for what he or she cannot, in all senses or reality, prepare for. When you know Christ, you will find out that he enables you to prepare for the reality that you cannot prepare for. When Noah was building the ark, his neighbors thought he was a foolish man. But he ignored them and was able to prepare for something they could not prepare for, because he believed in God. He was in that space where it does not make sense. They laughed at him, saying, "Why is this man building an ark? There is no flood. It is not even raining." He ignored them because he was in a different space, for he believed in God.

When we call ourselves believers today, but we are looking to stand on the firm shores of the senses of this world, looking to stand on the foundations of the world, then what we are saying to the world is that we are not ready to know the God that Noah knew and served. Frankly, we do not have the belief that was in Noah and the men and women like him in the Bible. We do not have the belief that enabled them to prepare for things that in all senses they could not prepare for.

We do not have this kind of belief because Christ is not the substance of our belief, the evidence of it. Paul says in Hebrews 11:1, "Now faith is the substance of things hoped for, the evidence of things not seen." What does substance mean? It means something that holds things up, something that undergirds you. What does hope mean? It means things that are not there, as Paul explains in Romans 8:24–25. He says no one hopes for what he or she has. Thus by definition, hope means you are hanging on nothing; that which you are looking for is not there. Hope means something that is not there. When something is not there, it is what? Nothing!

Once again, we have come to the idea that Christ or the knowledge of him always brings us to the middle. Paul is saying in Hebrews 11:1 that once you are in this middle, this space of nothing, the abyss, belief in Christ is what will undergird you. This is what he means by faith being the substance of things hoped for. Here substance is not your usual or normal assurance. You can hope for something until the gray hairs come—even until you die. Hope is not a magic wand. Hope does not mean that what you are expecting will come. All that you are really putting forth with hope is this: "I am going to jump into the space where there is nothing, and I expect that God will show up"; and eventually your belief becomes the everlasting arm of God that holds you up. This is what the word *substance* means, to undergird and firm you up. So, when you hope, it means you are going into that space where there is nothing. You are going into a site where you are not seeing things, but you are willing to hang in because Christ is already there. But if you are not willing to go into that space where there is nothing and you are only living in that space where everything is set, where everything makes sense, brother Paul is likely to ask you, "Why then do you have hope?"

Once you get this revelation about belief, you will notice the different ways it occurs in the Bible. This realization will transform your understanding of this statement: *It does not make sense, but it makes spirit*. It will no longer sound like a nonsensical statement to you, no longer seem to you the stupid talk of "ordinary Pentecostals." You will grasp what believers like Pastor Elsie Obed mean by *it does not make sense, but it makes spirit* if you are determined to fully engage what Paul means when he says faith is the substance of things hoped for, the evidence of things not seen—or with what he says in another place: "God calls those things which do not exist as though they did."

They do not exist means: there is nothing. If I go to your fridge, Pastor Elsie, and you say to me, "Get me a bottle of water," and I say, "There is no bottle of water," what does this mean? It means the bottle of water does not exist in your fridge. I see only an empty fridge. Then you say to me again, "I hope that something will come up." What does this mean? You are asking me to join you in hoping on nothing based on the empty space in your fridge. But now let us listen carefully into her statement of hope. If she believes that there is a God that undergirds her hope and who says to her, "There may be nothing there in the empty space, but look very well. Are you looking? There is something there." When she obeys and looks, the face that will confront her is not the face of a bottle of water, but the face of Jesus Christ. In that moment of nothing, in that space between abundance and scarcity, that is where you meet him. And God will tell you something like what he told Hagar when she said there is nothing for me to do, my son is about to die of thirst. There is nothing. God answered her and said, "Lift up your eyes, there is a well where you can get water" (Gen 21:15-19).

Hagar was in that space of nothing—the skin of water that Abraham gave her when he drove her out of his house with her son Ishmael at the instigation of Sarah had been emptied. She looked everywhere for water, and there was nothing. So, when God said "lift up your eyes" and she did, she saw water and broke out in praise.

Our misstep in faith today is that we do not want to be in that space that Abraham, Paul, Noah, and Hagar occupied. We do not want to be in the space where we are totally dependent on the foolishness of God's wisdom (1 Cor 2:1-12; 1 Cor 1:18-31). This is one reason we do not really know Christ. Today, God is saying to us that we should begin to look in the cracks of the world, to look where things appear to be cracking. In the midst of the cracks there is God; in the spaces of existence where it does not make sense, it makes spirit.

In conclusion, let me say I have learned a lot from this sermon. The major revelation I got from this session of the conference is this: in all things that I do I should ask myself this question: Am I willing to find the space in between the somethings of the world so that I can dwell with God? In other word, Can I find the space that does not make sense and looks foolish to the world and its powers, but that will confirm in me the hope that I have in God? My prayer is that God will always give you and me the grace to look for him not in the midst of the world, but where the world is not expecting.

Off-Pulpit Remarks: Looking Forward to Chapter 2

The Pentecostalist characterization of Jesus Christ as a middle space is simultaneously extraordinary and ordinary. Extraordinary or innovative because he is portrayed in a bold new light, as a gap, a liminal site of creativity, the empty place from whence the new comes into existence, and a connector/disconnector of sense and *the other* of sense. It is also extraordinary because the Pentecostal conception of Jesus Christ appears to spring out of the gaps in our theological inheritances and conceptualities. It is ordinary because it draws from basic and long-standing human knowledge about how and where the new emerges in social existence or social practice. Here Derek Attridge's description of how the new or the other (that is, an *other* to the senses that comes from beyond the senses) to extant thought arises from within an inherited culture will be very helpful to ground the mundanity of the idea of Jesus Christ as a gap:

> The creative act, however internal it might seem, works with materials absorbed from what we can broadly call a culture or a melange of cultures. . . . The most innovative artists or scientists have usually had an exceptionally great capacity to incorporate cultural materials and have therefore been able to make the strongest impression on cultures. Nor is this merely a question of the richness and range of the stuff that the mind has to work on; what the inventor finds in the cultural field is not just material *but gaps* in the material, strains and tensions that suggest the pressure of the other, of the hitherto unthought and unthinkable.[4]

Indeed, the trope of gap (split) I have employed so far in this book to describe Pentecostal epistemology is made a little clearer with the passage quoted above. I can shed even more light on the trope. Conceiving existence as split or maintaining that there are gaps in reality means that the believer must "fill in something that is not given" in a situation in order to interpret it.[5] Situation or existence (considered as text or intertextuality) is always "gapped and dialogical."[6] The cracks and their pressures invite Pentecostals into the *tehomic* depths of sense-spirit hermeneutics.[7]

Let us now turn to chapter 2, which philosophically explores the key ideas in the lecture-sermon presented to a Pentecostal congregation. We turn to chapter 2 in the hope of philosophically "exegeting" the main arguments of this chapter, but not with the hubris that the paradoxical particularity of the sense-spirit epistemology that I have described can be cleanly conceptually assimilated into modern philosophy. For those who are not Pentecostals, the way of knowing described in this chapter will always remain a *scandalon* or "stumbling block" and a *source of offense*.

---

4. Attridge, "Innovation, Literature, Ethics," 23; emphasis added.
5. Boyarin, *Intertextuality*, 41.
6. Boyarin, *Intertextuality*, 14, 17.
7. For an excellent history of classical Pentecostal hermeneutics as expounded by academic theologians, see Oliverio, *Theological Hermeneutics*.

2

Exegeting the Sermon
Exploring the Depths of Pentecostal Thinking

INTRODUCTION

THEOLOGY, AS SOME WISE scholars say, is often personal and correlational. The Pentecostal theological theorization of Jesus Christ as the middle space says more about the religious and personal situations of Pentecostals than about the Son of God himself. The conceptual Christ is created in the image of humanity engaged in one of its earthly struggles. And as we learned in the last chapter, this conceptual Christ is neatly translated into decision criterion: "Accept if it makes spirit, otherwise reject." Wherever possible translate "it makes sense" into "it does not make sense, but it makes spirit." Yet it is very difficult for two Pentecostals to agree when a particular case makes spirit instead of sense.

Permit me to tell a joke that captures some of the difficulties involved in interpreting Christ as middle space between the wisdom of the world and the so-called supernatural wisdom. The joke is about a Pentecostal pastor and a female member of his church. In a case where she should have been referred to a professional marriage counselor, the pastor and his deliverance ministers decided to pray for the woman to "heal" her.

A married Pentecostal woman who believes that she is in love with her neighbor is taken to her church, where the deliverance ministers do their best to cast out the "spirit of adultery" from her. She is told that the demon troubling her has been destroyed by the fire of the Holy Ghost. No sooner has she left the church than she comes back, very worried, claiming that she is still deeply attracted to the neighbor, and afraid that the demon will deliver her to an oceanic bliss of illicit sex.

"Dear sister," says her pastor, "you know very well that the demon has been roasted by the fire of the Holy Ghost and your fear does not make sense."

"Of course, I know that," the woman replied, "but does the demon know that? My dearest pastor, my fear or caution does not make sense, but it makes spirit."[1]

Indeed, there is not only a void between what is interpreted as sense and what is considered as spirit, but a possible gulf between any two Pentecostals on interpreting any specific situation.

One of the tasks of this chapter is to investigate how Jesus Christ is capable of structuring faith suspended to a "space" between logic-sense and non-sense, the possible and the impossible, whose only "existence" stands out because the subject has declared it. Once this "opening" is declared in the name of Christ or conviction about his powers and promises, it becomes a *pure event*. This opening does not testify to the order of facts, arguments, or knowledge per se. The believer testifies to the fidelity of the possibilities, the expected transformation of impossibilities into possibilities opened by the event.[2] The person who declares open this space,

> [the] one dependent on an evental grace, properly speaking knows nothing. To imagine that one knows, when it is a question of subjective possibilities, is fraudulent: "He who thinks he knows something . . . does not yet know as he ought to know" (Cor I.8.2). How does one know when one is an apostle. According to the truth of a declaration and its consequences, which, being without proof or visibility, emerges at that point where knowledge, be it empirical or conceptual, breaks down. In characterizing Christian discourse from the point of salvation, Paul does not hesitate to say: "Knowledge . . . will disappear" (Cor. I.13.8).[3]

What is important for us is to know how to investigate the connection between a faith founded in the subject's enunciation (or subjective recognition of *a site*, path without support) and subject as a *universal singularity*. Pentecostals believe that the subject who has this kind of conviction is not limited to any particular ethnic, racial, or class identity. The subject of faith is without identity—he or she only needs to believe in Jesus Christ. This

---

1. This joke is a transformation of a joke in Zupančič, *Odd One In*, 15.
2. Badiou, *Saint Paul*, 45.
3. Badiou, *Saint Paul*, 45.

does not mean that the believer is no longer white or black, Asian or African. What it says is that to have this kind of faith or to have *split Christ* (that is, Christ as the middle space) is independent of one's identity or particularism. Faith is a subjective disposition. The person's focus is on God's presence in the world, on Christ's presence, which ruptures preexisting knowledge systems to initiate something new amid ongoing social processes.

The locus of God's presence is believed to be in the space that opens when born-again believers navigate the crack between spirit and sense. This is both a personal and communal space—more communal. A religious gathering or community collectively engages with the Bible and God's promises with covenantal passion, and in this process a space is created to experience God's presence, triggering a concentrated divine presence to rest in the in-between among them. This space that Christ's (God's) presence opens in the world, which also inhabits the in-between of the believers in a community, is the space between sense and spirit, and it is basically a fecund *void*, creative nothingness.

God chooses those things that are nothing, non-beings, in order to make nothing those things that are, beings (1 Cor 1:28–29). That the faith-event "causes non-beings rather than beings to arise as attesting to God" means that faith consists in the abolition of what all previous worldviews or regimes of discourse about orders of faith or conviction entail.[4] This gives us a measure of the ontological subversion to which Pentecostalism's anti-common sense or anti-majoritarian stance invites us.

Pentecostals are also glad to point out what Paul writes about the foolishness of God: "For the foolishness of God is wiser than human wisdom, and the weakness of God is stronger than human strength" (1 Cor 1:25). It is this belief that "foolishness" takes precedence over wisdom or weakness over power (strength) that creates the disjunctive space between sense and non-sense (un-sense), being and nonbeing, where things do not make sense but make spirit. It is what discourages active mastery of one's socioeconomic reality and encourages eventual declaration.

The Pentecostal split (the space between sense and spirit) is ultimately based not on emotion but, arguably, on age-old Protestant theory. The Reformers taught us that we are saved by faith and not by works, and those who believe in Jesus Christ are no longer under the regime of law but in the freedom of grace. For Pentecostals, the combination of faith, works, law, and grace enacts two subjective dispositions or paths of life. The path of sense correlates law and work, the everyday logic of existence. To succeed, a person masters the laws and logics of her environment, matching inputs

---

4. Badiou, *Saint Paul*, 47.

to outputs. Another person on the path of spirit, where grace and faith are correlated, gets results that are not (rigidly) connected to effort or work. The space of eventual truth, the path of split Christ lies between these two paths, which is the eventual site.[5]

The space that opens between sense and spirit is the space of grace.[6] Grace not only provides "ground" for this space, it also interrupts the chain of cause and effect. This is done not by shunting the chain into a separate non-human or non-phenomenal realm, but as a split within causation itself such that possibilities, which are either retroactively activated or become freshly legible, come together with ongoing automatism of social processes of the now to form a new constellation. Just as the split needs to occur over and over again as believers encounter multiple different realities, spaces of grace also open up as required. The grace that operated in split A does not automatically operate in split B; thus, the grace the Pentecostal possesses has a perishable quality, it is *amissible*. Grace is not only eventual, the knowledge it enables the Pentecostal to garner is also eventual. It-makes-spirit is an event of knowledge, a particular form of being able to know, an invention of a cognitive space that increases the possibilities of knowing. It is fidelity to this event that transforms the "want-to-know" into "want-to-know-something." This is a fidelity that transforms conditions of production of knowledge into coherent discourse or meaning.[7] Fidelity to this cognitive space is seen as fidelity to Christ, and this space of knowing is reflexive of some key dimensions of Pentecostal lived experience.

Section 1: Metaphor of Christ as the Middle Space

The void, middle space, in which Jesus Christ is placed, inscribed or represents, is reflective of the void every decision-maker must inhabit at the nearly imperceptible moment before a decision is made. At such a moment, such a "now," the decision-maker has sensible information, on one side, and on the other, the unknown, what-is-to-come, or inspiration. She must dwell in this gap, a space of promise between the island of security and the ocean of uncertainty; she must inhabit this temporal gap, the dark space, the night, where all cows are black.[8] To take a decision, to traverse this gap, the person must somehow act on herself; she must insert herself into the gap and cross

---

5. Badiou, *Saint Paul*, 75, inspired this paragraph.
6. Agamben, *Time That Remains*, 122, inspired this sentence.
7. This way of articulating my view was inspired by de Certeau, *Mystic Fable*, 2:222–23, 218–19.
8. Arendt, *Human Condition*, 237, informed the metaphors of island and ocean.

from one side to the other. The person and the space (the temporal gap) are acting on one another. Within this perspective, to act, to reach a decision, is to allow the temporal gap (the middle space) to speak with the *middle voice*, so to speak.

Note that the person trying to make a decision, the believer that is struggling between sense and spirit, sensation and aspiration (inspiration), the one who is inserted in the flow of time and holds both sides of the decision together, is not a beholder; she herself is the gap. The decision-maker does not merely observe the gap, the void, she becomes the gap, the battlefield of the two antagonists of sense and spirit, hard data and insight (inspiration, aspiration). It is her standing in the middle that keeps the gap in existence. The presence of the decision-maker in the gap is the real gap. Only because she is inserted in the flow of sense-spirit and only to the extent that she stands her ground does the flow of sense-spirit, data-inspiration break up into sense and spirit, data and inspiration (what-is-to-come). The void between sense and spirit, the time gap between what is and what-is-to-come, came into existence because believers (human beings committed to alternate epistemology) are inserted into decision flows, imperialistic operations of knowledge systems, or objective time to make a new beginning, to initiate something new.[9]

Insofar as the gap between sense and spirit is created by the insertion of the Pentecostal believer, our meditation must extend to the Pentecostal hypothesis. From the foregoing analysis, it is not a big step to reach the conclusion that the Pentecostal hypothesis is an embodied stance within this gap of decision-making whose basis is the event of *natality* (insertion, being born-again) and fidelity to Christ, to the Christ-event in history. It is also clear from the foregoing (including chapter 1) that it is not only Christology that influences Pentecostal epistemology but also epistemology (and/or socio-psychological forces of decision-making) that bends back on Christ, *who Christ is*, the conceptualization of Christology. The framing is, indeed, bidirectional.

The Pentecostal hypothesis is the capacity to constitute alternate ways of knowing. It is for the purpose of initiating a new beginning or something new amid automatic social processes. The generation and renewal of the hypothesis are constitutive of freedom, as individuals assert their politically concerted power of a new beginning or something new over ongoing social processes and structures undergirded by cognitive injustice that they view as concretely life-limiting or potentially destructive. Broadly conceived, the

---

9. Arendt, *Between Past and Future*, 11, inspired this paragraph. See also Wariboko, *Ethics and Time*, 127–35.

Pentecostal hypothesis is a mode or way of inhabiting the world. It is a fundamental disposition toward knowledge production, that is, naming how a group actualizes or enacts alternate epistemology, providing a meaningful framework to its existence in a particular way and grappling with the contingency of decisions that mark its humanity.

As a way of knowing that is different from, interrogates, and resists dominant or regnant knowledge systems, the Pentecostal hypothesis is not a property of Pentecostals alone. It flourishes in other spiritual communities, in ethnic groups, indigenous societies, ecological movements, or social groups that resist cognitive injustice and fight epistemological battles as they seek meaningful existence in their own ways. Sociologist Boaventura de Sousa Santos, in his book *Epistemologies of the South*, argues that social theories have not paid enough attention to cognitive injustice, "the failure to recognize the different ways of knowing by which people across the globe provide meaning to their existence."[10] He maintains that conventional epistemology, Cartesian rationalism, or the "character of the universal claim of modern science"[11] does not allow the world to recognize itself in its infinite diversity but functions to marginalize or deny the creativity of all those who do not agree with it and causes the death of knowledge ("epistemicide") of social groups that possess alternate ways of knowing. While not advocating for the discarding or discrediting of scientific knowledge, or even downplaying the "technological productivity of modern science,"[12] Santos presses for the recognition of other forms of knowledge. He writes,

> In many areas of social life, modern science has demonstrated an unquestionable superiority in relation to other forms of knowledge. There are, however, other interventions in the real world that are valuable to us today in which modern science has played no part.... Herein lies the impulse for copresence and for incompleteness. Since no single type of knowledge can account for all possible interventions in the world, all knowledges are incomplete in different ways. Incompleteness cannot be eradicated because any complete description of varieties of knowledge would necessarily not include the type of knowledge responsible for the description. There is no knowledge that is not known by someone for some purpose. All knowledges are testimonial since what they know of reality (their active dimension)

---

10. Santos, *Epistemologies of the South*; this summation is on the book's back cover.
11. Santos, *Epistemologies of the South*, 201.
12. Santos, *Epistemologies of the South*, 201.

is always reflected back in what they reveal about the subject of this knowledge (their subjective dimension).[13]

The Pentecostal hypothesis we are laying out in this book is one type of the marginalized, despised, and unappreciated epistemologies that should be recognized for the sake of global cognitive justice. In addition, for the sake of acknowledging the fact that "the reasoning mind," for many people in the world, is often complemented by imagination, spiritual insights, and emotion, especially in their private domains or their ways of being.[14] We argue that Pentecostals conceive Christ as the crack in the world, a creative space of nothingness that energizes the world and is emblematic of the crack between sense (rationality) and spirit (a different way of knowing and being in the world). This crack is a void, an abyss. The void schematizes the impossible search for knowledge emptied of Enlightenment rationality or sense data. Epistemology happens not at the edge of the void but by traversing it. Epistemology is the hope that this void is fruitful, and it is worth depending on. Traversing the void, which is an abyss, could be seen as dangerous, homely, or sheer belief in the virtue of the uncalculatable.[15]

One reason we say that the void is an abyss is that it is a zone (a site of incalculability, the point where the network of cause-effect breaks down) that can never be eliminated. When Pentecostals turn from it-makes-sense to it-makes-spirit, they cross it by means of trust. In this gray zone, the believer is not operating by knowledge (sense-certainty) or ignorance, but only *crediting* Jesus Christ and his consistency. Indeed, the trust in Jesus precedes every encounter with the void in every point of decision-making, and they also trust him with the decision. It takes redoubled trust to navigate the chasm between sense and spirit, and it is what creates the site for the spirit to eventually arise in the midst of it-makes-sense and turn it-makes-sense into it-makes-spirit.

Jesus is the ballast that enables Pentecostals to pin down the elusive *cut* in the decision, *de-caedere* in the ocean of uncertainty, and he is the light that

13. Santos, *Epistemologies of the South*, 201.

14. All this does not suggest that we should accept all knowledge claims because their proponents allege cognitive injustice. We should accept claims as plausible as determined by commonly accepted standards within a given context or tradition.

15. "The abyss is the schema-image of the infinite as not needing the finite, as prior to or unconditioned by the finite. The abyss is approached by stepping over the verge of the finite; it is a place (or non-place) we get to by going to the edge, or by imagining the world explicitly emptied of all things that give it definition. By contrast to the unconditioned abyss, we are conditioned by dependency on the fruitfulness of the abyss. Spiritually to step off into the abyss is to commit oneself to the indefinite, abandoning all means of self-definition. The abyss can be fearsome beyond measure, or true home." Neville, *Truth of Broken Symbols*, 94–95.

makes them grasp the truth of decision on nights when all cows are dark. (We could, indeed, at this juncture wonder if this "Jesus" is not a fantasmatic screen at work as Pentecostals interact with a world split between mechanical sense and fluid spirit). The trust in Jesus is "something" in the void more than the void. It is this treasure (which is less than nothing, as in quantum physics) that Pentecostals put in the void that activates the transition from sensation to *pneumasation* (that is, the intuition or feeling of making-spirit; pneumatic data or certainty as against sensation or sense-certainty).

At this point, someone might raise the objection that there is really no void between sense and spirit. For those who believe only in rationalist epistemology, there is nothing like pneumasation, so there cannot be a gap between sense and spirit. Even for Pentecostals, let truth be told, there is no preexisting void. What do I mean? The gap is only a retroactive effect of their presumed duality of sense and spirit, matter and spirit. But have we discerned the whole truth if we simply say Pentecostals encrusted onto reality a duality (whether retroactive or aprioristic)? Is reality itself not split, cracked, incomplete? Or will the split not emerge when sense is referred to itself, confronted (by means of its excess) "with itself as seen from the outside"?[16] The noncoincidence of sense with itself creates cracks in sense, in all that is called reason. It is germane at this stage of our argumentation to reiterate that the split in either sense or spirit that we are exploring remains "an intrinsic duality of *One*—that is to say, that it does not simply fall apart into 'two ones,'"[17] that we do not ultimately allow the split to disappear and in this way destroy their connection and unity.

The Pentecostal penchant to see and confront split reality with a split Christ, by an alternate cognitive space through conceptualizing a void, might well speak to a crucial dimension of the human will or to some ethics of the uncalculatable. The void is the abyss of nothingness that is entailed in every act of freedom. Freedom, as Hannah Arendt taught us, is the capacity "to begin something new and . . . not being able to control or even foretell its consequences."[18] Such a capacity must confront, tarry or engage the "abyss of nothingness that opens up before any deed that cannot be accounted for by a reliable chain of cause and effect and is inexplicable in Aristotelian categories of potentiality and actuality."[19]

The void separates or mediates between sense (pathological, empirical chain of cause and effect as per Kant) and the pure will (which wants to obey

---

16. Zupančič, *Odd One In*, 118.
17. Zupančič, *Odd One In*, 122.
18. Arendt, *Human Condition*, 235.
19. Arendt, *Life of the Mind*, 2:207.

or live by the dictates or imperatives of the Spirit).[20] The mediation works through two processes: Kantian and Sadean. On the one hand, the Pentecostal subject barrels through the abyss—the will to live by the spirit is not constrained by sense data since it is fueled by a sense of duty, like a Kantian ethical subject. On the other, like a Sadean subject, the Pentecostal subject avoids enchainment and enchantment of the chain of empirical cause and effect because she wants the pleasure, jouissance of the spirit, and she does not need to "rationalize" or "justify" her choice or desire. This is all about the capricious will of the acting subject. Lacan's "Kant avec Sade" comes to mind.

> Both the Kantian ethical subject and the Sadean subject of the unreserved will to *jouissance* want what they want unconditionally and pursue it without regard to any utilitarian "rational" considerations. In this precise sense, as was clear to Hegel, the utter caprice is the hidden "truth" of the Kantian ethical universality—no wonder that Kant himself characterized the moral law as "fact of practical reason," as an inexplicable unconditional demand which simply is there, exerting on us its unbearable pressure.[21]

Of course, there is another way to cross this void. And it is the way of gain in utility as espoused by either the eighteenth-century English philosopher Jeremy Bentham or the biblical Simon the sorcerer (Acts 8:9–25). Believers in this scenario want the translation of it-makes-sense (it-does-not-make-sense) into it-makes-spirit for pure financial gain. Oh, should you not call this the Pentecostal succumbing to mere utility, abandonment of true ethics, or—tongue in cheek—the religious suspension of the ethical? If you find the reference to financial calculation a little too much to bear, let me offer you a more palatable one. There is always a third party in the midst of sense and spirit, a fantasmatic supplement that powers the transition from sense to spirit. There is always the gaze of the *other* or others—an object-cause of desire. To be able to tarry in the void because of the spirit is a gift of desire; however, reliance on the senses comes by nature. There is always something such as "pretend to believe" and "believe to pretend," which sustains the desire to transform it-makes-sense into it-makes-spirit—something that teaches the person how to fantasize or desire. According to Slavoj Žižek, "To pretend to believe means that, even if belief is experienced as sincere, one wears it as a mask, one acts as if one believes; to believe to pretend means that, even if one experiences one's belief as a mere cynical game,

20. Žižek, *On Belief*, 139.
21. Žižek, *On Belief*, 140.

not taking it seriously, one falls into one's own game, one in effect believes in what one thinks is only a game of pretending."[22]

We have often used the word "translation" to mark the movement from it-makes-sense to it-makes-spirit. There are problems with the metaphor of translation—problems that we need to highlight to deepen our knowledge of what the movement from one side to the other aims to achieve. In typical translation, one hopes to render as faithfully as possible the original meaning into the new. There is always a gap between the original and the translated meaning. With Pentecostalism, the translation exercise from it-makes-sense to it-makes-spirit actually transposes the gap into the original meaning. The original, the starting point of it-makes-spirit, is already a fragment of a whole (human knowledge is considered part of the storehouse of God's wisdom). So the goal of the translation is to supplement the knowledge of it-makes-sense and not to achieve fidelity with it. Regarding the original as only a broken fragment of divine knowledge, the purpose of making the movement into it-makes-spirit "is to produce another fragment which will not imitate the original but fit it as one fragment of a broken Whole may fit another."[23]

Does all this talk about translation not bring us to the sphere of economics? What is the exact nature of the relation of translation, the exchange between it-makes-sense and it-makes-spirit? It is not a matter of exchange value as a quantitative relation in which value in one form of use is exchanged for that of another. If it is merely quantitative, then the relation has no intrinsic value, and is merely accidental and relative. Is the relationship a matter of use value based on the specific properties or qualities of each of them? The whole point of Pentecostal engagement in the translation exercise is to directly deny any similitude. The exercise is an act characterized by an abstraction from the "use value" of sense or maintaining a distance from the "use value" of sense (concrete properties of empirical data). So if we leave out the use values of sense-knowledge and spiritual-knowledge as the basis of the translation exercise, we have to look for a common property inherent in both forms of knowledge. The universal intrinsic in both is divine wisdom. It-makes-sense and it-makes-spirit are crystals of this divine substance. Both forms of knowledge have subjective (objective?) character as values insofar as they are fragments of abstract divine wisdom, or immanent dimensions of God's wisdom, hence the social dimension of God's knowledge, pure knowability.[24]

---

22. Žižek, *Incontinence of the Void*, 66.
23. Žižek, *Incontinence of the Void*, 169.
24. Žižek, *Incontinence of the Void*, 176–77, inspired this passage.

Just like Karl Marx's notion of abstract labor power that undergirds capitalist commodity exchange, the Pentecostal notion of abstract divine knowledge is the ultimate common basis or "substance" for the traffic between knowledge-commodity produced in the secular sphere and the spiritual knowledge created in the sacred sphere. Like Marx's, the Pentecostal "theory" is soaked in a variety of tensions. For instance, is value not what the market decides at the intersection of the forces of demand and supply? Is value not what the market decides it is? Why look for the "ought" of value in some rarified labor theory of value? Is the Pentecostal theory of knowledge or exchange of knowledges not riddled with similar questions?

The presentation of Jesus Christ as the *middle space*, the in-between of sense and spirit, and as the one who embodies and energizes the creative void between the knowledge systems of the world and divine wisdom, reflects a basic tension in various forms of Christian spirituality. The Pentecostal everyday conception of Christ we saw in the previous chapter is an ethical ideal that arises from the tension between the symbol of the "is" (what is already) and the "ought" (what ought to be realized) in the directedness of human flourishing (meaning-fulfilling, existential relationships) toward better future alternatives, toward freedom. This tension is the dialectic of the stimulus of the Christianity-wide Pentecostal principle, which never allows faith to come to rest in the extant wisdom and constraint of the current order of knowledge. At the same time, Pentecostals aspire to see the unity of the "is" and the "ought" in Christ, to have an unbroken capacity to move from the "is" to the "ought" in their decision-making.

Pentecostal epistemology is both a yearning for, a conformation into, identification with, and a claim regarding their nature as an inter-people, as persons who inhabit a hybrid space between flesh and spirit. It is like a prayer in certain respects. To adapt theologian Brian Bantum's perspective on the act of prayer, the epistemology of Pentecostals as an articulation of identity and confession of the hope of translating the "what is" of existence to "what ought to be" of spirit-filled life is "an articulation of [their] relationship to and in Christ made possible through Christ's calling to them, through the indwelling of the Spirit which stirs them to recall the promises of God and the promise of God which they are."[25]

Jesus Christ as the middle space, as a cognitive space that speaks to the to-come, can also be represented graphically as Jesus-hyphen-Christ. The Man-God or God-Man is not only a wholesale and coherent mapping of divinity onto humanity but also the structural underpinning of the interpretative claim that he is the middle space, the hyphen between sense and

---

25. Bantum, *Redeeming Mulatto*, 175.

spirit. The internal hyphen in the hyphenated Jesus-Christ is transformed into a positive epistemological condition. Pentecostals have transformed a positive ontological condition (or question) in the nature of Jesus Christ into an epistemological one. The hyphen of Jesus-Christ is reconceived or reconceptualized as a hyphen in the texture of reality. Their incomplete knowledge of the Jesus hyphen becomes a positive feature of reality, all worldly knowledge systems, or decision-matrices, which are in themselves incomplete.

Human life is suspended within the flow of Jesus's hyphen. And Christ as the middle space is also a hyphen within the lives of his followers. The middle space (the hyphen) designates by itself and as itself a syncope between the present and the to-come. It also designates the space through which Pentecostal spirituality is constructed, articulated, and deconstructed decision by decision. Everyday decision opens within the hyphen as an *outside* that is not beyond the hyphen but the *truth* of the hyphen. This a truth that exceeds knowledge. Living into the space of this truth, fidelity to the hyphen demands efforts: deliberation, judgment, and resistance to ongoing automatism of social processes and to popular validation of sense. For Pentecostals, the hyphen in reality or in sense-spirit always marks a contestation of the authority of modernity's knowledge paradigms or the legitimacy of secular humanist decisions, an ongoing conflict that liberal scholars or mainline Christians attempt to paper over with discussions of the distinction between the phenomenal (things) and noumenal realms (things-in-themselves).

Jesus as Christ here symbolizes a medium between sense and spirit. He enables Pentecostals to pass over an epistemological bridge spanning the shores of beclouded senses to the sweet fields of delightful spirit, to walk from the phenomenal into the noumenal. This pass-through is an art form, a poetics crafted (sometimes carefully, other times irresponsibly) to interpret epistemology christologically. It is christological not merely because their thinking about knowing is emblematic of Jesus as straddling two realms. It is also that the pass-through is an act of grace enabled by the personal relations of believers with Jesus. In the reckoning of the Pentecostals, Jesus is the one traversing the distance between sense and spirit, just as he crossed the distance between heaven and earth, divinity and humanity, "like the shuttle on a loom, weaving a continuous fabric joining [them] with God."[26]

The pass-through itself is a moving image of Jesus as the way, the truth, and life of knowing (John 14:6). As the path of knowledge, he leads them deeper into the full presence of the triune God where there is fullness of joy

---

26. Neville, *God Who Beckons*, 116.

and pleasures evermore. As the truth, he brings to light the inner dimensions and the future unfolding of the situations that call for decision. Finally, as the life, an epistemology anchored to him generates data and decisions that lift the believer's life more fully into God's glorious life and into her own life more abundantly.[27]

In all this, the ethicality of epistemology is in play: What knowledge production or acquisition or what decision constitutes a good Pentecostal life? It-makes-spirit is a consideration that tells us that a decision is right over and against the rival it-makes-sense. In (Charles) Taylorese, epistemology (the nobility of Pentecostal epistemology) is a "constitutive good."[28] What is the exact nature of this good? When does it seem right to say a particular decision makes spirit, or how does any Pentecostal know that his decision to live into the middle space named Christ is the right one?

Chapters 3 and 4 offer responses to these questions in a straightforward academic style. In the remainder of this chapter I will endeavor to give the reader greater insights into (or "feel" for) the Pentecostal conception of Christ as a middle figure. For Pentecostals, the answers to the questions I have just raised flow from the practice and performance of Christ as the middle space of existence and knowledge system. The answers are goods internal to the practice of faith rooted in Christ as the middle space of infinite value between sense and spirit. The answers are achieved in the course of trying to achieve the lifestyle, the spirit-filled life, which is appropriate to and definitive of the practices, the cooperative human activities of a spiritual community, entailed in being faithful to Christ, listening to him, and making personal and social decisions based on the interpretations of his instructions.[29] Perhaps we can better anticipate these answers the more we get an intuitive understanding of the metaphor of the middle space.

Section 2: Parables of Christ as Middle Space

Grasping the Pentecostal metaphor of Christ as a middle space may be difficult for people encountering it for the first time. How can I describe the metaphor of Christ as a middle space, as an in-between? What parables or stories should I use to illustrate it? It is like a silence, which is in the small spaces between words in any sentence.

---

27. Neville, *God Who Beckons*, 105, 116, inspired this paragraph.
28. Taylor, *Sources of the Self*, ch. 4.
29. Pardon me for echoing MacIntyre, *After Virtue*, 187.

Parable of Silence

The split between sense and spirit is like the silence, the spaces between words in a spoken sentence that enable us to understand the meaning of a sentence. There is a silence that inhabits all that has been spoken or written, and every new word or sentence speaks from the silence that follows the full stop (period). Creativity or innovation usually springs from the dwelling place of silence. Every act of renewal, innovation, or fresh perspective wells up from the silence of the last achievement (understanding) and the ones before it and allows (craves) for emptiness. The void, the no-thing-ness, the silence, the margin is the source of the new. It is the place where the artist, the painter, the scholar, the dancer, the musician, the priest, the scientist can touch the *prima materia* of the eros of creativity.

Without the split between words enabled by silent spaces, we would not understand what a speaker is saying to us. The silence, it seems, is the fecund void from which meaning floats out, from which the sense of the statement emerges. The silence here is the silence of breath (wind, pneuma, air, spirit) and words as the audible representations of the invisible breath manifest silence as sounded breaths. In a sense, silence (breath, spirit) and sense (meaning, understanding) enfold from an invisible space, the void we can name as "sense-spirit."

When spirit and sense emerge from this primordial void of sense-spirit, they (still) carry the traces (cracks) of silence that engendered them. For Pentecostals, sense (reason) could not be experienced or interpreted as a double—a combination of sense plus spirit—or as a sufficient stand-in for the void or a substitute for the traces of sense-spirit. Reason or sense is not sufficient unto itself; rather, in order to properly discern a situation, reason has to be added to, energized by the believer's spirit, by her breath offered in prayers and praise to God, the Holy Spirit, the Holy Word, the sacred breath. The spirit, the invisible breath is needed to animate reason, to make it come alive and reveal its hidden dimensions, to reveal how to surpass it without escaping it or transcending materiality. Reason is never complete in itself; "it has to be actually engaged by [the believer] who, by this engagement, [gives] rise to a particular interpretation," and who by this engagement finds the cracks between sense and spirit in which she can insert herself and her situation (problem).[30] Reason is "not some otherworldly essence that comes to house itself inside [the human mind or] physiology. Rather, it is instilled and provoked by the sensorial field, induced by the tensions and

---

30. Abram, *Spell of the Sensuous*, 243.

participations between the human body" and the reality it encounters.³¹ Somewhere in the deep-rooted connection between this worldly reason, material body, sensorial field, and encountered reality, there is always a crack, which is where the light that is the split Christ is. Reason, sense for Pentecostals, is something that remains overtly dependent upon spirit, breath—both are needed to reach that space we have called split Christ.

We are indeed describing the underlying matrix that engenders both spirit and sense, the collective tissue from which spirit and sense function and flourish together. This is the primordial dimension of "sense-spirit" of the sense that is spirit and the very spirit that is sense. It is a matrix that is neither wholly "sensuous" nor wholly spiritual, from whence "sense" and "spirit" have been derived by a process of subtraction.

Pentecostals lend their imagination to objective reality in its encounter with the "promiscuous creativity of the sense" to fully see into this matrix and discern its hidden or invisible cracks.³² The meaning of a situation, its epistemic density, is found not in sense or spirit taken singly but in the intervals between them, in the system of differences.

Usually spirit and sense are opposed to each other, as qualitatively heterogenous. The explanation of the split might give the impression that opposition between the two is all there is to the relation between them. What do Pentecostals mean when they say, "It makes spirit and not sense"? Since they must always operate in the phenomenal world with their senses, this statement must be interlacing spirit and sense even as it seems to render them as absolutely heterogenous. Spirit is not devoid of sense and sense is not emptied of spirit. Sense is that in which there is spirit, and spirit is that in which there is little sense.³³ Spirit does not have another *sensori motor* of human beings to communicate with them at its disposal. In other words, when a decision-maker "makes spirit and not sense," when a believer indwells that gap between sense and spirit, she is not seizing another sense, an in-human sensorium, but a contracted, refined, attuned sense that shatters the coordinates of the phenomenal realm. Thus, the spirit that splits reality is nothing more than seized sense; the spirit happens through sense. The spirit is a cut within sense. The spirit is not another principle of another world, but our phenomenal world itself "with a slight adjustment, a meager difference. But this ever so slight difference, which results from my having

---

31. Abram, *Spell of the Sensuous*, 262.
32. Abram, *Spell of the Sensuous*, 58.
33. Agamben, *Time That Remains*, 68–69, inspired this idea.

grasped my disjointedness with regard to [phenomenal reality, hard reality] is, in every way, a decisive one."[34]

The shift from sense (rationality) to spirit (it-makes-spirit)—this almost imperceptible shift—does remind us of the slight adjustment in things or human behavior that will occur with the advent of the Messiah or what it means to live in the messianic time. Philosopher Giorgio Agamben in *The Coming Community* points to the slight shift in perception that occurs when the Messiah comes.

> There is a well-known parable about the kingdom of the Messiah that Walter Benjamin (who heard it from Gershom Scholem) recounted one evening to Ernst Bloch, who in turn transcribed it in *Spuren*. "A rabbi, a real cabalist, once said that in order to establish the reign of peace it is not necessary to destroy everything nor to begin a completely new world. It is sufficient to displace this cup or this bush or this stone just a little, and thus everything. But this small displacement is so difficult to achieve and its measure is so difficult to find that, with regard to the world, humans are incapable of it and it is necessary that the Messiah come." Benjamin's version of the story goes like this: "The *Hassidim* tell a story about the world to come that says everything there will be just as it is here. Just as our room is now, so it will be in the world to come; where our baby sleeps now, there too it will sleep in the other world. And the clothes we wear in this world, those too we will wear there. Everything will be as it is now, just a little different."[35]

Parable of Langue and Parole

It bears to emphasize that the distinction between spirit and sense in Pentecostal epistemology is not that of dichotomous poles. The two are bound together like *langue* and *parole*. The spirit (it-makes-spirit) is the *langue*. *Parole* (it-makes-sense) is the grammar of modernity and rationality. The two are exposed to each other, in a relation of *ex-position*, as Jean-Luc Nancy might put it. Each is exposed to the other and to itself. Language is nothing but this *ex-position*—the co-appearing and sharing of *parole* and *langue*.[36]

Ex-position[a]. *Parole* (the "ex-") is always already displaced toward position. To speak is to fall into a position, place, site of understandability,

---

34. Agamben, *Time That Remains*, 69.
35. Agamben, *Coming Community*, 53.
36. Nancy, *Inoperative Community*, 25.

to fall into grammar, as if retroactively creating its conditions of possibility. The ex- is signifying that what is outside (what is about to be spoken) is not to be set in opposition to what is within, what is at hand. What is already is always related in a certain sense to what is not-yet. The ex- is the essential ingredient of the meaning of the already, of the margin that is at the center of all that there is in *langue* and the margin that is the emptiness that allows words and grammar to come forth. To have *langue* is to endlessly "fall" into this emptiness. *Parole* is not finally and fully subject to langue, but *langue* arises from and is ultimately subject to the *parole* which precedes it. The "fall" (*parole*) is at the origin of language so that it precedes the very possibility of the *langue* arising from language and makes possible the creative force of human speech.

Ex-position[b]: Langue (the "position") is like retroactive causation. The moment I speak, it is as if I had already spoken or the language is speaking through me or speaks me. *Langue* does not mean some grammatical structures are eternally sealed or set in place in advance to live outside of everyday speech, but that a temporal decision to speak, to make utterance, is capable of retroactively creating or/and changing the grammar. *Langue* that is created by *parole* retroactively caused *parole* to be. *Langue* is akin to the market, objective spirit (Hegel), or social fact (Durkheim): any one of these is a product of collective action that in turn affects the individuals and groups that created it and continue to create and renew it. The process is the product and the product is the process.

Parole is the process that creates and renews *langue* as well as drawing from and being guarded by langue. *Langue* does not exist apart from *parole* and *parole* is dependent and functions on langue. *Langue* is common and is *a common* in a community. This means it is a dynamic framework that is available to all speakers in that specific community, and it is a common in the sense that it belongs to all in the community, created and renewed by all. There is always some kind of tension between *parole* and *langue* in any language, and this tension is somewhat akin to that in F. W. J. Schelling's Godhead, the maddening tension between expansion and contraction.[37]

Parable of Genes and Epigenetics

Let me explain the connection between rationality and spirituality in the sphere of decision-making in terms of a crude analogy to genes and epigenetics (environmental signals). When a decision is needed, it appears, a

37. Žižek and Schelling, *Abyss of Freedom/Ages of the World*. See also Wariboko, *Split God*, 33–36.

signal from the spiritual belief system—which is not considered by Pentecostals as an emergent property of rational logic—activates the *rational* decision-making process. The character of decision is determined not by the logic of rationality but by responses of the rational-logic system to the belief system, spiritual energy-based environment. If the rational logic is the "gene" of the Pentecostal epistemology, then belief is the environmental signal that trigger the genes. Biologists have coined the word *epigenetics*, which means "control over the genetics," to capture the impact of environmental signals on the proteins that switch on and off genes (DNA).[38] In the same way, might we coin the word *epilogics* to capture the idea of a believer's spiritual context, environment conditioning her logic of rationality in (moral, ethical) deliberations?

The "dark matter" of the spiritual energy provides mechanisms, some kind of "algorithm" by which *environmental information* can be used to modify the "readout" of rationality-encoding logic. The epilogic mechanism of the dynamic belief system interprets, translates, and controls the requirement of the rational-logical codes of modernity, post-Enlightenment society.[39]

The question that arises at this point is this: What is the procedure or means by which the rational coding system transmutes spiritual energy-based environmental signals into decisions or behaviors? We will attempt to address this question in subsequent chapters, where we demonstrate that the process of it-makes-spirit is a form of social ethics and a search for normative standards for justification of reason in the Pentecostal public. It-makes-spirit is not limited as a gesture to the Holy Spirit but extends to the ethos of the Pentecostal spiritual community and to concrete social and historical considerations. The phrase stands as a symbol of their desire to find an alternate epistemology that is at once beyond the division between rationality and irrationality and beyond subordination to the five-sense imperium, and is thereby beyond such wasting away of belief that comes about when it becomes subjugated to the exclusive order of materiality or normative rationality.[40]

It-makes-spirit is also a gesture of critique of rationality's conceptualization of reality. It-makes-spirit pushes for a notion of reality that includes the sense of excess, of superabundance, of an energy in which reality is too complex and simply beyond the constraints and harnesses utilized by rationalistic logic to comprehend and interpret "what the matter is going on at

---

38. Lipton, *Biology of Belief*, 43–47.
39. Lipton, *Biology of Belief*, 51–52, inspired this passage.
40. Nancy, *Inoperative Community*, 1, inspired this sentence.

any place or time."⁴¹ What the matter is going on is also a matter of the self, the observer and her belief system.

Section 3: Christ and Faith as an Opening

It is germane to pause at this juncture and ask why Pentecostals are so concerned about theorizing, theologizing and philosophizing Christ as a middle space, as a cut or split in the dense fabric of existence. It is a way of instructing the self to hear, feel, and imagine the world differently. It is to attune and place the self at the points of crossing between the expected ordinariness of existence and the elemental, miraculous depths of extraordinariness so as to transform almost all phenomenal perceptions into experience of caesural moments. The whole point of the cultivation of the self is to make the outcomes of all these instructions into a sustained way of life and thought. Does the attunement required by this spirituality reject rationality? What kind of relationship exists between the rationality of drawing inference from sense data, the rationality of acting on experience, which can be verified or affirmed by the five senses of self and others in a given tradition or context, and the spirituality of attuning to a supposed cut in the fabric of hard reality? The relationship that exists is full of tensions.

"The basic tension is not so much the tension of reason versus [belief], but, rather, the tension" of a direct belief in reason that is subjectively fully assumed versus belief in reason-through-distance.⁴² Pentecostals maintain a distance toward post-Enlightenment rationality. They practice, perform, or enact reason without really believing in it, that is, believe in reason through a distance. While they do not reject reason, many see immediate direct belief in reason or see those who lack distance toward modernist rationality as ultimately a threat to spirituality. Such stance or persons miss the "secret" of Pentecostal epistemology. In the words of famed Catholic writer G. K. Chesterton, from a different context, this secret could be nothing but this:

> That man can understand everything by the help of what he does not understand. The morbid logician seeks to make everything lucid, and succeeds in making everything mysterious. The mystic allows one thing to be mysterious, and everything else becomes lucid. . . . The one created thing which we cannot look at is the one thing in the light of which we look at everything.

---

41. This way of putting the matter was inspired by Castelo, *Pentecostalism*, 176.
42. Žižek, *Puppet and the Dwarf*, 5, 6.

> Like the sun at noonday, mysticism explains everything else by the blaze of its own invisibility.[43]

Holding reason at a distance is akin to participating in the world of reason through an attitude of suspension. It is not totally an escape from the world of reason, nor simply to accomplish a spiritual revolution, replacing the demands of reason with those of faith, but to continue to be in the world of reason with a Pauline *as-if-not* stance (rejoice as if you are not rejoicing).

> Let each of you remain in the condition in which you were called. . . . I mean, brothers and sisters, the appointed time has grown short; from now on, let even those who have wives be as though they had none, and those who mourn as though they were not mourning, and those who rejoice as though they were not rejoicing, and those who buy as though they had no possessions, and those who deal with the world as though they had no dealings with it. For the present form of this world is passing away. (1 Cor 7:20, 29–31 NRSV)

In another vein, which is in line with the Bakhtinian dialogic and polyphonic approach to social analysis, Pentecostals argue that the problem with post-Enlightenment rationality is not that it is "too reason-oriented" but that it is not "reason-oriented" enough. There is something (precious treasure, *agalma*) in the believer that escapes the subjection of reason. "Spirit" is "the very intimate resistant core on account of which the subject [the Pentecostal believer] experiences its relationship to [Reason] as that of subjection; it is that on account of which [Reason] has to appear to the subject as a foreign power crushing the subject."[44]

Enlightenment rationality will lose its "'alienated' character of an external force brutally imposing itself on the subject the moment" it addresses itself to the subject's core that feels threatened by the rule of reason.[45] It can address itself to this core of the subject by turning itself to its own core, the belief or attachment that deep within itself (within Reason) there is a precious treasure (*agalma*) that cannot work with or submit to an authentic inner experience in which the subject recognizes herself. Reason appears too weak to address its core. The point here is that the inner treasure of Reason cannot engage the "interior" of humanity, the exposed innermost intimacy. Reason considers the externalization of the innards as externalized "shit," formless shit, formless spirit, which not only threatens it but also reflects its

---

43. Chesterton, *Orthodoxy*, 14.
44. Žižek, *Puppet and the Dwarf*, 117.
45. Žižek, *Puppet and the Dwarf*, 117.

foundational-less excesses. Does this reflection not remind us of what the psychoanalysts say: shit and *agalma*, excrement and hidden treasure, are parts of the same thing? Beneath the hard mask of Reason's exquisite image there is a weakness. And beneath the soft public identity of Pentecostal spiritual enthusiasm there is a core of resistance.

There is another Bakhtinian twist. Has someone not noticed that the whole opposition between sense and spirit is somewhat stuck in the dialectics of law and its transgression? Actually, there might not be real opposition between sense and spirit, but dialectic interdependence between reason (sense) and its transgression. The passion for the spirit (it-makes-spirit) relies on *prohibition* put in place by modern rationality (reason). The prohibition or the system of rationality generates its excess, the transgressive desire to experience the impossible as a way of being authentic to the Christian life-in-spirit.

What this attitude to enjoy the excess pleasure of transgressing the rationality of modernity reveals is that it is reason itself that is the absolute excess. Reason intervenes in the "homogenous" stability of the Pentecostal spirit-pleasure-oriented life "as the shattering of absolute destabilizing 'heterogeneity.'"[46] Thus in a certain sense sticking to reason itself is the highest subversion, and transgression of rationality a conformist act. I am tempted here to quote Chesterton's observation about the detective story:

> [It] keeps in some sense before the mind that fact the civilization itself is the most sensational of departures and the most romantic of rebellions. . . . When the detective in a police romance stands alone, and somewhat fatuously fearless amid the knives and fists of a thief's kitchen, it does certainly serve to make us remember that it is the agent of social justice who is the original and poetic figure, while the burglars and footpads are merely placid old cosmic conservatives, happy in the immemorial respectability of apes and wolves. . . . [The police romance] is based on the fact that morality is the most dark and daring of conspiracies.[47]

It-makes-spirit: Is this really revolutionary in the light of Chesterton's reasoning? It-makes-spirit might not be all that subversive as it fights to conserve the homogenous stability of a spirit-pleasure-oriented life. It may well be an anxiety about the overwhelming presence or orthodoxy of Reason, which necessitates carving out a space where the Pentecostal can gain a distance toward reason, to inhabit a breathing (pneumatic) space.

---

46. Žižek, *Puppet and the Dwarf*, 5–6.
47. Chesterton, "Defence of Detective Stories," 35.

If it-makes-spirit is reason held at some distance, then it can also be interpreted to mean that spirit is sense "in becoming": the break, rupture, with "old substantial" Reason as the condition for creation (generation, production) of new reason, a new form of pentecostalized reason. The gap between sense and reason is here transposed into reason itself.[48]

Pentecostals have multiple other ways to react to the intrusion of Reason or metaphorize the interplay of sense and spirit as they struggle to distance spirit from sense. When you listen carefully to Pentecostals talk about it-makes-spirit, you learn that there are two kinds of reaction when a situation or decision awaiting to be deciphered or made suddenly "makes spirit." The point where suddenly the light flashes, where the spiritual intuition acting as master-signifier retroactively fixes all elements in a decision matrix, comes along lines or directions unexpected, eliciting a surprise. The person may then just play along this surprising yet pleasant path as the "Spirit leads." Or the person may retroactively formulate the sensible path that led to the satisfactory outcome. In the first type of reaction, it-makes-spirit *supplements* sense-certainty; in the second it *complements* sense-certainty, an answer to a well-crafted demand (prayer).[49] The two forms of reaction are ways of managing the homogenous stability of spirit-pleasure-oriented life. To use the words of philosopher Alenka Zupančič from a different context,

> The supplement of pleasure [satisfaction], instead of allowing the release or production of more pleasure, could be retroactively transformed from supplement into complement. That is to say: every [pneumasation] encounter brings with it the temptation to reinscribe the surprising, accidental and bonus-like dimension of the satisfaction into the linear or circular coupling of demand and (its) satisfaction or, in other terms, of desire and *jouissance*.[50]

Concluding Remarks

We have used the theme or framework of split, crack, space and spacing, evental breaks in ongoing situation, order of being, to comprehend one of the ways Pentecostals interpret *who Christ is* in their lives. We explored the crack between sense and foolishness, sense and spirit in connecting Pentecostal epistemology and Christology. We argued that Pentecostals

---

48. Žižek, *Puppet and the Dwarf*, 88, inspired this passage.
49. Zupančič, *Odd One In*, 134.
50. Zupančič, *Odd One In*, 134.

conceive Christ as the crack in the world, a creative space of nothingness that energizes the world and is emblematic of the crack between sense (rationality) and spirit (a different way of knowing and being in the world).

The deployment of the theme or theory of split in this book makes it the third time it has been employed to interpret dimensions of the "economic nature" of the Christian Trinitarian God.[51] In my 2018 book, *The Split God: Pentecostalism and Critical Theory*, I extracted from everyday Pentecostal practice the notion of God the Father as split, the split itself. Pentecostals understand God or aspects of God as the ontological incompleteness that drives creation, creativity, and the world. The epistemological obstacle that prevented them from knowing God was transformed into a positive ontological condition. The split in their vision or gaze of God in his noumenal splendor is now transformed as a positive feature of God himself. The unknowability of God is not an obstacle to their disposition to combine the attributes of God or to deploy them as partial organs in ways that affirm their view of reality and how to transform it.

If the notion of split God deals with the ontological dimensions of the deity and deeper underlying structuring of reality, then the notion of Pentecostal hypothesis (precisely the christological framing of epistemology, the split Christ) deals with the ontical, the concrete issues of making decisions against hard reality. In this crude analogy, God the Father is dealt with at the ontological (noumenal) level, and Christ at the ontic level. Christ is the physical embodiment, the express image of the split at the phenomenal level. The Pentecostal believer becoming this gap, having an embodied stance in this gap, is a way to mimic Christ, who is the "original" gap. Those who are baptized into Christ Jesus are "baptized" into his split, so that they may live a new life, initiate something new amid ongoing social processes.

---

51. This trilogy on the three persons came about randomly. I did not plan it this way. I am recognizing a trilogy only after the fact. Now that I am at the point where I can look and recognize the emergence of a trilogy relating to persons of the trinity, I must not claim more than the little blessings that have come my way. With hindsight, I can also say there is a trilogy relating to economic ethics that also deploys the notion of split. So far I have *Economics in Spirit and Truth: A Moral Philosophy of Finance* (2014), and *The Split Economy: Saint Paul Goes to Wall Street*, which is scheduled to be published in 2020 by State University of New York Press; and if one is to follow the pattern, then I owe my readers a book on economic ethics that can creatively explore an aspect of economic life as this book has done on an aspect of Pentecostal life. There is a sense in which a trilogy of split as a philosophical theory that an organizes my thought was planned. This book, *The Pentecostal Hypothesis*, was to be named "The Split Christ." The earlier books in the "split lineage" are *The Split God* and *The Split Economy*. The *Pentecostal Hypothesis* completes the trilogy on the split theory, though it bears a different name. I decided against "The Split Christ" as a book title at the last minute because I thought it might be conflated with Jesus's hybrid divine-human nature.

This book, *The Pentecostal Hypothesis: Christ Talks, They Decide*, is to enable us to comprehend all this.

My 2012 book, *The Pentecostal Principle: Ethical Methodology in New Spirit*, focuses on the Holy Spirit as the freedom and capacity to initiate something new amid automatic social processes. In the book, we interpreted God's Spirit as the interruptive and inaugurative power of the split, which has no origin, no foundational point, and no end. The Spirit is the active principle of its renewal; the sustenance of the gap is constitutive of freedom, the capacity to begin. The Pentecostal principle is the capacity to begin:

> It encapsulates the notion that no finite or conditioned reality can claim to have reached its destiny. The movement of every existent to its destiny (full realization of potentialities) remains ever incompletable because it is "rooted" in the abyss of divine freedom. Every end has an option: to be a new beginning. . . . Because of the demand of new beginning, more is expected from every moment and every life, and there is radical openness to alternatives and surprises.[52]

I have studied the three—God, Christ, and Holy Spirit—always in the context of a social problem or an academic concern to explicate an everyday religious practice or experience. The Holy Spirit was investigated within the context of a search for an appropriate methodology for social ethics. The study of God the Father came enveloped in how Pentecostals use God as a framework to interpret and manipulate reality. Now Christ is analyzed as a frame for understanding epistemology, the construction and validation of knowledge as Pentecostals struggle against what they see as oppressive and exclusionary Enlightenment rationalism.

I have always believed (maybe because of my doctoral training in religion and society and not in systematic theology) that pneumatology (about the Spirit), theology (about God the Father), and Christology (about Christ) are best approached not as abstract academic topics but as they are experienced in everyday spirituality, as sieved through the nets of practical concerns of ordinary Christians, and as vehicles that believers can board in the ocean of uncertainty in order to land on islands of security that promise human flourishing. I strongly believe philosophies or theologies of God, Christ, and Holy Spirit must always touch the ground, that is, clarify how they affect, intersect with, and are influenced by the practical living conditions of real people. They must tell us how they are or will be appropriated by everyday folks. They must inform practice as they are pre-formed and in-formed by past and present practices. Every good theory of social ethics

---

52. Wariboko, *Pentecostal Principle*, 1.

must follow the grammars and scripts of ordinary people in their daily lives, interpret the practices of those excluded and discriminated against by the upper reaches of society or the academy, and make common cause with those who out of necessity must always anticipate a better world than the given one.

Chapter 3 presents an understanding or conceptualization of Christ based on how ordinary Pentecostals deploy him to frame an alternative epistemology and resist well-defined official Christologies that do not challenge any regnant knowledge system. To use the words of Santos, the "Christology" in the next chapter, unlike erudite academic Christologies even from Pentecostal scholars, does not see "itself as a vanguard theory that excels in knowing about, explaining, and guiding rather than knowing with, understanding, facilitating, sharing, and walking alongside" those who need cognitive justice.[53]

---

53. Santos, *Epistemologies of the South*, ix.

3

This Is Not a Christology
Writing Epistemology as the Christological Turn

INTRODUCTION

ALTHOUGH PENTECOSTALISM UPHOLDS AND celebrates Jesus Christ in its everyday practice, it works with a radical Christology that cuts into orthodox Christology. It slightly shifts Christology from the nature and work of Christ to Christ as an epistemological framing of reality that causes a shift in perception. Pentecostalism is the slightest shift in perception that occurs when Christians consider themselves as living in a messianic time. Christology as a category might be read not as dialectical interplay of the nature and work of Christ, but the new reality subtracted or displaced from the messianic event. For Pentecostals, Jesus represents a new possibility of knowledge, a new correlation of spirit and world that makes the regnant episteme nugatory or, at least, unsatisfactory (1 Cor 1:10–25; 2:1–4). This is to be actualized not only in the positive act of faith but also in the negative act of splitting hard reality in the radical cut of interrupting human knowledge systems without creating absolute disjunction between spirit and sense. The cut connects and disconnects. This cut articulates the discursive or operative separation of spirit and sense and presents their strong relationship. Spirit constitutes the *limit*, the outside of sense—and sense is also the limit, the outside of spirit.[1] This is "an outside that may appear inside the [other], at any moment and anywhere."[2]

---

1. Reinhard, "Political Theology of the Neighbor," 456.
2. Reinhard, "Political Theology of the Neighbor," 456.

This supreme act of cutting reality recalls the Trinitarian, monotheistic debates of early Christianity. Christianity as the religion of the Son has to make sense of the place of Jesus Christ as it finds its place beside Judaism, the religion of the Father. Is the Son a new God alongside the old God that is Father? What the sages did was to divide God from within. Without diminishing the role of the old God the Father, they found a space within the Godhead, not beyond, not before, not beside but *between* the narrow breathing spaces of God. The split Christ as a new epistemic framing of possibilities within the old world's (pre-Pentecostal shift in) perception does not diminish the role of rationality and its extant laws/principles, but works to "create a breathing space, a realm of living in the narrow place, not beyond but *between* the laws."[3]

Liberal theology presents Christology as a believer's subjective self-awareness of Christ, as a symbol of meaning. Conservative theology presents Christology as Truth (of and what God is) embodied in the way God or the Real is. Pentecostal Christology includes the subjective self-awareness, the symbol of meaning, and fiction or illusion in the embodied faith. The reality of who Christ is includes a fantasy of Christ's work opening a crack in being. The conservative directly sees God; the liberal sees God (sublime or godlike qualities) in a human being; and the Pentecostal sees God against the background of the void of desires or desires "transubstantiated" into the dimensions of God.[4]

In this chapter, we will discuss how the desire to know, to forge an alternate epistemology, conditions the conception of Christology or results in some kind of play with the dimensions of Christ or established features of academic Christology. There is a lot the masters of the theological guild can learn from everyday folk on the matter of Christology not as argued and debated but as lived by people on the ground. As much as I am persuaded by the rigors and constructiveness of academic Christology, I am equally persuaded that teaching and thinking about Jesus and human existence require the radical inventiveness of everyday Pentecostal rejiggering and implicit critique of received theological wisdom.

Yet, neither this chapter nor the book itself is a work of Christology. It is a text on a particular belief in Jesus Christ. This is not a study of the life and work of Jesus; it is an investigation of Pentecostal enframing of Jesus as a worldview. This is not a study of the mystery of Christ but a glimpse of the mystery that emerges when the basic assumptions of who Christ is are challenged. This work is an inquiry into the conceptual deposit of a material

---

3. Reinhard, "Political Theology of the Neighbor," 460.
4. Inspired by Žižek, *Event*, 95–96.

religion on everyday orientation to life. It does not aspire to be an academic pointer to a particular Christology in the present or the past. Rather, it is a defiance of the academic or doctrinaire Christ. Pentecostalism, as I will demonstrate in this chapter, makes us see Christ in an entirely different way.

The important thing about this book is to bring a (particular) Pentecostal framing of Jesus Christ into the open. This unveiling may annoy some Christians and upset some scholars. But to others, it is an aroma of life, a systemization of deeply held beliefs about their ownmost world. By daring to lift the veil, I am hoping to comprehend the Pentecostal capacity to make sense of the world in tangible day-to-day traffic with life. Pentecostals hold Christ not only as Lord and Savior but also as a hermeneutic of existence. For them, the question of *who Christ is* is not fully answered by a theological or philosophical interpretation of Jesus the Christ, but by the construction of a hermeneutic, which not only makes sense of Jesus Christ but explains how the world works in absolute correlation with him. It is no good asking a chicken-and-egg question here. What is important for our immediate purpose is that Jesus is simultaneously a divine person and a point of view, a lens through which the world appears to them, makes sense to them, and feeds back into who they think Jesus is. Deciphering the logic, ethos, and pathos of this *hermeneutic-ized* Jesus is the task of this chapter, and I believe it is the starting point for a proper or new Pentecostal Christology. Thus, this book is a not a work of Christology; it is only a clearing, a bush-clearing for a Christology that would take seriously the Pentecostal fundamental interpretation of existence. The book is an interpretation of Christ that takes as its point of departure Pentecostal epistemology as a particular reading of existence.

This interpretation—no doubt awkward and not academically kosher—locates Christ in a crack between sense and spirit. Jesus is perceived as a *split* or as dwelling in a split between rational logic and faith. In this space or void, all the issues of his person, creativity, spontaneity, and faith (e)merge. Just as God molded the world out of the void, the fecund void, the crack of not-yet, Pentecostals are daily fashioning an image of Jesus-in-the-world. Their task and their agony, their hope and their limitation, are to figure out—conceptually and pragmatically—how to comport themselves understandingly toward this Jesus-in-the-world, who and which is the human encapsulation of the inner working of reality.[5] Indeed, we are offering here a glimpse into a daring folk theology of Christ, which cannot be categorized as Christology as defined by the gatekeepers of the theological guild.

---

5. Pardon the allusion to Martin Heidegger here.

Indeed, what we are grappling with here is not about the person and work of Christ in the received, respectable orthodox sense. Neither is it about the being of Jesus, or the relation of Jesus the Son to God the Father. It is about the reality of divine presence that is perceived as underlying, defining, or creating the reality of believers' experience. Where these realities (spirit and sense) meet or intercept they create an *other-being* where the ensuing third space-time, emergent reality does not make *sense* but makes *spirit*. The space-time where reality makes spirit is a split-reality, an in-between located between the hard physico-socioeconomic reality and spiritual (noumenalogical) reality. As much as Pentecostals affirm both Jesus's divinity and his humanity, they also affirm a Chalcedonian twist of reality of sense and spirit, rational logic and faith. It is this peculiar lens of reality, which is anchored to a strong belief in Jesus Christ, that we have here named *split Jesus*.

Split Jesus is a language to capture the reality of divine presence in the Pentecostal community. It stands for the reality that enables Pentecostals to transcend the strict limitations of logic and recalcitrant existence.[6] To follow Jesus or to be led by the Spirit of God is to accept the significance of divine presence breaking everyday existence into "what is" and the not-yet, or the present and the future, and creating an in-between space for life-in-the-spirit. Jesus is present in this space and is the reality of liberation.

A Theory of the Split Christ

Split Christ, for me, does not signify primarily the unique nature of Jesus as both man and God, nor even a description of the Godhead, but only a way of talking about Jesus Christ as appropriated or deployed in the crack between spirit and hard reality. Split Christ is a metaphoric description of the Pentecostal Christian in active relation to divinity, especially Jesus Christ and using such relatedness to pry open phenomenal reality to enact a way of being in the world. Thus the notion or the nature of split Christ "will in what follows be understood first in historical and ethical, rather than metaphysical [doctrinaire or Trinitarian], categories."[7] Put differently, this study is a religious (if you will, christological) interpretation of empirical, historical practices of Pentecostals with regard to the active power and presence of God's Spirit, which is the Spirit of Christ, in their experiences, in their life-worlds. It is an inquiry into practice and discourse relating to

---

6. Cone, *Spirituals and the Blues*, 43, inspired this way of describing split Christ.
7. Lodahl, *Shekinah Spirit*, 3.

Pentecostal subjective appropriation of Christ's work.[8] There is the work of Christ as stated in the Bible and as known in Christian history, and there is a Pentecostal-current Christ as the principle of the subjective appropriation of that historical Jesus the Christ. These two Christs are one, bound up in inexhaustible spiritual presence "in which they are present with one another, for one another and in one another."[9] This duo-logical Christ somewhat stands in a split-off position from the orthodox Christ.

For Pentecostals, Christ is the constantly recurring space between the recalcitrant world of existential conditions and the imperfectly understood world of the spirit. This space in a different metaphor is the fixed point of assurance at the intersection of the phenomenological and noumenological. In this way, Christ is not only the son of God, the second person of the Trinity, but also the optimism or ethos that uses the hard, rational observable reality as raw material to create a robust counter-imaginaire. The notion of split Christ expresses and formalizes a consciousness already present in the teaching of the complex body of Christ, which rejects any sharp (docetic) distinction between matter and spirit, the human and the divine.

Note that this gap between sense and spirit is inherent to the notion of reality. It is not something that happens to reality or adds anything to it. We should be very careful in distinguishing sense (material, matter) from spirit (immaterial) when it comes to interpreting this gap as conceptualized by Pentecostals. Though as scholars we make sense of a Pentecostal worldview by invoking a division between spirit and matter, noumenal and phenomenal in everyday practice, the world is not exactly divided by Pentecostals in this way. Things are not necessarily material or immaterial but are both material and immaterial. Every part of reality is thus split from within, and what attracts a spiritual or speculative attention to a thing is its unusualness, strangeness, its difference from the commonplace, and thus the question will arise as to what special powers engendered or are sustaining it. By this difference the object stands out as a specific exemplar of the composite nature of reality, a special embodiment of categories.[10] Jesus as a composite being, a gap-figure, indicates power, excellence, and exceptionalism. The drive toward the middle, the gap, is how Pentecostals attempt to impose a system on an inherently chaotic experience, to transcend common-sense observations, to transcend the limited vision of cause-and-effect relationships

---

8. Lodahl, *Shekinah Spirit*, 36, inspired the description here, though our points of view regarding the Holy Spirit are different.

9. Moltmann, *Trinity and the Kingdom*, 198.

10. This way of understanding reality is also common in other religions. See Wariboko, *Patterns of Institutions in the Niger Delta*, 339–60; MacGaffey, "Dagbon, Oyo, Kongo," 151–52.

provided by common sense, as anthropologist Robin Horton might put it. The two-natures of Christ provide some kind of epistemological ballast for a Pentecostal explanatory system. Christology or epistemology is an orientation toward a kind of doubleness where one term is actually exposed or grasped to be the two terms in relation, and a slight adjustment of perception is what metaphorizes (*metapherein*, transfers) one into the other.[11] In this sense, Christology is a movement of immanence, a zone of indiscernibility between phenomenon and its interpretation, between the world as it is and the wished-for world.[12] There is a crucial theological point to all this, even though many of us will not agree with it. Following Giorgio Agamben, we venture to aver that the point is that the only theology or orientation to the world that can be robustly claimed in the context of messianic calling and in entrainment of liberation is an attempt to engage reality from the standpoint of the Pauline *as not* (*hos me*), a gap site between living in this world as if it is all that matters and rejecting the world for the eschatological future world to come.

Christ therefore represents the split between reality and its inner depth, for reality is divested of the logic it is covered up with, now revealing itself as inside exposed to the outside, now exposing reality's so-called logical core as mere accident.[13] For Pentecostals, Christ incarnates this split in itself and lays bare, as it were, the contingency of each and every logical connection and every configuration of reality; nevertheless, he "alone is capable of abolishing this division and emancipating" persons from the vise grip of reality and its ironclad causal chain.[14] Christ represents the dissolution of all social realities or logical premises that hold human beings captive (Luke 4:18–19; 2 Cor 10:5) and also the emergence of a split between the individual believer and her own social conditions, juridical-factual conditions, that inhibit human flourishing.[15]

In the light of the preceding discussion, we need to turn to the distinction between reality and the depth of reality to clarify the gap between them. We do not identify the depth of reality through a transcendental principle that will always clearly mark out or name the difference as such in reality. The depth of reality is an operation of a subjective position that divides reality itself and hopes to render inoperative its perceivable phenomenal "face" to find an alternative behind or within reality without ever reaching

11. Kaufman, "Saturday of Messianic Time," 297.
12. Agamben, *Time That Remains*, 25, 30, inspired this paragraph.
13. Agamben, *Time That Remains*, 30.
14. Agamben, *Time That Remains*, 30.
15. Agamben, *Time That Remains*, 30–31, inspired this idea.

an ultimate ground of reality. There is no depth that can be found in reality, but only the realization that no reality or thing can fully coincide with itself. The Pentecostal mindset separates every reality from itself, engendering a tension within reality, without ever transcending reality.[16]

This notion of reality not coinciding with itself connects with our earlier position that Christ dissolves all social realities. What does this mean for Pentecostals? What this means is that all realities are fundamentally subject to interrogation and possible overturn by the power of Christ, for no particular wrong needs to be alleged, because wrong is generally invoked in a fallen world dominated by Satan (non-Christian worldview)—it is always already perpetuated against believers, Pentecostals argue. In this sense, Pentecostals as a group are the bearers of a wrong that conceives reality as a *configuration of dispute*.

Pentecostals (not as academic Pentecostal theologians) see Christology not as a systematized discourse discerning the objective character of the person and work of Jesus Christ but as a radically subjective position. Christ is the living embodied split between reality (ordered, structured patterns of society or existential conditions) and the Real. As in many other areas of theology or doctrine, everyday Pentecostal practice does not approach Christology as already constructed but as in the process of being constructed in practice. Put in another way, the constructed (inherited) Christology is referred again and again to operations of lived experience in which it is reconstructed.

The everyday Pentecostal notion and practice of the split Christ is deeply rooted in the Christian ideas of grace, faith, hope, and love. Grace here refers to the quality of an event or encounter with reality that cannot be explained by the coordinates of the given situation. It is in this sense irruptive, a rupture. Faith is a response to grace; it is belief that a space between sense and spirit does exist and its dynamic is grace. Hope is the disposition or existential attitude toward the gap such that all problems and difficulties can be effectively addressed by the split Christ, by the power of the medial space. Love is the ethical struggle and practice to remain faithful to the meaning of the split Christ or to abide in hope. To love Jesus is to be ideologically interpellated by the split Christ. Truth or the true life-in-the-spirit is to have one's everyday life plaited by the elements of grace, faith, hope, and love.

The Pentecostal true life-in-spirit—a way of being under the hammer of the notion of the split Christ—upturns a basic understanding of the universality of Christ and the particularity of grace. It used to be that the

---

16. Agamben, *Time That Remains*, 52–53, inspired this idea.

work of Jesus Christ was considered as universal—that Christ accomplished a universal task for all human beings and thus all potentially come under his saving blood. Pentecostals reject this or at least maintain that it has a particular dimension. The salvation wrought by Jesus on the cross always imposes specific duties, commitments, rights, and privileges, and those who are under this imposition constitute a specific community, excluding all others. Christ's work is specific to one set of human beings—to Christian believers, to born-again followers of the man of Nazareth. Pentecostals domesticate the universality of Calvary in the name of subjective attitude. The radical nature of the event of the death and resurrection of Jesus is hijacked. Here the universal work of Christ becomes a particular appropriation. But grace (in some theological paradigms), which was heretofore taken as a particular blessing available to the redeemed, is available to all human beings everywhere to access the power of the split Christ and destabilize the extant order of being. In place of this radical nature of the cross and the empty tomb, the radicality of grace is asserted.[17]

Christology in this context is not the work of Christ but the belief in Christ. Christology is a mode of enframing. Belief is the mental attitude or the fundamental frame that structures how a person or a group relates to reality.[18] Christology is not an assemblage of the best theologies, philosophies, or doctrines about the person and work of Christ but an attitude toward reality that a follower of Jesus Christ assumes when engaged in everyday practices. Christology is the way reality discloses itself in the daily confrontation between logic (modern, rationalist epistemology) and spiritualist hermeneutic (alternate epistemology). The disclosed reality is split—the split being a space in which the effect of a thing exceeds its cause.[19]

Split Christ names an epistemic space Pentecostals occupy. The name is constructed not only to show what Christ means to them but also to point to how their way of knowing straddles two critical realms, two ways of being in the world, two ontological divides. The terminology shows how theological and pragmatic structures mesh and reveal the matrices, connections, and processes through which a body of episteme is formed.

This acknowledgment of the narrow epistemic focus of this book means that it does not lay claim to the jurisdiction of Christology despite its title. It stands separate, banished from this lofty subject matter. It is devoted to a "christological" view of epistemology in everyday Pentecostalism, but its own discourse as a philosophical or theological text does not share the

---

17. Jacobsen, *Thinking in the Spirit*.
18. This way of putting across my thought was inspired by Žižek, *Event*, 29.
19. Žižek, *Event*, 5.

status of Christology. It emerges from an unexplored connection that a particular understanding of Christ provides a bridge between sense and spirit in Pentecostals' encounter with reality or decision-making.[20]

The epistemological gap or split between knowing reality through the senses/rationality and through some "spiritual apparatus" is converted into an ontological feature that symbolizes Christ. The Bible says Jesus Christ is the wisdom of the world. Pentecostal Christology is the figuring out of the wisdom nestled in the interstices of the world, within the crack between sense-knowledge and *belieful* spiritual knowledge. Jesus in orthodox Christianity is an incarnation of God, the unique site of connection between the divine and humanity. For Pentecostals, Jesus is also an *intelligence*. He embodies the out-of-jointness of intelligence, for he is at once the precursor and ongoingness of interstitial intelligences. Taking him as a model, intelligence for Pentecostals is not encompassed within the limits of rationality; its place is at the edge of reason, mediating between accessible and repeatable human wisdom and the larger community of beings upon which creation (or the more-than-human world) depends for its movement, sustenance, and renewal.[21] The split Jesus is the Pentecostal spatialization of faith—the making of the faith into a space, or a site, a liminal space, an in-between. It is somewhat similar to the "personhood" of faith. John Milbank, following an exegetical reading of Galatians 3:23–25 and Romans 3:25–26, argues that Jesus's personhood is a hypostasis of *pistis* (faith, trust). "Indeed Galatians clearly implies that *pistis* is an eternal hypostasis that has now been 'revealed' and that has 'arrived' with Jesus (Gal 3:25–26). Thus it is legitimate to conclude that Jesus is, in one respect, the arrival in time of the 'personhood' of faith."[22]

The Christology of this chapter is a Christology written in the mind—the pattern of thought of a people. This is like "an epistle written in our hearts, known and read by all men; clearly you are an epistle of Christ, ministered by us, written not with ink but by the Spirit of the living God, not on tablets of stone but on tablets of flesh, that is, of the heart" (2 Cor 3:2–4). The idea of a Christology written in something that is intangible, invisible, and airy seems exciting, but it is also fraught with dangers. When we say that Christology is written in the heart rather than on paper, it raises for some scholars a concern about backward movement, not progress. The power of Christology is moved from paper, ink, and bytes (from "congealed life" or

---

20. This way of articulating my view was inspired by Certeau, *Mystic Fable, Vol. 1*, 1.
21. Abram, *Spell of the Sensuous*, 6–7.
22. Milbank, "Paul against Biopolitics," 49.

of any mediating thing) to the community, into the dynamic fluidity that is the vibrancy of life.

It is a Christology that is habituated to produce and sustain the virtue of practical reason. It is Christology as habitude. Indeed, it is a form of Pentecostal habitus—a feel for the game of knowledge (proper thinking, behavior) in a crooked world. Christology becomes a worldview, one that is juggling sense and spirit, the personal rational will and God's will as perceived and contextually interpreted. The high point of the juggling is to reach the point where the believer can say, "Not my will, but let your will be done." This mimics Jesus Christ, who said similar words in the garden of Gethsemane at the point of deciding whether to follow through with his salvific mission or to postpone (abandon) it. He was the one in whom sense and spirit, human flesh and divine presence, human will and God's will were literally constitutive of his being. Pentecostals in their garden of Gethsemane (in this world of many decision points) look up to and (hope to) mimetically follow the person whose being bodily reflected sense and spirit (in their nonconflictual relation) as literally walking on the streets of Galilee.

Pentecostal epistemology as we are defining and studying it in this book is about translating the life of Christ into a framework for the interpretation of human existence, relationships, and the meaningful determination of personal choices and clothing such historical choices (or one's decisions in life) in spiritual truths.[23] Christology is the substance of epistemology and epistemology is the form of Christology. So in the "style" of Pentecostal epistemology we can read the expression of Pentecostalism's Christology. This is so because they are dimensions of the same life-view (in the philosopher Søren Kierkegaard's sense of the term, a conception of the meaning of life and its purpose, what is good for human flourishing and how to live it).[24]

Epistemology works out as a *life-view* grounded in and directed toward Christ. Epistemology is an experience of everyday Christology. Epistemology here does not mean holding on to an idea of knowing; rather, it means that the Christology of the Pentecostal's Christianity is expressed in her existence. Pentecostals find their true epistemology not in the abstractions of academic philosophers or theologians but in conformity to norms of their Christology. These norms are criteria for knowing and justifying knowledge in the established social practices of communities directed toward Christ, the Spirit of Christ. For them, it makes no sense to ask in the abstract, "How must I know or justify knowledge?" They ask instead, "What must I know or

---

23. Rae, *Kierkegaard and Theology*, 84, inspired this sentence.
24. Kierkegaard, *Either/Or*.

how do I justify the knowledge behind my life's choices to be a good disciple of Christ, given the values imposed upon me by virtue of my membership in a particular church (congregation, denomination, or community)?" Epistemology "is not some abstract notion but a predicate attaining to" identities, attunements, and life-views within a particular community of Christ.[25] Worldly wisdom is of the ilk that portrays knowing (or decision-making, for that matter) as a relationship between a person (a subject) and her object (situation, goal); but Pentecostal epistemology teaches that knowing (deciding) is a relationship between a *person, Christ, and her object* (situation): person—Christ—her object. That is, Christ is the middle term that both connects and separates the person and her situation.[26] This book is an attempt to provide an intelligent account of this epistemology and to situate an inarticulate and nonuniversal pattern of Pentecostal thought within the framework of philosophy broadly defined.

Christology and Epistemology

This is an invitation to think about Christ subjectively—to have a personal encounter with Christ in a Pentecostal context in ways that lead you into the "guts" of Christology, into Christology epistemologically defined, and the "logy" of Christology displaced by a playful yet profound intuition from day-to-day experience sidling against the jagged edges of the positive sciences. Where others see religious fanatics working against rationalist culture or trapped in a parochial world, I want us to see or discern the intellectual subtlety and the profound philosophical maneuvers of this set of creators of epistemes even as we encounter crude thoughts. The intellectual subtlety I have in mind here is not about the monological constructiveness of a theology that pretends to be systematic, sweeping, and all-knowing. I am only offering the beauty of fragments, a running splash of plain Pentecostals' mundanity and brilliance, flung and scattered in everyday practices like glittering pieces of diamond in the sun.[27]

The perspective on Christology being developed here does not pretend to bring into focus all the dimensions of Pentecostal understanding of Christ, but it does illuminate the epistemological aspects of Christology that have been regularly left unattended. This is not a complete account of Pentecostal epistemology but an outline of its principal features as can be possibly discerned in the form of an analysis of Pentecostal christological

---

25. Rae, *Kierkegaard*, 86.
26. Kierkegaard, *Works of Love*, 111–12.
27. This sentence was inspired by Clark, "Ibadan," 14.

thinking. This partial account of Pentecostal epistemology brings into focus how Pentecostals gather together "sense" and "spirit" to forge a framework of knowing (a disruptive mode of knowing and being in the world) as they live into the promises of God through the power of grace. In bringing these two principles of sense and spirit together, they traverse a space that binds the two together without blending them or making them to disappear. This insight points us to the "inter" character of Christ's transgressive identity. Brian Bantum in his analysis of the mulattic identity of Jesus points us to how Jesus's Sermon on the Mount (Matt 5) even exhibits the disruptive character of his identity. His analysis is worth quoting at length:

> The Sermon on the Mount's apparent dichotomies (the poor will inherit the kingdom, those who mourn will be comforted, the meek shall inherit the earth) point to the first important aspect of Jesus's ministry and person. The kingdom of God is that in which notions of power and entitlement become inverted through a certain conflation of high and low. Thus poverty and inheritance, weakness and power become bound to one another in Christ's person, and through him those who dwell in the "lower" are bound to the "higher." Such a binding of higher to lower is not a transformative reality where low and high are blended so as to create a redemptive middle. Rather Jesus becomes the space in which high and low are present and presently bound to one another. This confession of God's presence on both sides in Christ is not a discourse that requires the rendering of one to make another intelligible. Both are present.[28]

In this fragmentary theology of articulating how Pentecostals bring together sense and spirit to forge a mundane christological framework of knowing, there are several practical questions that we must address. These are questions that will help us to approach the depths of the connection between Christology and epistemology in everyday Pentecostal practice. What role does Christology play in indexing Pentecostal everyday epistemology? Does Christology (or Christ as a "union of flesh and spirit," an "inter" existence[29]) hold any key to Pentecostal conceptual thought or religious legitimation of the way of knowing reality? How does religious belief (or movement) largely forged in the fires of the rationalist modernity of the twentieth century snatch strands of thought on Christology, bend it, process it, strengthen it, and weave it smoothly into "mystical" epistemology?

---

28. Bantum, *Redeeming Mulatto*, 124. Later he writes, "Jesus occupies or *becomes* this space so as to create a communion of neither/nor . . ." (129).

29. Bantum, *Redeeming Mulatto*, 99.

Precisely, we should name it *hybrid* epistemology. Pentecostal epistemology is not found within a "pure," modernist, religious, or theological notion of epistemology but rather within the spaces "that such claims create and the performances of [epistemic practices] that make those spaces possible."[30] Pentecostal epistemology is articulated within the spaces contested by the various ways of knowing, making it disruptive to each of these other articulations of epistemology. Is this destabilizing force—in the case of identity or personhood—not integral to understanding the two natures of Christ as defined by the Chalcedonian formulation or, at least, its rhetorical power? As Bantum puts it, "Chalcedon presents Christ both as an assertion and a refusal. The definition seeks to suggest how Christ is and is not, thus problematizing notions that bind Christ to a particular way of being in the world that is static."[31] As we will demonstrate later in this book, the Pentecostal it-makes-spirit is a binding of assertion and refusal of it-makes-sense. Indeed, the Chalcedonian formulation speaks powerfully to the reality of Pentecostal epistemology as we are trying to formulate it in this book. "While the claims concerning the constituent aspects of [Christ's] identity were different" from those of Pentecostal epistemology, "the process of identification and differentiation" that grounds its "neither/nor" also constitutes the conception of epistemology in Pentecostalism.[32]

The split Christ hybridly epistemological character of "neither/nor—but" echoes "a profound (though distorted) christological moment."[33] The Pentecostal epistemological framing that moves every decision from "sense" to "spirit," from "it makes sense" to "it makes spirit," displays the neither/nor hybridity that resonates with what Bantum argues is the fundamentally mulatto character of Jesus's nature.[34] "He was mulatto not solely because he was a 'mixture,' but because his very body confounds the boundaries of purity/impurity and humanity/divinity that seemed necessary for us to imagine who we thought we should be."[35] This work demonstrates that it is important for scholars to pay serious attention to Pentecostals' epistemology not solely because it is a mixture of sense and spirit, but because the very identity of this epistemology confounds the boundaries of street philosophy/pure academic philosophy that seem necessary to imagine what rigorous epistemological claims should be. Besides, the alternate epistemology of

30. Bantum, *Redeeming Mulatto*, 94.
31. Bantum, *Redeeming Mulatto*, 95.
32. Bantum, *Redeeming Mulatto*, 96.
33. Bantum, *Redeeming Mulatto*, 90.
34. Bantum, *Redeeming Mulatto*, 90.
35. Bantum, *Redeeming Mulatto*, 98.

plain Pentecostals should remind some scholars who have forgotten that the Christian faith was founded on epistemology (or epistemologies) that, at least, have some family resemblance with plain Pentecostals' epistemology.

Hoc est enim corpus meum: this is my body. Jesus said this before his disciples as he took the Passover bread. Now imagine the void immediately opened between sense and spirit, carnality and spectrality. The physical unleavened bread is (metaphorically or not) his physical body. How did it make the transition? What transported it across the chasm of plant body to the flesh body of a divine being? The poor bread, in making that journey (from humus to heaven?), not only exchanged one physical body for another physical body but also acquired a dual nature. Behold, Jesus *ob-jected* his body against himself. Lo, the bread acquired an identity, a reality beyond itself.

What way of knowing or what principle of (un)reason did Jesus presuppose when he made the declaration and expected his disciples to believe him and take him seriously? And to eat the "mulattic" bread that the "mulattic" body served as a meal? Does Jesus here not have two bodies? Split bodies: bread as stand-in and, if we believe the Catholics, a transubstantiated bread-body, and his physical Jewish body. Yet the bodies are not mixed-up or confused. He, the enunciating subject or the enunciated word of which he is a hypostatization, somehow stands in the gap between the two great bodies. Or is he, as the Word, the gap? This split Christ renders the "poles" of sense and spirit incoherent, disrupting their separateness through his contact (unity?) with either side. He performs one into the "life" of the other. Pentecostals' it-makes-spirit, as a way of departing from and entering (returning) into sense, performs sense (rationality) into a new way of being in the world, thereby performing modernist epistemology into life-in-the-spirit, into pneumatic existence, into living in pneumatic contamination, if you like.[36]

The resurrection account of Jesus, especially when it is told that he visited his disciples humbled behind a locked room, which he entered in ghostly form through walls, speaks to the split nature of Christ or calls us to pay at least some minimal attention to the character of Pentecostal epistemology. Despite Jesus's ghostly form, Thomas was invited to put his finger into the physical wounds, supposedly on Jesus's spectral skin. Jesus in the room was ghostly and carnal, and the resurrection is the void, rupture, or the site that connects spectrality and carnality, spirit and sense. In his resurrected form, as the Bible (John 20) relates, "he is both recognizable and unrecognizable to those whom he meets, and it is the process of coming to

---

36. Bantum, *Redeeming Mulatto*, 112–13.

recognition through the strangeness—and misrecognition—that makes this narrative of resurrection both consonant with [Pentecostal epistemology] and open to reinscription of it in [the epistemology-inflected Christology]" that we are crafting in this book.[37] Is the resurrection not the ultimate split (the resurrected body is not only sensorial and material but also spectral and ghostly)? The resurrected figure (which is spectral and corporeal) is located as inhabiting the space between spectrality and materiality. There is a crossing of sense and spirit that takes place in the resurrected figure.

Jesus's encounter with Thomas and the other disciples takes place in the Upper Room. Following the display of his wounds to Thomas and the latter's confession of faith, he breathed on them and said to them, "Receive the Holy Spirit." He appears to be giving them strength, restoring their energy (breath, spirit, life force), which must have been drained due to his crucifixion and the consequent fear that engulfed them. They needed to be reoriented to life in the spirit with the invocation of breath (spirit). The words of my colleague Shelly Rambo are worth quoting here:

> The Upper Room is often depicted as a space of transformation in which the disciples come to terms with their lives following his death. They are concerned with their future, and the room depicts a meeting of past and present that will determine how they move forward. And yet this room is under the grip of an old logic that has a hold on the disciples.... When we meet the disciples, there is no possibility of [transformation] there, unless new air is breathed into the space. When it is, new terms are set, and the force of an old logic is exposed.[38]

Pentecostals hold that they also need invocation of breath, new air to be breathed into the house of modernity, the regnant space of sense (rationality) to transcend or expose the logic that so easily besets them. If those in the Upper Room could need some intake of "spirit" to reorient them, to subtract them from the subjective path of death, they—who live in the crooked room of modernity/postmodernity—also need to infuse some spirit into sense in their path of life. Here we have borrowed the language of Melissa Harris-Perry, who argues that black women in America are living in a crooked room (constructed by racism) that deeply distorts their images and projects a negative image of them to society through stereotypes.[39] One of the effects of living in such a room is the distortion of one's perception of oneself by the structures of society, practices, and stereotypes that constitute

37. Rambo, *Resurrecting Wounds*, 9.
38. Rambo, *Resurrecting Wounds*, 84.
39. Harris-Perry, *Sister Citizen*.

the infrastructure of everyday life. Reality is distorted. Pentecostals hold that many citizens who live in the crooked room of modernity think that they are perceiving reality correctly when in fact, owing to the logic of the (post-)Enlightenment rationalist gaze, they are not. They therefore plead that an invocation of the spirit, a breathing of the spirit into everyday decision-making, is necessary to expose the distorted logic, to complement the rationality of modernity, or alter the way people "see."[40] Pentecostals thus need to breathe the spirit into the crooked room of modernity or to receive the Holy Ghost as Jesus's disciples to strengthen and enable other citizens to see things they would not otherwise see.[41]

Enough of the foray into the New Testament to help us understand that ordinary Pentecostals are not crazy, mere throwbacks to a bygone era. As we shall see in chapter 4, their fascination with it-makes-spirit has something to do with justification of reason for action or behavior in the Pentecostal public. That chapter will help us to understand all this without burdening us with a political philosophy of Pentecostalism. We already have enough on our plate.

Our concern about Christ remains epistemological insofar as we are interested only in how attitude toward Christ affects our perception of reality. How do Pentecostals make personal decisions from the position of the existence of Jesus Christ? How do they assume the abyss of an act on the support of the wisdom of the spirit of Christ?

This study proposes that an episteme-Christology, a model oriented to philosophical reflection on the role of knowing in Christology proper, is more relevant to constructing a Pentecostal Christology. This model is to be considered as an everyday-theology assist to other paradigms of Christology. It is not articulated to serve as a complement of any need or demand in them; rather, it is a supplement. It satisfies something in themselves that they did not even demand to be satisfied. As a supplement it is an excess that their symbolization (theologization) of Jesus's divinity and salvific work cannot capture. What do regnant (Pentecostal) Christologies leave out in what they constitute as Christologies when they themselves are constituted? Episteme-Christology is the gap, the split at the heart of regnant Christologies. Once a theology makes a cut into the preexisting primordial conception of Christ in a given social imaginary to establish Christology, the two parts (social imaginary and Christology) are "inherently linked and cannot be completely separated, but also that, hard as they might try, the two can

---

40. Rambo, *Resurrecting Wounds*, 85–87, inspired this paragraph.
41. Rambo, *Resurrecting Wounds*, 82, 84.

never fuse ('back') into an unproblematic One."[42] In short, when in a theology a social imaginary splits in two, "the sum of these two parts never again amounts to the inaugural One; there is a surplus that emerges in this split, and constantly disturbs the One."[43] Episteme-Christology "puts another division to work, one that does not coincide with the preceding ones but is not exterior to them either."[44] It is a cut within a cut, imposing upon regnant Christologies a further cut like the cut of Apelles. Below is a diagrammatic representation of episteme-Christology within regnant Christologies.[45]

Episteme-Christology, which is a philosophy of split, attempts to theorize the excess that is the split in the symbolization of Jesus Christ. It interprets the split (excess) as a supplement that disturbs Christologies, which ignore the surplus-enjoyment, satisfaction from the alternative ways of knowing that Pentecostals hold dear in their everyday practices. Christology is here analyzed or interpreted as an epistemological lighthouse giving directions to believers at sea about how to make specific decisions.

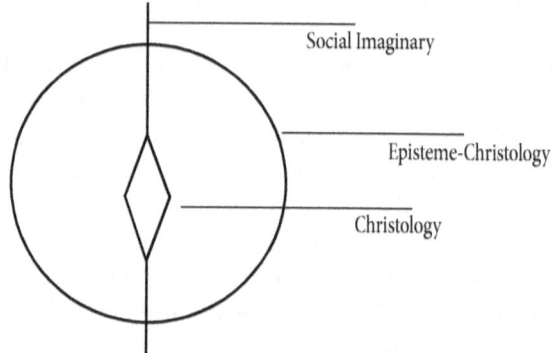

Figure 1: Diagram of Episteme-Christology within Current Christologies

To study Pentecostalism seriously is to learn to give credence to the Pentecostal excesses that disturb regnant interpretations of Christianity or cannot be symbolized within the reigning academic theologies. Take, for instance, speaking in tongues (uninterpretable tongue-speech). It is an excess on human language. It cuts into human language and disturbs it from within. Although many Pentecostal theologians have written about doing theology that takes seriously the distinctiveness of the experience of speaking in tongues, they have only focused on it as part of the symbolic

42. Zupančič, *Odd One In*, 185.
43. Zupančič, *Odd One In*, 185.
44. Agamben, *Time That Remains*, 49.
45. An adaptation of a diagram from Zupančič, *Odd One In*, 163.

structure—just a language that needs (awaits) to be deciphered. In this way, they have ignored its nature as an excess or split language—that human language does not coincide with itself. How do we as theologians take seriously the excess that is the tongue-speech that cannot be symbolized and begin to investigate its ethical and other implications? I have begun on this endeavor elsewhere.[46]

In addition, by paying close attention to how Pentecostals know, understand, explain, and experience reality through Christ as mediated by the Holy Spirit, episteme-Christology recognizes the centrality of the experience of the Holy Spirit in Pentecostal theology. I always wonder why Pentecostal ways of knowing (explanation, prediction, and control of their environments) have never been deemed worthy of christological reflection. Pentecostals' epistemological imaginations are connected to their christological imaginations in its pneumatological orientation (inflections). In Pentecostal epistemology, Word and Spirit as articulated by Lady Wisdom (Prov 8:22–31) are always at play. Pentecostal theologian Jean-Jacques Suurmond writes that "the book of Proverbs opens with an introduction from which it emerges that in Lady Wisdom there is both a 'spirit' which wants to pour out, and 'words' with which she calls out loudly in the streets."[47] As he explains these two: word and play (analogical to order and dynamism) in scriptures are "always thought of together."[48] He added that both "Word and Spirit are present at every level of creation, and work towards the eternal sabbath which has already become visible in a unique way in a man from Nazareth."[49]

In the light of this insight, Pentecostal epistemology, which is organized by the interplay of word and spirit, can provide a useful input into the construction of a framework of Spirit-Christology (or wisdom-Christology) if such a theology is oriented toward practical Christian living and is willing to take as its point of departure the knowledge practices of plain Pentecostal people. The aim of Pentecostal epistemological praxis is to equip believers with a way of relating to the world—to provide a worldview—that will enable Pentecostal Christians to transform their communities into the kingdom of God. Christology, therefore, that is relevant to the living conditions of Pentecostals in these communities must result from analyzing this praxis, which in turn may lead to refining of the praxis.

---

46. Wariboko, *Split God*, 21–44.
47. Suurmond, *Word and Spirit at Play*, 38.
48. Suurmond, *Word and Spirit at Play*, 40.
49. Suurmond, *Word and Spirit at Play*, 41.

Everyday Pentecostals are *living* their Christology, and the *thinking* of it by scholars should touch the ground of their life-worlds. In this *lived Christology*, pneumatology and Christology are related and interpenetrate each other. Christ is Spirit and the Holy Spirit is the Spirit of Christ. Whatever Christ does in the life of the believer he does through the Holy Spirit, and the work of the Spirit in the believer's life is the work of Jesus the Christ. Let us turn to Pentecostal theologian Sammy Alfaro for an explication of this viewpoint in Hispanic theology: "Hispanic Pentecostals juxtapose the presence of Jesus and the Spirit.... Jesus' presence is manifested through the Spirit."[50] How then do we construct a Christology characterized by the epistemology of everyday Pentecostals and their pneumatological perception of Jesus as the *ground* of thought, or as the light that dissipates all shadows of ignorance, or as the ethos by which their thinking or knowability organizes itself and interprets the world? Such a construction of lived Christology must be aware of itself as a behavioral Christology (theology), if such a term even exists.

René Girard's Christology, like the one we are crafting here, is focused on behavior. The core of his Christology is that Jesus's death changes the kernel of human violent behavior (rooted in rivalistic desires) by splitting its core belief. His death exposes the innocence of the victim and offers a remedy for group violence that abates only by means of the sacrifice of the other in their midst. In order to bring peace to the community caught in internal violence that threatens to destroy the group, the community scapegoats someone, marking the victim as guilty and deserving of death. Jesus's death exposes this ritual as a fraud, reveals the scapegoat mechanism as a generator of unjustified murders, exposes the social violence for what it is, and offers possibility for communities to turn away from mimetic rivalry and the associated violence.[51]

There are two key points about Girard's Christology that I want us to pay attention to as a way of entering the model we are developing in this text. First, following the insight of his model, the praxis of Christology is to imitate Christ in eschewing violence. Second, Girard's model is also not a debate or theory of the ontological status of Jesus Christ, and does not begin with the historical Jesus but with the effects his life could have on his followers or structures of human existence. In our model of Christology, we are concerned with the impact of Jesus's life on the deep structure of Pentecostal epistemology. We are deeply interested in the practical effects of

---

50. Alfaro, *Divino Compañero*, 139.
51. Girard, *The Scapegoat; Violence and the Sacred*

Christology on the lived experience of Pentecostal Christians, which engenders the Christology in the first place.

Of course, Christology all through Christian history has had practical effects on the behavior of Christians and the church as an institution. The line of cause and effect is usually from a formulation of Christology (whether high or low) leading to certain practices. This does not mean certain inherent tendencies of a culture did not get to influence the formulation or conceptualization of Christology. Our method differs in that we start from existing human behavior (that is, our interpretation of certain behavior) of a people who have not explicitly formulated a Christology and work out the implicit Christology in their social practices, behaviors, or common utterance. In the strict case of this book, we are drawing out everyday street-level Christology from the mundane epistemological practices of plain Pentecostal folk.

Christology for them in this respect is an immediate consciousness of the being of Jesus (as a special revelation of God and in its ethical fullness) beneath and beyond all their experiences and interpretations of the world. It is a profound, primal awareness of their total dependence on Christ.[52] In this way, Pentecostals hope to embody the same attitude toward the world as that of Jesus and enlist themselves into this task of transforming the world into the kingdom (kin-dom) of God and into their desire for human flourishing. This is what it means for them for the body of Christ or a person-in-communion to exist pneumatologically. Or to put it differently, this is what it means for church communion and believers to conform in varying degrees in their everyday life to the power of creative transformation in Jesus as revealed in each situation he encountered.

This way of being, this way of relating to the world, others, and Jesus Christ, is not a personal achievement apart from the Pentecostal life or being as a communion. To borrow the words of John Zizioulas from a different context, the Pentecostal Christology we are laying bare here is "an event of *communion*, and that is why it cannot be realized as the achievement of an *individual*, but only as an *ecclesial* fact."[53] The goal of this Christology is to determine what exactly the Christ-ness of Jesus says to Pentecostals who are trying to discern a path between modernist rationality and the imperatives of their spirituality in their decision-making in order to uncover the truths they need for human flourishing.

In discerning the Christ-ness of Jesus, Pentecostals try hard to discern what they make of him as the light of the world, as the light that can help

---

52. This way of expressing my ideas was inspired by Kärkkäinen, *Christology*, 80.
53. Zizioulas, *Being as Communion*, 15.

them uncover the worlds of possibility in their decisions and guide them in their behaviors. Jesus is a light that they can "split" through the prism of faith to gain a better epistemological footing in the uncertain and crooked world that they encounter daily, to reveal hidden worlds. Pentecostal epistemology is a heavy gravitational movement around the sun of Christ, whose light splits sense beyond senses and divides light into light and darkness (Luke 11:35). When light goes through the prism of Pentecostal faith, it splits or appears as a rainbow spectrum of realities in the noumenal and phenomenal worlds.

> When a beam of white light goes through a prism, the prism's crystalline structure refracts the existing light so that it appears as a rainbow spectrum. Each color, though a component of the white light, is seen separately because of its unique frequency. If you reverse this process by projecting a rainbow spectrum through the crystal, the individual frequencies will recombine, forming a beam of white light. Think of each human being's identity as an individual color frequency within the rainbow spectrum. If we arbitrarily eliminate a specific frequency, a color, because we don't "like it," and then try to put the remaining frequencies back through the prism, the existing beam will no longer be white light. By definition, white light is composed of *all* of the frequencies.[54]

The mystical mind or the sensation of the mystical enables mystics to experience God, the whole light in different frequencies. Yet no one can experience all the individual frequencies constituting the holistic beam of light. The person not so inclined to the mystical will only experience God as the simple white light. The mediator between the sense and spirit is the mystical mind or the superconscious mind. It-makes-spirit means the mediating mystical mind is able to act as a prism's crystal structure that refracts the "light" of reason (or sense data) into different frequencies, a rainbow spectrum, which splits the "universe" of reason into "many worlds," a "multiverse," a range of possibilities wherein sense makes spirit in an overlapping universe and spirit appears *rational* within a specific frequency.

Concluding Remarks: Temporality of the Pentecostal Split Christ

What is the temporal structure implied by the notion of the split Christ? Unlike received or orthodox Christology that principally speaks to the past

---

54. Lipton, *Biology of Belief*, 212.

and/or future, the split Christ primarily speaks to the present, the time of the now. It is an announcement or appropriation of the good of the Christ as a present fact, the enacting (preference) through faith of the presence of Christ in the present lived experience. Christology in everyday Pentecostalism is therefore not merely a discourse that posits something about Jesus of Nazareth independent of the power that binds or sutures splits in reality and of the subject who through faith performatively enacts such power.[55] Faith here is simply the trust in Jesus Christ—the credit believers possess and enjoy in him, and acting on it. There is more to unveil in the Pentecostal understanding of temporality of the split Christ. There is a formidable philosophical weight behind their identification of Jesus as the gap between sense and spirit.

There are remarkable conceptions of time and temporality that undergird the Pentecostal understanding of the middle space as indicative of the relation of sense and spirit, pre-decision and after-decision, and Christ as archetypical mediator, the embodiment of the middle space. Pentecostals believe that there are always cuts in the fabric of reality, that is, there are ruptures of preexisting temporal conditions taking place not in a mythic world, but in contemporary social orders, and they are created and sustained by a certain kind of agent in every generation. Put differently, Pentecostals believe that there are *time gaps* in temporality—gaps that mean that there is always a new temporality in the flux of the past, present, and future by which human beings (prayerful and spirit-filled believers) can insert themselves between the infinite past and the infinite future, thereby exercising their uniquely and supremely human capacity to begin something new and display the distinctiveness of each individual "who" or destiny.

Hannah Arendt taught us that human beings do step into the continuum of time to create the gap between the past and future where they change the meaning of the past and stop or redirect its perceived evil trajectory to help life better flourish.[56] In this gap humans do not wait for the future as such to come to them, but rather create it by the will's projects that negate the given.[57] It was Augustine who said that every newborn is an insertion into the world, into time, so that there may be novelty, a beginning made. Since actions cannot be undone once done, and since their consequences are unpredictable, caring for the other and for the self may mean stepping into the continuously flowing stream of actions and counteractions in order to defend all that sustains both biological and social life. Rituals,

---

55. Agamben, *Time That Remains*, 91.
56. This section of the chapter is drawn from Wariboko, *Ethics and Time*, 127–30.
57. Arendt, *Life of the Mind*, 2:36, 158.

institutions, and social practices may be the way humans insert themselves in this relentless flow; the insertion of humans, "fighting in both directions, produces a rupture which, by being defended in both directions, is extended into a gap, the present seen as the fighter's battleground."[58]

Arendt's notion of the time gap is a constituted time and a relational and discontinuous order (medium) of temporal events. Her source of this notion is Kafka's parable of the "He." The parable describes a scene where a man is caught between two antagonists. "The first presses him from behind, from the origin. The second blocks the road ahead. He gives battle to both. . . . For it is not only the two antagonists who are there, but he himself as well. . . ." The dream of the "He" is to jump out of the fighting line.[59]

Arendt interprets this parable to convey something about time. The two antagonists are past and future. Thus interpreted, the parable is said to convey the idea that human beings are not just borne along in the flux of time but insert themselves in the battle between the past and future in order to create a space where freedom could appear. She writes,

> Seen from the viewpoint of man, who always lives in the interval between past and future, time is not a continuum, a flow of uninterrupted succession; it is broken in the middle, at the point where "he" stands; and "his" standpoint is not the present as we usually understand it but rather a gap in time which "his" constant fighting, "his" making a stand against the past and future, keeps in existence. Only because man is inserted into time and only to the extent that he stands his ground does the flow of indifferent time break up into tenses; it is this insertion—the beginning of a beginning, to put it into Augustinian terms—which splits up the time continuum into forces which then, because they are focused on the particle or body that gives them their direction, begin fighting with each other and acting upon man in the way Kafka describes.[60]

This is a remarkable intellectual insight into time, and we should all be grateful to Arendt. She reached this brilliant insight by linking Kafka's parable to Nietzsche and Heidegger. Nietzsche had his own parable of the "now" (*Augenblick*), which is represented by a gateway between two paths. Heidegger interpreted Nietzsche's image of now (eternity in the now) to say that this view of the now is not granted to a beholder but only to "the one

---

58. Arendt, *Life of the Mind*, 1:205.
59. Arendt, *Between Past and Future*, 7–12.
60. Arendt, *Between Past and Future*, 11.

who *himself is* the now . . ."⁶¹ For Arendt, humans do not merely observe time; they *become time* or the battlefield of time. There is no option of abandoning the fighting lines. Human beings cannot walk out of it to go into the past or to flee into the future.⁶²

Arendt argues that (real) time occurs where humankind is inserted between the past and the future; the *presence* of humans in the gap is the (real) time. One cannot help remembering the argument of her teacher, Martin Heidegger, in his essay "Time and Being," where he offers that there is a *presence* behind the usual linear sequence of *nows*, referring to the experience of the present as presence, the place of real time. As he puts it,

> Obviously, time is not nothing. Accordingly, we maintain caution and say: there is time. We become still more cautious, and look carefully at that which shows itself as time, by looking ahead to Being in the sense of presence, the present. However, the present in the sense of presence differs so vastly from the present in the sense of the now. . . . [T]he present as presence and everything which belongs to such a present would have to be called real time, even though there is nothing immediately about it of time as time is usually represented in the sense of a succession of a calculable sequence of nows.⁶³

In this essay, Heidegger conceives of time's hidden powers that approach human beings from outside of them and offer them the gifts of presence. These are the powers of the past and future that are hidden from the open presence, which they mutually enact or make possible. The future (that which is to come) conceals itself by *withholding* its presence and the past (that which has been) by *refusing* its presence. Heidegger explains further,

> What has-been, which, by refusing the present, lets that become present which is no longer present; and the coming toward us of what is to come which, by withholding the present, lets that be present which is not yet present—both [make] manifest the

---

61. Arendt, *Life of the Mind*, 1:204.

62. From a philosophy of life perspective, human beings are in the middle because the future is a potentiality that has the power to become actual. The present in which humans are always resident is the place of "actuality of time." The present of time is always at a *presence* (see below). The past, though essential, does not have this power and thus cannot subject itself to existence and finitude. Humans are the structure of time's existence. Humans and their socialities constitute the structural condition of time. (*Presence* is used in the archaic sense of a site where there are sovereign or high dignitaries. See Tillich, *Systematic Theology*, 3:107.)

63. Heidegger, "Time and Being," 11–12.

manner of an extending opening up which gives all presencing into the open.[64]

Whence the refusing and withholding powers? Where can we catch a glimpse of that source? For Arendt it is the human being that makes sensuously present the past and the future as *absences*. The powers are inscribed in the human body (a form of materialized space) and are in embodied action that functions as a horizon that gradually discloses its hiddenness as an observer approaches the curvature. Such actions as the initiation of the new gradually open the hidden horizons of our common existence and the distinctiveness of our individual "whos." Action is the means by which human beings standing in the gap come to the presence, to bring forth (about). That is to say, the presencing of the "who" is given or enacted in the presence of others. This means that action is the modality of being that enables concealment of presence within the gap itself to be lifted.[65]

It is important to state that for Arendt the gap has no origin, neither in the past nor in the future. It is founded in the interstices of the past and the future and not grounded in any of them. The gap is produced in a moment of deflection. From this point of deflection, there is no simple movement backward into the past, the repetition of the past or the automatic initiation of the new. In this deflective and disjunctive gap, movement is founded on human actions that can only open up new possibilities. The temporality of this gap is iterative. Peg Birmingham, an interpreter of Arendt, comments on the iterability of this gap in which Arendt's actor is located:

> The repetition of iterability is interruptive and inaugurative—it is the temporality of the deflected [gap] in which the actor seeks reinscription and revision of the web of relationships in which he or she is immersed. The process of reinscription and revision—the insertion or intervention of something that takes on new meaning—occurs in the temporal break of the deflected [gap].[66]

Arendt argues that this gap is hidden from view by tradition, which functions to pave the way from the past to the future. Tradition makes thought and action appear regular and repetitious; it thus creates the illusion that the movement from the past to the future is linear.[67] This work

---

64. Heidegger, "Time and Being," 17.
65. This interpretation of Heidegger and Arendt was inspired by Abram, *Spell of the Sensuous*, 205–17.
66. Birmingham, *Hannah Arendt and Human Rights*, 23.
67. Arendt, *Between Past and Future*, 12.

of tradition (*nomos*) grates against the very meaning of being human that Arendt holds: beings inserted at birth between the past and future as beginners. With this thought Arendt put her "thinking ego" and her actor (the fully embodied version of the "thinking ego") into the same gap.[68] This merger also suggests ways of thinking about temporal orientation:

> Most important for our discussion, insofar as the gap between the past and the future is created by the insertion of beginners, Arendt's analysis extends beyond a consideration of the temporality of thinking and judging to include the temporality of action and, by extension, the temporality of natality itself, which she defines as the insertion in linear time of unique beginners.[69]

From here, it is not a very big step to reach the conclusion that temporal orientation is an embodied stance within this gap of involvements whose basis is the event of natality (insertion) and individual distinctiveness. In Arendt's theorization, the clash of the forces of time, the middle of the *absences*, becomes a place where a human being, an actor stands or dwells. The human being is actually the place, the battlefield. This gap between the forces names the place of be-ing. Then she converts man/woman or the dwelling place into a force, a force of action that transforms existence. Not only this, man/woman becomes time itself or the most precious time, since he/she is the only active principle of its renewal. Time is because man is. Arendt presents man as the *typos* (location and motor) of time. In other words, all that is infinite time relates to itself at a distance from itself owing to the place of insertion where man is.[70]

I have given us a philosophical explanation of the Pentecostal conceptions of time and temporality that undergirds the middle space. This middle space is important for understanding Pentecostal subjectivity and the theologization of Jesus Christ as the middle space between sense and spirit. The Pentecostal subject (actor) emerges from the rupture in time and articulates his subjectivity in it. The subject punches a hole in historicization, his actions blocking the infinitude of the repeatable, to allow for the advent of the new—thus perpetuating the rupture. Belief in Christ or the capacity to access the hidden realm of the noumenal or intensified phenomena is what the Pentecostal actor uses to pierce through time or make a hole in time

---

68. Actually, Arendt did not do this clearly or consistently. The "thinking ego" was really what she preferred to put in the gap.

69. Birmingham, *Hannah Arendt and Human Rights*, 19.

70. Here I have adapted for my own use Alain Badiou's statement in another context. Badiou, *Theory of the Subject*, 8, 341.

to insert himself in it. Just as man/woman becomes place of the temporal gap, Pentecostals transpose Christ into the gap and he becomes the gap itself. Jesus in a sense becomes the man/woman in the gap *writ large*. One of the assumptions about their mission (destiny), that is, what difference they want to make in the world, and one of the assumptions about their core gifts (endowments) needed to accomplish their mission and thus to transform their (this) world, is the capability to think of this time gap as a "space" to pry open and animate the void between sense and spirit, or as the juncture where an alternate epistemology bursts forth into modernist rationalism. Chapter 4 focuses on the dialectic and dialogism of sense and spirit as created and sustained by the Pentecostal hypothesis.

4

Sense and Spirit
The Dialogical Imagination in Pentecostal Thought

INTRODUCTION

WHAT DO PENTECOSTALS AFFIRM when they say it-makes-spirit and what do they deny in uttering this statement? It is the task of this chapter to show that the statement carries no straightforward, single meaning but has myriad significance that brings it into the borders of secular justification of arguments. The chapter challenges Pentecostals to consider that the real animating force of the statement may lie in the inherent exchange of defeasible reasons in a democratic culture. It-makes-spirit, as it will be demonstrated below, is a path to public reason, at least in the Pentecostal community. The ethical community that is Pentecostal, which we find in many congregations, sustains a discursive practice that "imposes on each of its members the necessity of keeping track of the normative attitudes and entitlements of their interlocutors."[1] And it is within this tradition that communication about divine encounters takes hold. The statement (or aphorism, as in concise statement of a religious principle) it-makes-spirit is one way of publicly espousing "reasons" for one's actions—saying it is justified because it respects the norms of grounding one's action in divine approval. Whatever else we may think of Pentecostalism, it serves us to always remember that it is also a discursive practice that moves and has its being in

---

1. Stout, *Democracy and Tradition*, 280.

the social practice of giving and asking for "ethical" godly reasons for one's (or its members') deeds. (More on this later.)

It-makes-spirit appears solipsistic when it is taken out of this communal ethos and context of understanding and ongoing debates within the tradition. Always uttered by an individual to support her action, it comes across as an expression of self-generating and self-defining "I." But properly understood, it is an utterance that opens and reopens a dialogue with (and within) a community, with other individuals in an ongoing process of reciprocity and exchange through mutual recognition.

It is also wise to consider it-makes-spirit as "addressing" the community of believers and nonbelievers. It is implicitly or explicitly saying to the secular society in which the believer uttering the aphorism lives that this is my option, my way of proceeding or making a decision. This is all good and fair until you realize the very forceful enunciation of the statement as a marker of specific identity that signifies that the religious option is just one possibility among many others in a secular society, and as such it is contestable. It-makes-spirit as an option indexical of belief in God is not axiomatic in our contemporary society.[2] Thus, the significance of it-makes-spirit is not limited to the sacred, religious, or private sphere of believers but is entangled in the "immanent frame."[3]

Overall, what this chapter is doing is simple: prompting attentive thinking on plain Pentecostal life. The philosophical treasures of this life, believed by many secular scholars to be dumb and useless, "are being made to speak, in the course of which it turns out they propose things altogether different from the familiar, worn-out trivialities they had been presumed to say."[4] There exists a Pentecostal world or cultural and linguistic treasure that can, perhaps, help philosophers to think of the wonder in the life of an everyday "stupid" believer (peculiar Christian). If only we are willing to pay close attention to this world or treasures, we might discover that some of the issues relating to public reason in democratic societies are also being played out among the so-called God-drenched, "Precambrian" Pentecostals.

It-makes-spirit is a form of justification that is rooted in communal standards of plausibility and fidelity—an exercise in social exchange of "reason," and a self-conscious awareness of the process and demands of the exchange. It-makes-spirit somewhat functions as the Hegelian "absolute

2. Taylor, *Secular Age*, 3.

3. This last point is not a contradiction of everything that I have been saying, but the beginning of the process of pointing out that it-makes-spirit is a path to public reason, at least within the Pentecostal community, as I stated in the introductory chapter of this book.

4. Arendt, "Martin Heidegger at Eighty," 295.

spirit" (self-sufficient standard) in its social-ethical dimension. We see how Pentecostals use it-makes-spirit as a self-sufficient standard to justify or assess their beliefs, norms and practices in their own communities or in personal decision-making. As Molly Farneth, an astute interpreter of Hegel's *Phenomenology of Spirit*, puts it, "absolute spirit . . . is the self-sufficient standard generated by a community that is engaged in the process of creating, sustaining, challenging, and transforming its norms and judgments over time."[5] In a Hegelian sense, it-makes-spirit becomes public reason when the Pentecostal believer is conscious of it as a normative justification of actions in her own Pentecostal community, and conscious of it as shaping such community.

Section 1: It-Makes-Spirit as Social Ethics

I am going to demonstrate that the Pentecostal it-makes-spirit is a way to internalize the norms that will authenticate a person as follower of Jesus Christ, or what Jesus Christ himself would count as following him. In this view, it-makes-spirit translates into internalizing Christ's normative spirit. Pentecostals through this performative utterance or formula are trying to reach the spirit implicit in what Jesus counts or recognizes as persons and performances that conform to his image. Next, we will explore how this recognition has been transmitted from the time of Christ himself to the present Pentecostal era through the process or chain of intersubjective recognition. Thus, the key Pentecostal ethical interest here is this: How can their persons and performances be recognized as going on in the same way as those that were recognized by Christ, thereby carrying on the normative Spirit of Christ's recognition?[6]

It-makes-spirit is about conformity to the Spirit of Christ, the alignment of decisions and everyday activities to the standards of Christ. At first glance, these standards or commitments appear fixed, not subject to change. But Christ as a standard is a theological concept whose meaning and content are altered through use, social practices, and the processes of dialectical reasoning. Sure, Christ or Holy Spirit is the theological (or social-ethical) standard against which decisions or behaviors are judged, "but it is the members of the [Pentecostal] Christian community who are the finite and fallible judges of whether a [decision or behavior] carries on in conformity to Christ [or the Holy Spirit]."[7] Conformity to Christ is split between

---

5. Farneth, "Hegel's Sacramental Politics," 185.
6. Hector, *Theology without Metaphysics*, 262–64.
7. Farneth, *Hegel's Social Ethics*, 107.

seemingly fixed foundational commitments and the believers' participation in generating and sustaining the standard of commitment and ground of authority. Conformity to Christ or it-makes-spirit properly understood cannot stand outside of the members of the community, their narratives of who they are and want to be, their relationships, and social practices.

In the Pentecostal distinction between it-makes-spirit and it-makes-sense, there is a clear-cut separation between the actual *decision-act* and the (abstract) system of epistemological standards, norms internalized by the decision-maker. They are separating what is social from what is private, personal, or individual. The private is deemed essential, while the social is seen as auxiliary, a mere backdrop to the decision-act. Our argument is that the decision-act and common rational system (the systems of perceptions, norms, and practices of justification) are indivisible; one cannot be studied in isolation from the other. The abstract common epistemological system is always deployed to execute or birth the concrete decision-act. The "spirit" cannot be divorced from its material base, from the concrete forms of sensorium. Decision-act is always a dialogical act.

Another dimension of the thesis is that the creative novelty of the decision-act is not private or individual but social. The emphasis on the individual character of the it-makes-spirit is a wrong attempt to relate the decision-act to the inner (individual) psychic life of the Pentecostal decision-maker. We show that it-makes-spirit is best viewed as a social structure insofar as we hold to the social character of inner thought and individual consciousness. It-makes-spirit, which is a salute to an alternate epistemology, is a form of social ethics—at least, an incipient one, arising from the specific concern of the Pentecostal public.

Two of my books on Pentecostalism—*Nigerian Pentecostalism* (2014) and *The Split God* (2018)—have tried to theorize the connection between epistemology and social ethics, knowledge and living well. How is Pentecostal knowing connected to how they think, how they (their communities) ought to live? How does Pentecostal epistemology, their theory of knowledge, influence the ways they think and construct relationship, cultivate social practices and virtues, and build institutions for human flourishing?

In this chapter, I study the ground of authority claimed for Pentecostal decision-making, the authority of norms and norm-generating practices of Pentecostal Christian life. In doing this, we journey through what Pentecostals call "makes-sense" to discover "makes-spirit," move from *sense-certainty* to *spirit* (in crude Hegelian language).[8] It is like traversing a path that moves from the "sense-certainty" of general modernist rationality that

---

8. Farneth, *Hegel's Social Ethics*, 2–3.

is assessing the truth or falsity of claims or experiences to a more complex specific "communal context" in which Pentecostals' knowledge claims are attuned to their form of spiritual life—to the spirit. Here spirit has a double meaning: Hegelian and Pentecostal.

In the Pentecostal construct, spirit refers to a personal (determinate) supernatural being. It is a recognition of the authority of God the Spirit and of accountability to God's spirit, even as there is an intersubjective process of affirming, denying, or contesting normative judgments. Such recognition and accountability are socially and historically situated. Judgments that can be safely regarded as rooted in it-makes-spirit emerge from the practices of a worshipping and liturgical community. More precisely, the judgments are grounded on the appropriate standard of knowledge or decision-making matrix a Christian in a Pentecostal form of life would be entitled to hold or manipulate. This standard is not conceptual; rather, it is an embodied form of norms, practices, language, and expectations deemed integral (essential) to a Spirit-filled social life.

In the Hegelian construct, spirit refers to—as Molly Farneth has put it— "the collection of norms and norm-generating practices of a form of life."[9] One of the arguments of this chapter is that the metaphysically sounding Pentecostal it-makes-spirit can be nicely translated into a nonmetaphysical one, into norms, practices, and laws that characterize the Pentecostal form of social life. Thus what the Pentecostals name as it-makes-spirit—or, at least, in their translation of it into a pragmatic, everyday judgment-making process—is transformable into the Hegelian notion of spirit as not only "the collection of norms and norm-generating practices that characterize [their] community,"[10] but also how members of community "create, sustain and transform [their] collection of norms and norm-generating practices."[11]

The Pentecostal process of normative judgment can be viewed as (a) registering a problem or situation intellectually—"does it make sense or not," and (b) an awareness of the problem's spiritual dimension or an awareness of the need to subject its resolution to specific norms of the spiritual community that transform an abstract reason (Enlightenment matter) into a visceral ethical consciousness, into reason for itself, into an "ethical substance" that animates and binds the community. This is how it-makes-sense becomes it-makes-spirit. This is not an abstract movement but one involving the subjectivity of the believer—the transformation of substance into subject, so to speak (in the "tongues" of Hegel).

9. Farneth, *Hegel's Social Ethics*, 3.
10. Farneth, *Hegel's Social Ethics*, 6.
11. Farneth, *Hegel's Social Ethics*, 6.

The movement from it-makes-sense to it-makes-spirit is a process of self-emptying. It takes three steps to accomplish. The self-conscious Pentecostal believer (subject) empties herself or relinquishes her self-certainty (self-sufficient knowledge) to submit to what she (or the community) considers the judgment of the Holy Spirit. Second, it is a movement from the universality of sense-knowledge or reason to the particularity of personal religious experience. This particularity returns (through self-emptying) to the unity with universality that is rooted and proceeds from communal practice and scripture. This third movement is the it-makes-spirit. The Pentecostal subject is conscious of herself in her self-emptying, admitting of sense (reason, human) fallibility. It-makes-spirit unifies sense and subject; its truth value is in suturing *substance* and subject, self-sufficient reason and self-consciousness.

We can again discern two concepts of spirit operative in the movements. Pentecostals believe that it-makes-spirit is enabled by the Holy Spirit, but they have largely not reflectively grasped the fact that it is their beliefs, norms, practices, and institutions that also generate and sustain the "shape" of the spirit or the community of self-conscious believers. They therefore miss the working of the Hegelian absolute spirit, that is, "the self-sufficient standard generated by a community that is engaged in the process of creating, sustaining, challenging, and transforming its norms and judgments over time."[12] Of course, Pentecostals viewing the Holy Spirit as set apart from their practices and community never quite go far enough to recognize their participation in creating the aura, the transcendental matrix, the representational entity they have come to call it-makes-spirit.[13]

There are other forms of twoness in the perpetual movement from it-makes-sense to it-makes-spirit. The practice of it-makes-spirit is at once an attempt to (better) know God and create or sustain a standard of knowledge and ground the normative authority of knowledge. The Pentecostal distinction between it-makes-sense and it-makes-spirit involves two ways of conceptualizing truth. In it-makes-spirit the truth is carried over, embodied in flesh and blood. For it-makes-sense, truth is correspondence between fact and its interpretation. This is about the imperative of acting according to the dictates of hard reality, according to facts as detectable and confirmable by more than one person. The latter is about manipulating the data (facts). The former is about "praying the ultimate," being grasped by what one considers as truth arising from ultimate reality.[14] Truth, Robert Neville argues,

12. Farneth, "Hegel's Sacramental Politics," 185.
13. Farneth, *Hegel's Social Ethics*, 96–97.
14. Neville, *Ultimates*, 287–300.

is not whether a form is repeated but whether what is of worth in the thing is grasped by the interpreter. The form of that grasp in the interpreter's experience might be quite different from its form in the object interpreted. Surely the interpreter's form will be influenced by the purposes and contexts of interpretation, as well as by the forms of the interpreter's body, culture, and semiotic systems. . . . Truth is the carryover of value from the object into the interpreters' experience by means of signs, as qualified by the biological, cultural, semiotic, and purposive contexts of the interpreters.[15]

The Pentecostal subject is grasped by truth of the experience of faith in Christ as the middle space between sense and spirit. Subjectivity is what makes the transition from the sense to the spirit possible. Subjectivity—that split, antagonism, inconsistency that traverses every substance to render it non-all, ontologically incomplete—is the vehicle. Without the subject (subjectivity) the two principles of it-makes-sense and it-makes-spirit will combine into a substance, and "we get the traditional cosmological vision of reality characterized by the eternal struggle of the two 'principles,' masculine and feminine (yin and yang, light and darkness, form and matter, etc.)."[16] Pentecostalism posits a Christian's subjectivity of excess, split reality, pragmatic contradictions, and rupture or opacity of the link between cause and effect, and *these* condition Pentecostals' everyday traffic with life and reality.[17] It-makes-spirit happens when it-makes-sense (reason, empirical data) is captured in the positing or dream of a religious human subjectivity. It is "the *nightmare* of [reason] (its nightmarish disturbance)," since reason wants nothing of a dream or deeper meaning, but to be left to its own devices.[18] But like all dreams there is often confusion between dreamland and reality on waking up. There is a story of a Chinese philosopher who dreamed that he was a butterfly. On waking up, he thought to himself, What if I am a butterfly dreaming to be a man? Reason (sense) may have been captured in a dream of spirit, but it is not too far afield to imagine spirit as (or is) reason on waking up.

If the spirit is ultimately knowable through the senses (broadly defined); if it-makes-spirit is in the end a superior "reason"; if it-makes-spirit takes contextual hues (as any careful reader of the biblical book of Proverbs will note, with its changing or dynamic counsels); and if Pentecostals

---

15. Neville, *Truth of Broken Symbols*, 240.
16. Žižek, *Incontinence of the Void*, 1–2
17. See Wariboko, *The Split God*.
18. Zupančič, *What Is Sex?*, 97.

believe that all human reason (of believers and nonbelievers alike) is part of the storehouse of God's wisdom, that the generation of reason and other material happenings are all subject to the interruptions of unexpected contingency, then the "spirit" (or what is appropriated as spirit or what is considered as the ultimate justification for decision under uncertainty) is not a positive entity with a fixed formation external to, hovering over, or beyond the transient dynamic world of reason. It-makes-spirit is nothing but the process of the rising and passing away of all particular reasons.[19] Now if two Pentecostals can come to different interpretations of a specific situation while claiming to rely on the same it-makes-spirit, and such difference in interpretation, as often occurs, is attributed to a disparity in their levels of spiritual maturity, then we might infer that spirit (precisely it-makes-spirit) is self-unfolding, not an absolute entity external to the spirituality (subjectivity) of the believer. What displays, manifests, expresses it-makes-spirit is nothing other than the path of discernment that is its method. The decision arising from it-makes-spirit is the effectuation of it-makes-spirit. It-makes-spirit as the whole of the discernment process, the delicate movements within the decision-making process, is the immanent arrival of its own it-makes-spirit. Indeed, this is the subjective nature of it-makes-spirit. More importantly, the entrance into the "mindset" or milieu of it-makes-spirit by the Pentecostal believer involves or presupposes the transformation of the person's being as subject of the spirit or truth. How can I transform myself, what conditions must I endure to have access to the truth? One of the fundamental premises of Pentecostal spirituality is to contest reality as the conditions and limits to access knowledge and truth, while endowing it with spirit. The spirituality of Pentecostalism seeks to raise self-conscious subjects who can do something to themselves in order to access the noumenal realm for knowledge. Pentecostals believe that the subject, by working on her self (techniques of the self on the self), can modify the conditions and limits of her access to knowledge and truth.[20]

Where is this information coming from? Is the intuition or input of information (idea) supposedly from the Holy Spirit, unmediated? Does it escape the influence of social, constructed appearances or subjective representations? Put differently, is it-makes-spirit another term for mental immediacy? How does God, in reaching the believer's mind, bypass the complex fabric of beliefs that the person employs to live her life as a Christian or to apprehend her world? For instance, if we took it-makes-spirit as the human spirit's journey into itself or into the Holy Spirit that dwells within the

19. Žižek, *Less Than Nothing*, 368, inspired this sentence.
20. Wariboko, *Nigerian Pentecostalism*, 41–44.

self, we could still aver that it-makes-spirit is not an immediate presence of divine information. The information coming as divine light within the self still needs to be interpreted, shaped by mediating cultural (religious) symbols or signs. Yes, the information as experienced can be considered as direct, but also mediated. Whether peering into the soul to see the spirit within or looking at the starry heavens above, Pentecostals like human beings everywhere (must) engage the ultimate dimensions of life in certain respects through a system of signs. They interpret life, God's actions, human actions, and situations in the respects that are important for their commitment to Jesus Christ, life-in-the-spirit, and human flourishing.[21]

The point I am making is this: the movement of it-makes-sense to it-makes-spirit is both subjective and social in the shaping of the dialogue between a Pentecostal and her reality. The sense of the situation or predicament is always in concrete context. Let us call this the human word, the worldly word that must be transcended. The word, situation, or data must be transformed, shed its sense-ness, give up all that pertains to it, undergoing a process of emptying or kenosis that will result in its *spirification*. Owing to this process, the human *word* has become a word from the Holy Spirit, a divine word, so to speak. In this "transfiguration" the human word at the minimum becomes what they believe Jesus Christ will approve, and its existential consequences he will bless. This transformed sense data has to rejoin the human context, interpreted and appropriated by a person in dense human context, in order to make a concrete decision or enable an action. The spiritual word of knowledge must become "flesh." The naked human word is enfleshed or re-enfleshed so that it can now perform "miraculous" feats. If you believe the Pentecostals, such a re-enfleshed word can "resurrect" dead businesses, dead careers, dead wombs, and even raise a mighty army from dry bones.[22] In one certain sense it-makes-spirit is a bisected unity of two "natures" of "flesh" and "spirit" without confusion and without separation. And if the believer seamlessly (that is, without sense confusing or contaminating spirit) received the word of knowledge from (or in) it-makes-spirit, as Pentecostals maintain (and this is how it should be, that is, without confusion or contamination, if it is not to be a fortuitous

---

21. Neville, *Defining Religion*, 139–41.

22. One question that arises when Pentecostals make this kind of claim is this: What are the limits to such beliefs, or are there none? What are we to make of such claims? How do we separate actual "makes-spirit" from pure nonsensical invention? All this goes to the heart of the issue of discernment of spirit that we raised earlier in this text. Unfortunately, Pentecostals do not have an easy way of addressing this question. In this chapter, we are pointing to some ways of "authenticating" it-makes-spirit when a decision is interpersonal.

mongrel), then some kind of "interpenetrative and perichoresical mutual relations between words," between human and divine words, exist.[23]

We have just described the subjective, inner movement at the individual level in its Chalcedonian ideal of two natures in bisected unity. (There is something carnivalesque about all this, that is, in its contact of upper and lower realms, strata, in its boundary-crossing motion, and in its norm-disrupting flux of the privileges of rationalism. It-makes-spirit is the sense's second life, organized on the basis of carnival.[24])

There is also the social level in the shaping of the dialogue between the believer and her reality (situation). This refers to the communality of all those interacting with her in the Pentecostal circle for whom she needs to justify her actions (behaviors) or explain herself—this community has standards for justification. Note that she might not be called forth by any person or panel, but she interprets and acts on God's word always in relation to, in view of and aware of, the communal standards for justifying a believer's claim to "hearing from God." Let us not forget that the believer is not in a solipsistic, isolated world. She is linked to members of her community by Christ (Holy Spirit indwelling of her consciousness) and commonly shared norms.[25]

We, therefore, have two forms of it-makes-spirit: the inner form, which we named as the "divine word," and the outer form, the "human word." The latter is the expression of the former in action and into the ever-expanding body (collection) of God's words (or interpretations of divine words) in a community where it acquires social meaning. The inner form of the word also has existential consequences. The two together form an indivisible structural whole. This is why Pentecostals understand "the ethical life as the union or harmony between one's word [the received, transformed word that started as sense data] and deed."[26] In this way Pentecostal ethics is aesthetics: action and behavior depend on the vision (seeing or hearing the word), "where to see is indeed to be. All of this is cast in the form of a [double] transubstantiation." The human word becomes naked and *spiritized*, while the divine word—naked, *spiritized*—in turn becomes clothed in flesh and dwells in the density of human deeds.[27] The deed is the physical incarnation of the thought, it-makes-spirit. This is the kind of fundamental unity between

23. Mihailovic, *Corporeal Words*, 27.

24. Bakhtin, *Rabelais and His World*, 13. I have adapted his definition of carnival to my purposes here.

25. Mihailovic, *Corporeal Words*, 70–71, inspired this sentence.

26. Mihailovic, *Corporeal Words*, 39.

27. Mihailovic, *Corporeal Words*, 46.

ethics and aesthetics that the Russian philosopher and literary critic Mikhail Bakhtin talked about.[28] He argued that those who think participatively do not separate their word, thought, or act from its product. This is so because the "ought" of their ethical system or reasoning is not "activated by forces external to the act."[29] The Pentecostal performer of deeds is fully answerable for her acts, having no alibi for herself; she cannot claim to be elsewhere, in another place to her actions. Alexandar Mihailovic, drawing from Bakhtin's thought, enables us to better understand what the absence of alibi means for ethics.

> To have an alibi or an excuse for one's actions means not only to lack a definite or rooted place in existence [or in faith], but also to living speechlessly, which for Bakhtin means to have no awareness of value, either one's own or of society at large.... Not to have an alibi in life therefore means to come to an awareness of one's own rootedness in existence, which is also to reinforce and concretize that space around the self.[30]

In all this emphasis on and efforts toward endlessly experiencing it-makes-spirit, there is the inclination to link spiritual principles to life "so that they may render to themselves an account of their possible application.... The emphasis on praxis is the indispensable condition for the productive mastering of" Pentecostal spirituality.[31] Since there are always multiple situations and events that require the believers to resort to it-makes-spirit, and there is always a multiplicity of believers making such a move, it-makes-spirit is in a certain sense a multivoiced discourse on social reality.

The foregoing should not be construed to mean that it-makes-spirit is studied here to tell the story of the use of revelation as a legitimate basis for public deliberation and decision-making. This is a topic for another time or for another scholar. It-makes-spirit is only being investigated as the salience of religious worldview or religious commitment in private deliberation, decision-making at the moment. We seek to grasp decision-making through the use Pentecostals make of religious language in their effort to bridge the gap between "matter" and spirit.

The syntagma of it-makes-spirit is used to justify or explain decisions (actions, aims), which are deemed good (or bad) for a person's flourishing. This suggests "practical wisdom" without reason. Aristotle defines practical wisdom (*phronesis*) as a virtue "that is bound up with action, accompanied

28. See Mihailovic, *Corporeal Words*, 51–85.
29. Mihailovic, *Corporeal Words*, 53.
30. Mihailovic, *Corporeal Words*, 58.
31. Mihailovic, *Corporeal Words*, 98.

by reason, and concerned with things that are good and bad for a human being."[32] It appears that the Pentecostal "it makes spirit and not sense" removes sense (a stand-in for reason) from the Aristotelian conception of prudence. The question here is this: Is reason absent from the Pentecostal notion of prudence (practical wisdom)? Does sense not include "conceptual and critical thinking . . . creative reasoning, which expands possibilities, and social-emotional intelligence, which perceives what others are feeling so that one can act appropriately and sensitively"?[33] When sense or reason is considered in this way, it-makes-spirit cannot be devoid of reason. It-makes-spirit creatively involves reason as that social-emotional intelligence that enables a person to act appropriately and sensitively in a given situation.

Now if we take into further consideration Martha Nussbaum's understanding of practical reason as the capability of a person to form a conception of what the good life is for her own flourishing and then plan her life pursuit accordingly, then the Pentecostal it-makes-spirit includes some reason too. In her list of ten capabilities that a person needs to flourish, practical reason and affiliation are of central importance.[34] Affiliations and memberships in groups (communities) are important for a person's wellbeing. The Pentecostal spiritual identification, her special relationship with Jesus Christ (the Holy Spirit) as defined in communal relationships that drive her quest for it-makes-spirit, enables her to act appropriately and sensitively. Is the accent on it-makes-spirit in the context of decision-making or initiating actions not about human flourishing, which always includes "exercising human capabilities in the domains of body, mind, character, and relationships"?[35] Yes, it is about human flourishing (wellbeing, the good life). It is important that we do not forget that the goal of disciplining oneself for or the utterance of it-makes-spirit is to promote human flourishing of the believer. It is always part of the believer's efforts to deliberate and decide on actions that will promote human (personal) flourishing in specific circumstances. Spirit is also a quality of the mind or a certain disposition, the possession and exercise of which tends to enable the believer to make decisions, initiate actions, and achieve the goods of life that are internal to the practice of Holy Spirit–filled living, and the lack of which effectively prevents believers from living a flourishing life, as Pentecostals broadly understand it.[36] Seen in this light, it-makes-spirit is an integral part of the virtue ethics of Pentecostals,

32. Aristotle, *Nichomachean Ethics*, 1140b5–7.
33. Stiltner, *Toward Thriving Communities*, 64.
34. Nussbaum, *Creating Capabilities*.
35. Stiltner, *Toward Thriving Communities*, 99.
36. MacIntyre, *After Virtue*, 191.

or should be considered as such in any scholarly analysis of the community's social ethics.

For virtue ethics to be supremely useful to the needs of Pentecostal communities, it must pay more attention to ontology than is typical with the scholarship of virtue ethicists. For Pentecostals, ethics and epistemology are never set apart from ontology; the possibility of living well and the possibility of knowing are always linked to their understanding of reality, the possibilities of existence. Epistemology is a strategy of managing risks that pertain to reality, to what things are. In light of the uncertainties and dangers of existence, epistemology is a response to contingencies within the temporal and finite world. Thus, it-makes-spirit is a way of limiting the risks posed by making decisions based only on empirical, phenomenal evaluation. It-makes-spirit becomes a form of an ethic of virtue aimed at overcoming what Pentecostals consider to be an etiolated *Moralität* by situating themselves within a tradition and accepting "its standards upon its own authority. . . . [They have placed themselves] within a 'narrative,' or the accepted and ever-to-be-repeated 'plot formation' of a particular [community]."[37] The sociolinguistic practices of Pentecostals constitute a tradition that rejects reason as an ahistorical universal, insisting that the tradition of life in the spirit affects their human reason and morality.

By way of conclusion in this section, let me state that analyses in this section have strongly hinted that it-makes-sense and it-makes-spirit are not two dialectically opposed ways of knowing. Rather, it is a movement from the former to the latter, attempting to bridge the subject-object divide. Pentecostal knowing is not a mere withdrawal into spiritual inwardness, cut off from sensory data or reason. On the other hand, it is not an absorption into the fabric or substance of reason, the objective world. Ultimately, it-makes-spirit—the practice and language of it—is to unify the objective and subjective sides of knowing through some form of self-emptying movement and construction of self-sufficient standard for communal discourse.

It-makes-spirit—apart from the particular sensible world, history, and context in which it is "revealed" or apprehended—is "as unknown and as unknowable as any sense-object apart from the sense-qualities in which it appears to us."[38] There is no way for Pentecostals to circumvent the historical situation or historical viewpoint in claiming direct access to the source of it-makes-spirit or in holding that it-makes-spirit and its interpretation are only matters of an inner life or depths of moral consciousness. As H. Richard Niebuhr once put it with regard to the meaning of revelation,

---

37. Milbank, *Theology and Social Theory*, 340.
38. Niebuhr, *Meaning of Revelation*, 52.

> We cannot speak of an inner light at all, save in ejaculations signifying nothing to other men, unless we define its character in social terms, that is in terms which come out of our history. The "true" seed within, the "right" spirit, can be distinguished from false seeds and evil spirits only by the use of criteria which are not purely individual and biographical. We discriminate between the light within and spiritual will-o'-the-wisps by reference to a "Christ" within. But the word "Christ" comes out of a social history and has a meaning not derived from individual experience.[39]

Do we still hold onto the view that in Pentecostalism spirit is dialectically opposed to reason? Do we still say that Pentecostals reject reason? What many scholars characterize as the rejection of reason by Pentecostals I consider the tragedy of reason. An event is tragic when two goods or rights conflict and the choice of one entails the abandonment of the other. Moreover, the choice is unavoidable—it seems to follow inevitably from the situation of the choice. Pentecostals do not consider reason evil, but the pursuit of the good of the life-in-the-spirit often (or occasionally) comes into conflict with the dictates of the good as prescribed by the path of reason. This is a tragedy born out of religion "as a state of being grasped by an ultimate concern, a concern which qualifies other concerns as preliminary and which itself contains the answer to the question of the meaning of our life," to quote Paul Tillich.[40]

Spirituality of It-Makes-Spirit

It-makes-spirit is the state of being grasped by that wisdom or horizon of knowability that concerns the Pentecostal unconditionally. It is the state of being grasped by the power of wisdom itself that promises ultimate fulfillment. The decisions and knowledge that daily shape the life of the person are considered to be of infinite importance for the wellbeing, the human flourishing of the believer. The believer seeks the infinite wisdom, so to speak, to rest her finite "wisdoms," to see their ecstatic fulfillment in the infinite. The grasping and promise are rooted and sustained by the demand, promise, and threat of the unconditional character of God as Spirit, the ultimate concern of Pentecostals.[41] This power of grasping does not destroy sense or nature but seeks to turn it to the infinite for fulfillment.

39. Niebuhr, *Meaning of Revelation*, 52.
40. Tillich, *Christianity and the Encounter*, 4.
41. Tillich, *Dynamics of Faith*.

In this line of reasoning, it-makes-spirit is not opposed to it-makes-sense. Sense is the presupposition of spirit, and spirit is the fulfillment of sense. It-makes-spirit as the state of ultimate concern is sense in ecstasy, going beyond itself.[42] It-makes-spirit, properly understood, is not to reject or despise sense perception or reason but to go beyond it. And this is not irrational. It is an endeavor or process to reach that which is present in every reason or framework of rationality, and yet hidden under the sense experience in which it is embodied.[43] It-makes-spirit is a way of recognizing it-makes-sense as a *symbol* and as such calls upon it to point beyond itself and participate in that to which it points. For Pentecostals that to which sense perception points is the ultimate concern of all human beings, which should infinitely concern all thinking and speaking beings. Given this orientation to sense perception, they hold that the personal and societal use of reason is inadequate if it is "determined by something less than ultimate."[44] Therefore, human beings "must always try to break through the limits of finitude and reach what can never be reached, the ultimate itself."[45]

For Pentecostals, this ultimate is God as Spirit, hence the syntagma it-makes-sense, reason, or sense participates in the Spirit. Put differently, sense or reason becomes a medium through which they are grasped by that which they consider holy, and in this way they experience a content of their ultimate concern. Is this not somewhat telling us that reason or sense has a "sacramental" character? If Pentecostals believe that reason (sense) is a place, a site where they encounter the holy, an avenue that has the possibility of mediating the ultimate itself, or is meaningful for asserting their faith, then (implicitly) they regard such as sacramental.[46] Let us not forget that they do not say driving a car or going to the toilet makes spirit, for these are not regarded consciously or unconsciously at the present as "sacramental."

Before proceeding further, we need to sound a note of caution. There is a major problem or tension with the Pentecostal impulse to move from it-makes-sense to it-makes-spirit. While it-makes-sense may be genuinely inadequate to the ultimate concern of the believer, it-makes-spirit might fall into the trap of identifying its ensuing decision with the ultimate itself. The decision or discernment resulting from it-makes-spirit becomes holy or spiritual in itself. The decision or discernment now represents the ultimate. It appears it-makes-sense has been "transubstantiated" into it-makes-spirit.

42. Tillich, *Dynamics of Faith*, 88, inspired this sentence.
43. Tillich, *Dynamics of Faith*, 71, inspired this sentence.
44. Tillich, *Dynamics of Faith*, 65.
45. Tillich, *Dynamics of Faith*, 65.
46. Tillich, *Dynamics of Faith*, 66–67.

If the decision or discernment is never more than a transparent medium of the divine—if we are not to fall into an idolatrous claim—then what makes it-makes-spirit special is that decisions are made in correlation to faith, a state of being ultimately concerned.[47]

We have stated that there is not much difference between it-makes-sense and it-makes-spirit. This is so because when it-makes-sense is "grasped" by the faith of the believer, when sense-certainty is integrated into the center of the personal life of the believer, it becomes it-makes-spirit. Following Tillich, I will argue that being "grasped" means sense and spirit are brought to the same place; sense is participating in the believer's ultimate concern. But spirit (it-makes-spirit) will cease to be what it is without some separation from sense (it-makes-sense). It-makes-spirit is (must be) separated from the object of it-makes-sense; otherwise it-makes-spirit will possess it-makes-sense; and decisions and situations will no longer require the process of discernment, deliberation, and struggle. In the state where it-makes-spirit possesses it-makes-sense, it-makes-spirit becomes a matter of sense certainty and no longer it-makes-spirit.[48] In such a situation or circumstance, "the 'in-spite-of element' of faith would be lacking. But the human situation, its finitude and estrangement, prevents man's participation in the ultimate without both the separation and the promise of faith."[49] It-makes-spirit ceases to be it-makes-spirit if there is no separation; it becomes an idolatrous, "demonic" utterance coming from a finite person claiming to be the infinite God. Out of being grasped by the ultimate concern or the Holy Spirit follows the certainty of it-makes-spirit; out of the element of separation, out of the irradicable distance between finite humanity and infinite divinity, follows the humility (caution, "doubt," circumspection) of it-makes-spirit.[50] Indeed, *an* it-makes-spirit once translated into a concrete decision is a lie. This does not mean that Pentecostals should stop questing for it-makes-spirit in their decision-making, only that they have to somehow build into their translation the awareness of what, by taking this decision (*decadere*, to cut off) and not that, they have stopped seeing or have started concealing options, possibilities, choices.[51] Every it-makes-spirit is at its most *ideological* in its decision-point, or cashing-out point, "in its

---

47. Tillich, *Dynamics of Faith*, 68–69.
48. Tillich, *Dynamics of Faith*, 116.
49. Tillich, *Dynamics of Faith*, 116.
50. Tillich, *Dynamics of Faith*, 116.
51. Williams, *Dostoevsky*, 45, inspired this sentence.

endings, those pretenses of closure and settlement," in its cocksure monological affirmations.[52]

Let us continue our discussion of the overlapping relationship between sense and spirit in a different register. The relation between the two exhibits what psychoanalysts call fetishist and symptomal modes of operation—symptom refers to the events or things that disturb the perfect dichotomous appearance Pentecostals want to maintain about the relationship between sense and spirit. There are always cracks in the fabric of their system of separation—things that they have repressed keep returning. In 1999, a top African Pentecostal pastor based in Washington DC called me to complain about a statement the leader of his denomination had made at a conference of ministers. He said, "The certainty with which our leader was making some statements as directly coming from the mind of God seriously disturbed me." He asked me, "Have we all not thought at one point or the other that God was speaking to us and it turned out not to be so? How can he [the denomination leader] be so sure?" The gripe of the DC pastor was that the famed denominational leader was speaking out of his human mind and reasoning but repressing that fact. This kind of symptom, the exception, the eruption of sense, which appears to disturb the fine (false) appearance of direct, privileged access to God, cracks the fabric of the religious lie that there is a fine distinction between speaking from sense and speaking from the spirit, even for those at the top echelon of the Pentecostal movement. Often Pentecostals working with so-called highly anointed men and women "repress" the role of earthy, messy, human frailties in the words and actions of such leaders. They try not to think of them.

Fetishism, on the other hand, "is the embodiment of the Lie which enables us to sustain the unbearable truth."[53] Pentecostals may rationally accept that their super-anointed leaders are mere human beings yet incline on the fetish that such leaders are always "organs" or "mouths" of God. Such followers cling to some "extraordinary" features, past actions, or past pronouncements of such leaders as embodiments for their denial of sense posing as spirit. This allows them to cope with the harsh reality that their leaders are flawed human beings and not angels. It allows them to pretend that all is well. It allows them to pretend that sense has been vanquished for the triumph of spirit, and thus they can accept reality the way it is. This view of their leadership enables them to participate in the frantic pace of church programs, to donate lavishly to acquire "prosperity," and to enjoy the subjection of Pentecostalism to capitalist logic, while telling themselves that they

52. Williams, *Dostoevsky*, 46.
53. Žižek, *On Belief*, 13.

are not really fooled, that they are aware of the whole spectacle. They say to themselves, "Look, I have inner peace—the Holy Spirit is inside me and my involvement in the game is nothing."[54] Indeed, "fetishists are not dreamers lost in their private worlds, they are thoroughly 'realist,' able to accept the way things effectively are—since they have their fetish to which they can cling in order to cancel the full impact of reality."[55]

As if the relationship between sense and spirit is not complicated enough, fetish and symptom can almost function together indiscernibly in many cases. A leader's body posture, tics, or pronouncements can function as a fetish. In it the leader is seen by the followers as having direct, immediate access to God and as a symptom (the disturbing detail that the leader is human and not divine).

Now the awestruck Pentecostal believer might reply, "True, the anointed pastor is a human being who does detestable things like regarding his opinion as that of God, 'but we should not forget that he nonetheless does noble things,'[56] like specially communicating the mind of God to ordinary folk (which produces confusion or hubris)." Your response should be, "True, the anointed pastor does some powerful and pleasurable things like passing off his opinion as divine and incontestable, 'but nonetheless, we should not forget that he has to pay for this by the boring'[57] charismatic rituals of 'holy' lying." This is the true stance and not even a version like this one: "True, the anointed pastor is able to elevate even the human function of speaking into the divine sphere, 'but let us not forget that ultimately'[58] he does have to accomplish the vulgar, unfortunate act of replacing God's voice with his own as a compulsion-to-enjoy."

Is anyone really surprised at this kind of rationalization by the followers of the so-called super-anointed Pentecostal pastors? If you are, I want to provide an interpretative lens to decipher what you have just read. First, one good way to interpret the quest for it-makes-spirit is to view it as a principle of thematic composition. Pentecostal believers are struggling to adequately map meaning (knowledge) onto sign (spirit, thematic meaning). The lack of fit between the two, the deviation is what is known as it-makes-sense.[59] When there is a fit recognized by them they say it-makes-spirit. The composition is not a strict system as in a tight philosophical system "built purely

54. Žižek, *On Belief*, 15, inspired this passage.
55. Žižek, *On Belief*, 14.
56. Žižek, *On Belief*, 60.
57. Žižek, *On Belief*, 60.
58. Žižek, *On Belief*, 60.
59. Spivak, *Critique of Postcolonial Reason*, 41, inspired this sentence.

rationally by following irrefutable laws of logic," but more akin to musical composition, which works by "repeating and varying a number of themes and presenting them in ever new combinations."[60]

There is no it-makes-spirit that is not at the same time it-makes-sense insofar as spirituality paradoxically carries with it the potential of both discursive self-legitimation and self-transcendence. Put differently, it-makes-spirit is also it-makes-sense because it-makes-spirit is always already an interpretation, a deconstructive proclivity of rationalism, and a meaningful (re)construction of "sense" that is dialogically embedded in everyday social intercourse. As an interpretation, it is also a transgressive and disruptive penetration into the logic of dominant (post-)Enlightenment discourses of knowledge production (authentication) and epistemological credentials. It-makes-spirit is a form of practical consciousness rooted in Pentecostals' own self-definition that is not outside the dialogical alterity of human and God, self and other, rationalism and spirit, and so on. This practical consciousness is also a tragedy born out of religion "as a state of being grasped by an ultimate concern."

The grasping by faith in the inside sets the drama between it-makes-sense and it-makes-spirit in the external realm of decision-making. Pentecostalism has externalized an internal struggle within the self. Pentecostals have projected their sense of self as a composite of spirit and flesh onto the external reality as an epistemological framework of noumenal and phenomenal. Reality is not one piece (layer); dimensions of it are seen as "little incomplete realities" in a fractured, ontologically incomplete whole. Pentecostals have projected their epistemological limitation about knowing their split self to reality. The limitation of their knowledge about the self, their own being, is simultaneously the limitation of the very reality they encounter. This is against the trend of monotheism,[61] and this is in line with the idea of *split God*, in which "each aspect of the divine personality [is] seen as a separate deity."[62] In the notion of the split God, "parts," dimensions, signature traits, and attributes of God are separated from Godself and treated as self-standing rather than being in an organic simple whole. Pentecostals have generated too many "powerful gods" from God the Father as a result of isolating certain qualities of God and treating them as deities. They have projected their epistemological limitation about knowing God, their

60. Steinby, "Concepts of Novelistic Polyphony," 46.

61. "Monotheism relocates conflict from 'out there' to 'in here,' transforming it from an objective fact about the world to an internal contest within the mind. This changes our view of God, and fate, and history." Sacks, *To Heal a Fractured World*, 177; see also 175–76.

62. Sacks, *To Heal a Fractured World*, 175. See also Wariboko, *The Split God*.

knowledge of ontological incompleteness to God. At their deepest level of philosophy, Pentecostals hold that there are gaps in knowledge, reality, and God; these gaps become the foundation for miracles in a universe that is itself incomplete.[63] In their reckoning, God and reality are not fundamentally indifferent to the existence of human beings (especially Pentecostal believers) and to their hopes and wishes.

Oftentimes what is considered as the work of the Spirit or it-makes-spirit is the presumptive operation of the gap. The spirit or *pneumasation* emerges from the unbridgeable gap between the beauty, sublimity, or out-of-jointness of an idea, action, or statement and the human, all too human, of the person(s) generating it.[64] Often what Pentecostals take to be the work of the Spirit is the explosive noumenal potential, "inner greatness" of sense, the liberatory potential of the density of the interaction ritual chains in any shared intersubjective contexts. Simply put, they are not always careful to differentiate collective effervescence from the Spirit of Christ. In my 2014 book, *Nigerian Pentecostalism*, I showed how spirit could be "manufactured" from sense—and Pentecostals often engage in this kind of production.[65] The obstacle to the *correct* perspective here (that is, both in the understanding of it-makes-spirit and in many cases of the generation of spiritual anointing in Pentecostal worship services) is that sense which has been used to generate the spirit or the numinous is not seen as part of the spirit it generates. Hence the gap is viewed as the spirit or the spacing of spirit—and not the reflexive appearance of *dense* sense.

It-makes-spirit may also refer to the inner contemplative self within a person that leads to insight on how to deal with natural events. Take the story of the prophet Elijah in the Hebrew Bible (1 Kgs 19:1–18). Elijah was afraid for his life and in dark despair after Queen Jezebel threatened him for killing hundreds of the prophets of Baal. He fled to the wilderness as he ran for his life. God instructed him to go to a mountain (Horeb) and await further instruction. While he waited in a cave, a wild wind came up and broke parts of the rock. Next an earthquake hit, and that was followed by a raging fire. In none of these catastrophic natural events did he hear the voice of the Lord. But the Bible says the voice came to him as "a still small voice" within him, as a gentle whisper. On hearing it he was reinvigorated with a renewed sense of mission. Philosopher of religion Donald A. Crosby states,

> This still small voice, I suggest, can be construed as the symbol of a contemplative, openhearted spirit that is able to attend to

---

63. Wariboko, *Split God*, xiv.
64. Žižek, *On Belief*, 38, inspired this sentence
65. Wariboko, *Nigerian Pentecostalism*, 124–41.

the natural, everyday events of the world—not just those of a highly unusual or unfathomable character—with empowering religious insight, faith, and conviction. Experience of the authentically miraculous can in such cases lie in keen discernment of the profound religious significance of commonplace things and occurrences. . . . [This happens because of the] cultivation of inward ways of experiencing, recognizing, and responding to the ordinary things of the world.[66]

How we interpret this inner voice should not be divorced from the splits and gaps in the Pentecostal understanding of reality. At the core of it-makes-spirit there is a split. As a process that emphasizes God's Spirit it bespeaks liberation, disruptions of ongoing automatism of social life, the initiation of new beginnings, and free action amid tradition. But as a model of decision-making, as an "ideology" believers live by, and as a premise to everyday life, it subjects the decision-making process or the mind of the believer to an inner compulsion. What goes for discernment or hearing the voice of God in the inner self becomes nothing more than deducing a conclusion from a pregiven spiritual premise or ideology. In this compulsion or deductive process of spiritual (ideological) thinking, the person in the decision-making process enters into what Hannah Arendt calls "the tyranny of logicality," which keeps the person's thought process away from anything that would question its assumptions or from new beginnings that will interrupt it.[67] According to Arendt in a different context, "The self-coercive force of logicality [of spirituality] is mobilized lest anybody start thinking."[68]

The spirituality of it-makes-spirit or the interpretation of an inner voice is also related to another gap, that between what the believer is today and what she thinks she ought to be. Pentecostal spirituality is "the sensation of being fully alive" that endlessly seeks to renew itself and unconceal the person.[69] It-makes-spirit is a process through which the Pentecostal believer discovers and discloses her unique destiny (her understanding of the central purpose of her life) and identity before her community.[70] Every utterance of it-makes-spirit gradually builds and displays a portrait of what she thinks is her true self. The process is akin to a "space of appearing" of who she is (her irreducible particularity) and who she is becoming. "New beginnings

---

66. Crosby, *Extraordinary in the Ordinary*, 4.
67. Kiess, *Hannah Arendt and Theology*, 60.
68. Arendt, *Origins of Totalitarianism*, 473.
69. The quotation is from Kiess, commenting on Arendt's observation on thinking. Kiess, *Hannah Arendt*, 213.
70. Kiess, *Hannah Arendt*, 143, inspired this sentence.

emerge out of this process of discovery,"[71] and the *Pentecostal principle*, the capacity to begin, becomes the art of being spiritual, the embracing and nourishing of one's natality.[72]

This quest for a "space of appearing" of the "who" of the believer often involves the dream of doing away with sense, crucifying the flesh, and only "walking in the spirit." "Good" Pentecostals aspire to eliminate the work of sense or modernist rationality in their daily life or decision-making. They want to be totally dependent on the Holy Spirit, transparent to God, as Jesus Christ was. All well and good. Their dream of eliminating sense and only having the spirit reminds us of Karl Marx's fantasy of obstacle-free capitalism. His dream of communism is an utopia where an economy will have all the self-revolutionizing potential of capitalism itself, without the periodic destructive economic crises, without the inherent obstacles or contradictions of capitalism. Let me quote Slavoj Žižek's gloss on this Marxian idea as we prepare to deploy it in the analysis of Pentecostals' dream of vanquishing sense forever in devout spirituality.

> What Marx overlooked is that . . . this inherent obstacle/antagonism as the "condition of impossibility" of the full deployment of the productive forces is simultaneously its "condition of possibility": if we abolish the obstacle, the inherent contradiction of capitalism, we do not get the fully unleashed drive to productivity finally delivered of its impediment, we lose precisely this productivity that seemed to be generated and simultaneously thwarted by capitalism—if we take away this obstacle, the very potential thwarted by this obstacle dissipates.[73]

Similarly, the very sense or rationality that seems an obstacle to "full" life-in-spirit, to the permanent self-enhancing spirituality, is the very condition of possibility of it-makes-spirit. By eliminating rationality or sense as an obstacle, the Pentecostal believer no longer exists as a living being functioning in a rational world, but also her very potential for spiritual growth thwarted by sense (rationality) dissapates. No spiritual life functions outside the flesh, its sense and its rational mind. The notion of a Pentecostal life of pure it-makes-spirit *outside* the frame of the senses (or empirical data and their logic of interpretation) is a fantasy inherent to spirituality itself.

Outside the realm of the extreme dream of elimination, it-makes-spirit works well as a good principle for decision-making within the Pentecostal tradition. What do I mean? This is the underlying (implicit) rule of the

---

71. Kiess, *Hannah Arendt*, 143.
72. Wariboko, *The Pentecostal Principle*.
73. Žižek, *On Belief*, 18–19.

operative decision-making "model" of it-makes-spirit: initial information (objective data) is modified by subjective belief. The Pentecostal moves from observation of the world to subjective assessment of its future state and/or abstractions about its inner teleology (final cause). This could be termed the inverse of Bayes' rule. Instead of initial belief being modified by objective new information we have the opposite move here.[74] It-makes-spirit is an (not) arbitrary method for utilizing both objective and nonobjective types of information for decision-making.

No doubt categorizing spiritual intuition as a *judgment or priori* (in the Bayesian sense) is a stretch, but Pentecostal believers often consider what comes forth from their minds as evidence of God's presence in their lives and/or in the world. And they (at least some of them) are willing to bet their material substance on such subjective belief as an index or degree of their confidence. This measure of belief is a basis for their decision-making. Indeed, the purpose of it-makes-spirit is to reduce uncertainty in decision-making, and thus singular reliance on it-makes-sense is to increase uncertainty, so they think. In practice, in the quiddity of everyday decision-making, the whole paraphernalia of it-makes-spirit is an attempt to bridge the gap of intuitive soft information of subjective nature and objective, hard information used in everyday life by all human beings.

The soft information is not derived from a sequence of repeatable events or repetitive experimentation but from mere subjective believability. What does it mean to generate a piece of information like eighteenth-century statistician Thomas Bayes' *prior*, information from a situation where there is no frequency of observations, conjuring "data" from what has not happened in the past? What does it mean to derive information on the basis of the assumption that the impossible can happen? While statisticians using Bayes' rule also deal with similar questions and generate hard, precise numbers and rational theories to facilitate decision-making, Pentecostals confront a harder barrier. They are unable to make their opinion (belief) or method precise. Not only is it that the impossible they are trying to figure out is not in the historical realm, there is no commonly shared way of calculating the probability of an event based on the frequency of a person's claimed "contact" with God. Every contact is not better than a *prior* or better than a highly improbable event that does not occur. This is so because the Holy Spirit is not predictable, cannot be an object of experimentation, and God is not an objectively attained data that believers can import (program) as knowledge into their decision matrices. Yet Pentecostals intuit something about this impossible God and *plug* it into their decision-making "models."

---

74. McGrayne, *Theory*, 11.

They are, in a sense, akin to business executives, relying on "managerial intuition" and "feel for a situation" to make decisions under extreme uncertainty.[75] On another note, their claims of repeated interactions with God, and claims of updating their (interactions') integrity and worthiness, are not exactly a case of no data; hence, they can form hypotheses about the expectation of God's behavior. All this notwithstanding, some sober outsiders to the Pentecostal movement may wonder if it-makes-spirit is not a spiritualization of ignorance.

Like the business executive trying to use techniques to help him make decisions under uncertainty, Pentecostals have invented the it-makes-sense and it-makes-spirit to manage their own worlds of uncertainty. The difference is that in one case, management is strictly viewed as a form of spirituality instead of a technique or symbol for engaging with recalcitrant reality or the sense world. Let us not forget that it-makes-sense refers to evidence of immediate sense perception that is undergirded or organized by logical and mathematical rules that express the structure of reality.[76]

It-makes-sense is a metonym for the mixed nature of reason and the sense in human beings. It-makes-spirit is an artful management of reason and the sense through the (so-called) elevating effects of spirituality, and it frees Pentecostals from immediacy of uncultivated senses (feelings and passions), from the arrogant reflective faculties of human beings, and helps develop their engagement with Jesus as source of true wisdom. While Pentecostals consider subjection to reason and the sense as conducing to conformity to this world, they regard submission to it-makes-spirit as invigorating their will in the experience of the Holy Spirit (Rom 12:2). Their point is that the power and lure of it-makes-spirit constitute an instrument for good Christian character formation, as it disarms the sensuous energy and douses the heteronomous power of reason.[77] It-makes-spirit as a decision model, a creative consciousness, is a play of material sensation and free contemplation—the *restraining force* in the empire of sense and reason.

Spirit restrains the "lawlessness" of senses even as at the same time it longs for what is already in sense that is more than sense itself. It-makes-spirit wants to uncover or regain the creative impulse in sense. Every sense contains an event, something astir in it, in its present conditions, contained in its logic, restless in its accumulated historical power, scholarly affirmation, or worldly prestige.[78] It-makes-spirit is a response to the call of

---

75. McGrayne, *Theory That Would Not Die*, 150.
76. Tillich, *Dynamics of Faith*, 39, inspired this sentence.
77. Schiller, *On the Aesthetic Education*, 139.
78. This paragraph is indebted to Caputo, *Weakness of God*, 2–7.

event harbored in the sense, to the promise in every conditioned sensible appearance. Sense reigns supreme, dominates understanding, or captures our imagination because it belongs to "conditioned and coded strings of signifiers. The event is the open-ended promise contained within a [sense], but a promise that the [sense] can neither contain nor deliver."[79] Pentecostal everyday decision-making or deployment of a theory of knowledge is principally about the

> hermeneutics of the event that is astir in [the sense, sensible appearance], for the event is what the [sense] "means." By a "meaning" I do not mean a semantic content but what a [sense] is getting at; what it promises; what it calls up, sighs and longs for, stirs with, or tries to recall.[80]

To assert it-makes-spirit in the face of sense is to gesture to the containable possibilities harbored in every sense, to solicit for the excess that is beyond the horizon of expectation that the balanced equation, the coded economy of the present condition, avers. In a certain sense, it-make-spirit is a cut into sense to release, liberate the event that is contained in sense. Sense is "conditioned, coded, and finite, whereas the event it shelters is unconditioned and infinite in the sense of being capable of endless linkings and endless productive dissemination."[81]

To-make-spirit is, therefore, to-make-sense under conditions that destabilize, improvise, or threaten to undo the sense we are thrown into as a matter of course, resisting our thrownness into the signifying chain of causation or regnant, accepted language game.[82] Put differently, to make spirit is to solicit (meaning also to shake, to make it tremble, *sollicitare*) sense out of its thrownness. This shaking eventuates in moving sense from its preferred or originary thrownness into a different spacing where like the Apostle Paul the things that are not are used to confound the things that are, the "spirit" that is low and weak and despised is used to reconfigure the strong, exalted, and celebrated sense (1 Cor 1:25, 27–28).

If to make sense, to be seen as reasonable or worldly wise is to work out one's decision within a rigorously systemic chain of cause and effect or rule-governed inferential system, then to make spirit is to consider the signifying chains of reason and reasoning not as "closed formalizable systems,

---

79. Caputo, *Weakness of God*, 2.
80. Caputo, *Weakness of God*, 6.
81. Caputo, *Weakness of God*, 3.
82. Caputo, *Weakness of God*, 24–25, inspired this sentence.

but open-ended, incompletable networks."[83] The power of spirit is neither pure reason nor pure irrationality. It is to hold the constructedness of reason or sense to the demands of the event of human flourishing. It is to sense the gap between what reason offers on the basis of the present order or being and what is to come, the order of the to-come (Rev 1:8). The only problem with this interpretation is that the Pentecostal effort to escape or transcend the fixed (fixing) order of the present to the (dis)order of the spirit is actually a search for power, a love of power. The love of power is packaged as dispersed spiritual orientation struggling against all celebrated sense and rationality in the name of human flourishing. This last sentence nicely sets us up for the next section, which raises more critical questions about the whole Pentecostal hypothesis of it-makes-spirit.

Questioning It-Makes-Spirit

One sensibility behind the preference for it-makes-spirit rather than it-makes-sense is the Pentecostal desire to escape the "metaphysics" of modern reason, to go beyond the conceptual violence of reason and the constraint imposed upon human decision-making by the modern human condition. The telos of this desire is to drive toward ownmost reality of objects or situations that figure in decision-making—hoping to transcend the historically contingent mediations of modern and postmodern epistemologies.[84]

But does anyone really believe that Pentecostals can eliminate the historical, anterior conditions in terms of which it is possible to think or understand objects and situations? When they speak of making decisions by the spirit (claiming to occupy God's point of view) they have not extricated their reasoning, discernment process from "all anterior conditionality. [They] have not gotten something unconditioned but something better conditioned to a religious sensibility."[85]

Even now a question forces itself upon us: Does this something conditioned by religious sensibility, experience, or predetermined framework necessarily represent the Holy Spirit's point of view? Is the conformity of a decision-making process to ideas of the Holy Spirit and God as Spirit, or any claim of direct discernment, not in some sense a way to underwrite Pentecostals' projects, garner spiritual compliments, and so on?

---

83. Caputo, *Weakness of God*, 24.

84. Hector, *Theology without Metaphysics*, 23–24, inspired this sentence and the following ones.

85. Caputo, "How to Avoid Speaking of God," 23.

Can anyone realistically hope to transcend the historically contingent mediations of modern epistemologies or escape sense to reach the realm of direct discernment, if such a site exists? Many Pentecostals speak about the spirit in their epistemological frame not only as if there were no sense in it, but as if there had never been any sense for it.[86] Such people have forgotten why they demand "spirit" as a frame in the first place and the fact that they continue to demand it. The spirit is not given to hide the awful shortcomings of sense, but to glorify, decorate, intensify sense already reasonable or acceptable. The Holy Spirit does not locate the believer in a spirit-matrix of decision-making or knowing because the believer is so senseless without it-makes-spirit. In a certain sense, make-spirit is sense cutting into sense. The it-makes-spirit is the silent swerving from the calculatable by slight adjustment that is the surprise element in every sense.[87]

It-makes-spirit is not a statement about epistemic certainty but, as Søren Kierkegaard is wont to put it, "an objective uncertainty held fast in passionate inwardness."[88] Considered in this sense, it is "a committed struggle to understand in the face of the palpable mystery of the world. . . . The struggle is not something that results from the incompleteness of some theory or from the fact that we don't know enough. Rather, it derives from the very nature of the various human attempts to encounter what I am calling the transcendent."[89] As Alfred North Whitehead once put it, "Religion is the vision of something which stands beyond, behind and within the passing flux of immediate things; something which is real, and yet waiting to be realized; something which is a remote possibility and yet the greatest of present facts; something that gives meaning to all that passes and yet eludes apprehension; something whose possession is the final good and yet is beyond all reach; something which is the ultimate ideal, and the hopeless quest."[90]

In the common religious struggle to understand in the face of uncertainty and the need to justify one's action to members of one's community, Pentecostals, as we have learned earlier, appeal to self-sufficient communal standards of justification. Their transformation of reason into it-makes-spirit also relies on another communal standard, *this is that*, which our earlier Hegelian discourse missed.[91] Pentecostals' justification of their de-

---

86. This is an adaptation of a sentence in Chesterton, Orthodoxy.
87. Chesterton, Orthodoxy, 51.
88. Kierkegaard, Concluding Unscientific Postscript, 171.
89. Crane, Meaning of Belief, 77–78.
90. Whitehead, Science and the Modern World, 192.
91. The following discussion of *this is that* is taken from Wariboko, Nigerian

cisions or affirmation of an event often draws from Peter's speech on the Day of Pentecost (Acts 2), which took the form of *this is that*. What you are seeing now is what was promised, prophesied, or done in the past. The miracles or the extraordinary events you are witnessing today are similar (if not identical) to what happened in the days of the Old Testament prophets, Jesus Christ, and his disciples. The *this is that* in a sense means there is virtually no distance between the past and now, between the *thisness* of the phenomenal realm and the *thatness* of the noumenal. The *this* is the transparent medium of the *voice* that enables the self-presence of the *that*. What is happening today, the current miracle (the *this*, the it-makes-spirit), speaks to and at the same time reenacts what transpired in the past, the *that*. The present, the *this*, in so doing, carries forward the past, the *that*. Thus, the *this is that* is both a remainder and an excess. What you are seeing today is the *latter rain* of the *rain* that fell in the time of Jesus and his disciples. *This* is the latter and surplus rain of *that*. The *this* points to an excess over phenomenality and jouissance of those privileged to see the *this* as *that*, to regard a new event as a replay of past event. The *that* is the fantasmatic support of the *this*. The *this* signifies the *that*. But the *that* is absent, empty, so the *this* is a pure signifier, a signifier without the signified. The presence of pure signifier, as Slavoj Žižek has taught us, is what allows meaning to emerge in the discourse of the new event.[92]

But the meaning that emerges from it-makes-spirit is (often) ambiguous. This powerful, provocative, and self-affirming statement of spirituality is caught within the blindness of rationality it professes to reject. It is ensnared by the opponent it tries to dish. It-makes-spirit set against "sense" suggests that spirit is an affirmation of a belief or decision beyond evidence, something a believer cannot defend, something not warranted by publicly acceptable standards of evidence or justification. This is precisely how modern Western rationality defines faith—always beyond reason or sense, a leap into irrationality. Why can't the "it" (whatever it is in the "it makes . . .") make both spirit and sense? Does the spirit of the believer, or the spirit in being-in-the-world of the believer, or the spirit connected to the *making of it*, not have a lived awareness of the physical world? How does the *making* spirit connect with the physical (flesh-and-blood) believer?

We need not to wait for good answers from the Pentecostals and their alternate epistemology. The epistemology of Pentecostals is in service, among other things, to set them apart from what they consider as the

---

Pentecostalism, 101. For a full discussion and critique of *this is that*, see also the rest of p. 101 and up to p. 103.

92. Žižek, *Indivisible Remainder*, 43–44; see also 212.

secular ways of knowing reigning supreme in the present world. They like to deny the importance of secular ways of knowing. They clamor for a turn from secular epistemology to biblical epistemology, whatever that means today. The irony here is that their very epistemology represents the confirmation of a world of Christ-loss by the necessity of the turning that it asserts. Paradoxically, Pentecostal epistemology or receptive knowing is a theological confirmation of worldly knowledge system that is increasingly becoming atheistic—and is a resistance against it. The resistance is not really a resistance of confrontation but that of *kenosis* of reason, the emptying out (finitization, spacing) of reason's divinity. This resistance means—at least in their own lives, decision-making processes, discerning moments—that Pentecostals open *within* reason an *outside* that is not beyond reason, but the *truth* of reason.[93]

The emptied-out reason means that the Pentecostal resistance to modernity's rationality or even Pentecostal epistemology is not theological. It is *atheological*. For reason is seen as *a-theos*, in the sense of not being divine, and thus resistance to it is not necessarily a defense of God, the transcendent, or dogma, but an affirmation of a particular vision of human flourishing or existence. Epistemology is existence. In the zone of the atheological, spirit (it-makes-spirit) is a self-conscious path of sense (*sentier*), sense of sense (it-makes-sense). It-makes-spirit is subjectivity making itself into its own sense: "It is the projection of an assumed interiority into the reality of an exteriority."[94] Put differently, it-makes-spirit is the signification of it-makes-sense. Signification subdues the practical, empirical data, sensuous observation to its genitive: it gives the sense *of* the data. It-makes-sense presents the data. It-makes-spirit refers the data to a different sphere of understanding, to a site of intensified engagement with existence than that of its "data-being," whereas it-makes-sense merely inscribes its difference (the data/context) within existence, registering it in the sphere of being.[95]

Many Pentecostals even go to the extreme of interpreting it-makes-spirit-and-does-not-make-sense to mean an effect is causeless, an effect arising without an obvious physical cause. This is when it-makes-spirit becomes a synonym for "divine miracle." This miracle is not a miracle of natality but of repetition, invariability: God does not change. The world of biblical Israel has not changed as it traveled to New York, Lagos, or Canberra. It-makes-spirit rests on one assumption: repetition. A repetition that can renew sense

---

93. Nancy, *Dis-Enclosure*, 79, inspired this sentence.

94. Nancy, *Dis-Enclosure*, 124.

95. I have borrowed the words of Nancy, *Dis-Enclosure*, 131, to express my ideas here. I am sure in the process I have mangled his ideas and style of phrasing.

or modernist rationalism. A repetition that makes all things new and fills them with life, vitality, power. The God that does not vary, does not tire of communicating with God's children, will keep on doing. Jesus Christ is the same yesterday, today, and forever. The Holy Spirit is always full of gigantic joy and unbroken strength. Individual creaturely life varies because its life, as we know, is always mixed with death. But God as life is the power of being that has conquered nonbeing, vanquished death. The Holy Spirit is the spirit of life; life is repetition, the spirit is the power of the repetition. Before we declare that our Pentecostals have all gone mad to think of the world in terms of repetition or to craft a spirituality that accents repetition when the Pentecostal principle demands something else, we should take a moment to reflect on the words of Catholic writer G. K. Chesterton. He taught us that repetition is not lifelessness but the rush of life itself.

> The sun rises every morning. I do not rise every morning, but the variation is due not to my activity, but to my inaction. Now, to put the matter in a popular phrase, it might be true that the sun rises regularly because it never gets tired. His routine might be due, not to a lifelessness, but the rush of life. The thing I mean can be seen, for instance, in children, when they find some game or joke that they specially enjoy. A child kicks his legs rhythmically through excess, not absence of life. Because children have abounding vitality, because they are in spirit fierce and free, therefore they want things repeated and unchanged. They always say, "Do it again"; and the grown-up person does it again until he is nearly dead. For grown-up people are not strong enough to exult in monotony. But perhaps God is strong enough to exult in monotony.[96]

This is a repetition with the promise of renewal and a better future, and Pentecostals are counting on God to deliver the goods in the future as he did in the time of Moses, Elisha, and Paul. The split, the gap between sense and spirit, is founded on split time, future anterior, that is, you project yourself to the future (as if it has happened). The gap is a gap of promise.

Temporality of Desire and the Promise of It-Makes-Spirit

The fundamental gesture of it-makes-spirit is promise, the promise of a better future. One engages in it with the promise of making a better decision. One adheres to it with the promise of getting closer to God. One invests in it with the promise of untold returns to one's prosperity (human

96. Chesterton, *Orthodoxy*, 35–36.

flourishing). In all cases it-makes-spirit embodies a type of dissatisfaction with sense-data and points to a future that embodies a type of satisfaction foreclosed to it-makes-sense. The promise of a better satisfaction ensures a sense of dissatisfaction of the ordinary visible phenomenal density of the world, with the present in relation to the future or the promise of a better future. This promise of a higher (authentic) satisfaction or a better future is the fundamental Pentecostal fantasy. The promise has a lot of psychic appeal to Pentecostals.[97]

While fully aware of the genuine faith of most Pentecostals, one cannot help imagining that every repetition of it-makes-spirit signals something beyond human-divine relationship. It seems a supplement, an excess attaches itself to it-makes-spirit. In the real world that Pentecostals inhabit with other human beings, it-makes-spirit is never just an it-makes-spirit. There is an excess that remains irreducible to it. The self-division of it-makes-spirit "enables it to signify something beyond itself," to embody something more.[98] The division of it-makes-spirit from itself means it is not identical with itself. There is a gap: the "name," it-makes-spirit, and what the name signifies.[99]

Is it too much to imagine that it-makes-spirit may be pointing to the "existence and repression of desires" that either the extant system of rationality or capitalism cannot gratify?[100] In any case, is the investment in the promise of a better future, in promise *as such*, not akin to the fundamental logic of capitalism, as Todd McGowan taught us in his 2016 book *Capitalism and Desire*.

The split nature of it-makes-spirit generates an important insight about pneumasation as an "object" of Pentecostal decision-making. It is not really a goal (object) that the believer hopes to attain (as no one can possess, acquire the mind of God or possess the Holy Spirit) as a mechanical decision-making algorithm, but a *limit concept* that the Pentecostal encounters. The believer "cannot overcome the limit but constitutes [herself] and [her] satisfaction through the limit. That is to say, the object that thwarts the subject's effort at obtaining it, retroactively creates the subject [believer] around the recalcitrance."[101] Rather than this failure to overcome the limit inducing the believing subject to abandon her goals like instinctual beings, she derives satisfaction from her inability to overcome the limit, to

---

97. McGowan, *Capitalism and Desire*, 11–13, inspired this passage.
98. McGowan, *Capitalism and Desire*, 23.
99. McGowan, *Capitalism and Desire*, 24.
100. McGowan, *Capitalism and Desire*, 18.
101. McGowan, *Capitalism and Desire*, 30.

attain her goal. Being in (or taking) this path of satisfaction without ever concluding the journey is interpreted as abiding in Christ; the finite being moving closer and closer to the infinite is considered as the proper ethic of not betraying one's desires. This failure (a mode of success) to overcome, the inability to reach the Spirit as possible possession, the failure to achieve revelation of ultimate truth, haunts the subject and constitutes her subjectivity. As a "true" believer she must endure the perpetual movement toward the object or her desire—and its constitutive loss. No wonder that the path (or the drive) that leads to an easy access to it-makes-spirit in *Pentecostalese* is called *crucifixion of the flesh*, a kind of "dead drive" of the human nature for the sake of a treasure believed to be at the core of the self. There is really no substantive content to be found because the believer's satisfaction is in how she desires and the promise of the future, and not what she obtains.[102]

With this kind of subjectivity and subject's desire, the believer's gaze on the sensuous, empirical data is distorted. The subject's desire distorts the field of empirical facts, the visual field of the phenomenal world in which it-makes-sense is rooted and legitimized. There is no longer a neutral field of vision; the subject's desire now disrupts her field of vision. "The visual field is not simply there to be seen but constituted around" her vision of it.[103] In fact, she becomes "present" in the field of vision, the stain that distorts or warps her field of vision. Under this scenario it-makes-sense is really not an alternative to it-makes-spirit; rather, it-makes-sense is conceived in spiritual terms. Perhaps we now have some understanding of why many Pentecostals see a ghost under every rock or reduce everything to the mere veil of a "deeper" spiritual essence. What they see as reality, object, or fact is always already distorted, stained, corrupted, or constituted by their spiritual vision of it.

Pentecostals love to talk about the impossible, focusing on what is beyond human capacity, and it is in this region that transcends human limits that they situate in general the power of the spirit. The impossible (or spirit) is in a sense a master signifier of all that existence implies beyond human conditions and limitations. This to the non-Pentecostal might mean they are always looking beyond history, or thick and coarse reality. To the contrary, they are well grounded. Like Jacques Lacan, Pentecostals believe that the impossible happens. The impossible is never seen as something that can never happen. Pentecostals sing, "Jehovah Jireh, he makes impossibility possible . . ." The impossible is just what resists full symbolization, rational apprehension, what has not been captured or "castrated" by

---

102. McGowan, *Capitalism and Desire*, 36, inspired this sentence.
103. McGowan, *Capitalism and Desire*, 79.

the socio-symbolic order, which can leak through the cracks of the system (order). The impossible is not something beyond history or even the finite but often the obstacle (antagonism) that distorts our vision of reality.[104] "It is simultaneously the Thing to which direct access is not possible *and* the obstacle which prevents this direct access; the Thing which eludes our grasp *and* the distorting screen which makes us miss the Thing."[105] When the impossible is interpreted in this way, it can happen.

Permit me to make a small detour about this case of seeing a spiritual form or an ideal form behind mere appearance, sense data, before continuing with our discussion. The issue of seeing a veil behind sense data or material reality is, perhaps, related to Pentecostals giving epistemological privilege to, or positing the ontological priority of, the ideal form. Like Plato, they believe that there are ideal forms of worldly appearances. They largely refuse to accept that appearance qua appearance is self-divided. It is the self-division of appearance rather than the external, eternal form that gives the illusion of an ideal form—something outside the limits of appearing. We see an object (especially if it has flaws) and we think that there must be a better one, a flawless one somewhere else outside history. The mere encounter with an object, according to Alain Badiou, produces the idea that it is out of place, that is, there is an ideal form of it. Why? He holds that "all that is relates to itself at a distance from itself owing to its place where it is."[106] This simply means every particular object is split "between its place and its being, which always exceeds the particular's position in the world. Every particular appearance suffers from this self-division in which universality manifests itself."[107]

Let us now return to subjectivity and desire. Often the advocates of it-makes-spirit fail to recognize that it has an internal limit (that is necessary and contingent) which it-makes-sense does not seem to have. It-makes-spirit is a retreat or reconfiguration or resituation of it-makes-sense so as to enter into the authentic, serene, or true realm of godliness, holiness, or spirituality. Therefore it-makes-spirit requires the world of it-makes-sense to retreat from. It-makes-spirit can only function by focusing on the realm of it-makes-sense that it disdains. It-makes-sense is a necessary obstacle to it-makes-spirit through the logical requirement of it-makes-spirit. This is another way of saying that it-makes-spirit is internally split.

---

104. Zupančič, *Odd One In*, 51.
105. Žižek, *Incontinence of the Void*, 114.
106. Badiou, *Theory of the Subject*, 8.
107. Eisenstein and McGowan, *Rupture*, 72.

Split Christ: Jesus Talks and Pentecostals Decide

We have demonstrated (in this chapter and the previous ones) that the Pentecostal hypothesis is an organum of Christ's talk and Pentecostals' decision on what to do. What exactly does it mean to say Christ talks? What we mean by this goes beyond the Spirit of Christ speaking to the inner spirit of believers. It goes beyond grasping the ideas in what may be called Christ's or the Holy Spirit's linguistic representations of realities. It exceeds rhetoric, narrative, and other linguistic practices. It includes Christ's living bodily activities, spontaneous reactions to events. Now you may be asking, How on earth can anyone know how the noncorporeal Christ body relates to other bodies in his talks? Christ talks through the bodies of his followers, through worshipers, and through the very individuals (supposedly) speaking as his mouthpieces. Christ talks by engaging the senses of his mouthpieces as they in turn engage their hearers' senses, precipitating a confluence, celebration, and conviviality of the known physical senses. The advice, the talk, the whisper of the spirit-content of the talking Christ is presented to his believers dialogically by the senses, by *his* bodily responsiveness to "others and othernesses" around him.[108] Christ does not just talk; he is in a dialogically structured relation with those with whom he is interacting, and his talk and their talk (and decisions) are "not shaped by [their] following of preexisting rules; [they are] unique and creative."[109]

To get some handle on how we got to know that Christ speaks through the bodies of his believers or devotees, we need to turn to the famous English-Nigerian anthropologist Robin Horton. He argues that we can know the unobservable underlying reality of gods and their actions by observing the words and deeds of their devotees who claim to be under their influence. Gods or spirits are defined as incapable of direct observations, but by reference to their effects. It is the behaviors of observable objects (bodies) that are assumed to be symptoms of variations in the unobservable (spirits).[110] The invisibility of the gods' bodies or the direct inaudibility of gods and spirits should not distract from the dialogicality of their interactions with human beings. Mikhail Bakhtin, the Russian literary critic and philosopher, calls interaction with nonpresent interlocutors "hidden dialogicality." He explains it in this way: "The second speaker is present invisibly, his words are not there, but deep traces left by these words have a determining effect on all the present and visible words of the first speaker. We sense that this

---

108. For the words in quotation marks, see Shotter, *Conversational Realities*, 7.
109. Shotter, *Conversational Realities*, 7.
110. Horton, *Patterns of Thought in Africa and the West*.

is a conversation, although only one person is speaking . . . for each present, uttered word responds and reacts with its every fiber to the invisible speaker, points to something outside itself, beyond its own limits, to the unspoken words of another person."[111]

So the Pentecostal hypothesis in the form of the utterance it-makes-spirit takes into account both the influence of Christ's voice that enters into believers and the already corporeally shaped dialogism from which it draws inspiration, to which it is a response, in whose chain of communication it is a link, and which it augments.[112] The Pentecostal hypothesis thrives only in this kind of dialogical interaction of a bodily engaged Christ and those who respond to him with their open and *ex-posed* senses.

This Christ we are talking about here is a metonym of a collective body receiving, performing, and reflecting (the sacred energies of) Christ to capture something eternal within passing present moments. Pentecostals have (or cultivate) the existence of *this* Christ in the middle of activities. The bodily engaged Christ is a middle figure, thrown in between the abstract, universal Christ and the Christ (Spirit of Christ) that dwells in believers. This figure is a dynamic unity of "unmerged" projected bodies of God and human beings "in the interplay occurring in a dialogically structured or chiasmically structured event."[113] Also imagine this figure as an in-between space (as we have argued in chapters 1, 2, and 3), a contact zone between divinity and humanity, a site of intensified encounter of believers with the transimmanent Spirit of Christ. As we stated earlier in this book, Pentecostals lend their imagination to objective reality in its encounter with the "promiscuous creativity of the senses" to fully see into it and discern its hidden or invisible cracks.[114] The meaning of a situation, its epistemic density, is found not in sense or spirit taken singly but in the intervals between them. Under the right set of conditions of intersubjectivity, attunement, common focus on an object in a passionate worship, and so on, the bodily engaged Christ flashes through, undulates on, and froths on the bodies of believers as a partner in the perichoretic dance of Christ's three bodies: heavenly Christ, bodily engaged Christ, and as the mass of believers (also known as the body of Christ).[115] The nisus of the Pentecostal hypothesis in this "living conversation is directly, blatantly, oriented toward a future answer-word

111. Bakhtin, *Problems of Dostoevsky's Poetics*, 197.

112. This way of putting across my ideas was inspired by Shotter, *Conversational Realities*, 5.

113. Shotter, *Getting It*, 17.

114. Abram, *Spell of the Sensuous*, 58.

115. For a theory of how intersubjectivity, attunement, and other factors can engender the "spirit," see Wariboko, *Nigerian Pentecostalism*, 124–41.

[from Christ]; it provokes an answer, anticipates it, and [its deployment] structures itself in the answer's direction."[116] The Pentecostal hypothesis formed in the context of a response to Christ's word and to Christ as the Word of God is constantly re-forming and in-forming "in an atmosphere of the already spoken" word and the still speaking word; it is, therefore, "at the same time determined by that which has not been said but which is needed and in fact anticipated" from Christ.[117]

The anticipation of Christ's answer-word, the expectation of believers located in the temporal time gap between the present and the future, and the traffic with the bodily engaged Christ are some of the driving forces that are in, through, and behind the gap between sense and spirit. We have been able to theorize these complex interconnections in the book not because we are smarter than the Pentecostal scholars who came before us but because of one distinctive assumption that guides our study. We turned away from taking "thoughts and thinking as basic in attempts to understand human activities, to taking [Pentecostal] activity itself as basic."[118] This is to say that what is basic to a proper study of Pentecostalism (Pentecostal theology or philosophy) is not thinking and thought but activities, the embodied practices of those trying to realize what it means to have life-in-the-spirit. Allow me to borrow the words of Ludwig Wittgenstein (from a different context): "If I had to say what is the main mistake of [the leading Pentecostal theologians] of the present generation . . . I would say that when [Pentecostalism] is looked at, what is looked at is a form of [doctrines, theologies] and not the use made of the form of [doctrines, theologies]."[119]

When I say that I am not, by any stretch of the imagination, claiming any superior insight into the proper method by which to conduct inquiry and corral reason to seek definite truth about Pentecostalism, it is to register my inclination to perpetually grope my way to understanding Pentecostals not as objects but as subjects.[120] So let me end this section by quoting what Albert Einstein said about Nobel Prize–winning quantum physicist Niels

116. Bakhtin, *Dialogical Imagination*, 280.
117. All the quotes are from Bakhtin, *Dialogical Imagination*, 280.
118. Shotter, *Getting It*, 94.
119. Wittgenstein, *Lectures and Conversations*, 2.
120. "The exact sciences constitute a monologic form of knowledge: the intellect contemplates a *thing* and expounds upon it. There is only one subject here—cognizing (contemplating) and speaking (expounding). In opposition to the subject there is only a *voiceless thing*. Any object of knowledge (including man) can be perceived and cognized as a thing. But a subject as such cannot be perceived and studied as a thing, for as a subject it cannot, while remaining a subject, become voiceless, and, consequently, cognition of it can only be *dialogic*." Bakhtin, *Speech Genres and Other Late Essays*, 161.

Bohr: "He utters his opinions like one perpetually groping and never like one who believes himself to be in possession of definite truth."[121]

Concluding Remarks: Key Findings Concerning It-Makes-Spirit

There are six key findings I want to highlight as we bring this chapter to a close. First, it-makes-spirit is neither anti-rationality nor obscurantism, neither metaphysical decision theory nor mysticism; rather, it is rationality made contextual and fluid through phronesistic investigation of the emotional dynamics that underlie rational decision-making.[122] It offers Pentecostal believers a helpful "framework through which to reimagine the possibilities" of sense data and rational decision-making theory.[123] It-makes-spirit is a reason to those who think they feel, an emotion to those that really feel.

Second, rationality may be made fluid with the decision-making technique of it-makes-spirit, but is the technique itself historically mutable? Does reality give feedback to Pentecostals that reinforces or problematizes the sacred canopy of it-makes-spirit that they have erected over their decision-making process? The answer is yes. There are always "repairs" going on the canopy. And there is also ongoing religious crisis among many of them as the canopy increasingly does not fit reality or deliver what it promises. This is a story that needs to be fully narrated, but this is not the time for it.

Third, having accented the dialogism of it-makes-spirit in this and previous chapters, we will be deficient in our thinking if we do not unconceal the "hidden wish" of many Pentecostal believers who turn to it for succor in their challenging modern world. For this group, it-makes-spirit carries the burden of logocentrism. Faced with the uncertainties of existence, perplexed by the polyphonic diversity of modernist thought patterns, and desirous of reaching out from the dividedness of secular self-sufficient thinking toward a way of being that might connect her to fellow believers, the Pentecostal seeks a unifying divine purpose or monological voice behind the sense-data that confronts her.

Fourth, this chapter frames the basic problem of Pentecostal thinking or everyday decision-making as a twin demand for justification—justification of revelational reason and justification of religious discourse in the Pentecostal public. The key insight from the analysis of this problem is that revelational reason is not self-sufficient or self-referential but always

121. Quoted in Shotter, *Getting It*, 119.
122. This sentence was inspired by Gribetz, "Jewish Response," 30.
123. Gribetz, "Jewish Response," 30.

points beyond itself or redirects spiritual understanding back to the empirical use of the senses (more on this in the sixth finding below). Herein lies the potential for it-makes-spirit to make contributions to the Pentecostal community's notion of public reason or Pentecostal social ethics.

Fifth, it-makes-spirit is both morality and ethics. It is universal and particular. Morality because it is a binding constraint on the believer as she pursues her own interests, and such constraint also governs the behavior of others as they pursue their own interests. It is ethical because it also applies to her concrete situation as conditioned by specific norms and ideals of her community.[124] These norms, among other things, are instantiated in social practices that are at various stages of working out the love of God and the love of neighbor. Believers, with all their faults, are summoned to infinite responsibility by God and the other. In this call to infinite responsibility, any form of social practice as an organization of responses to the summons or as a patterning of the infinite responsibility of relations between a believer and her others, or between believers and God, must always fall short. It must always be inadequate, always insufficiently manifesting the essential strangeness of the call and always concealing the responsibility in familiarity. This is so because the pattern must always miss what lies behind the patterning itself. Thus, the ethics of it-makes-spirit is always ethics-to-come.[125]

In the light of the summon to infinite responsibility, it-makes-sense always comes too late. It comes too late in two ways that remind me of the thoughts of Søren Kierkegaard and Immanuel Levinas. The Pentecostal believer in responding to the question of her decision is first of all put in a situation where she must evaluate the significance of her own life. The relationship she has with her own life, the content of her life, is indirectly communicated (as Kierkegaard is wont to say) by the situation within which she faces the question of the decision.[126] Second, the question of decision for which the existing individual believer needs to apply her panoply of reason, sense-certainty, is addressed to a person who is already a believer summoned to God and the other. The believer has to deal with God and the other before the question or burden of decision-making weighs on her consciousness (as Levinas is wont to say). "The ethical is one which [the Pentecostal believer] discovers [she] is *committed to already* by the

---

124. Weston, *Kierkegaard and Modern Continental Philosophy*, 58, inspired the definitions of morality and ethics.

125. Weston, *Kierkegaard and Modern Continental Philosophy*, 101, 161, inspired this thought.

126. Weston, *Kierkegaard and Modern Continental Philosophy*, 171–72, inspired this thought.

discourse [practice, habitude] through which" she lives her own life.[127] It-makes-spirit is thus prior to it-makes-sense as a response to the question or press of decision or deliberation on the structures of rationality. In the same vein, the "abstractness," the "universality" of it-makes-spirit is preceded by its particularity. The primacy comes from the passionate involvement in life of the concretely existing believer who is the subject (and not an object) of morality or conceptuality.[128]

Finally, it-makes-spirit is ultimately it-makes-sense. This happens in two ways: *licensing inference* and as surplus over sense which becomes *expanded sense*. After the believer has received the bit (byte) of information from the Spirit, the question arises, What sense could she make of such an input? What sense does she makes of it? The spiritual information makes sense only within the whole grasp of the believer's (receiver's) situation, which includes her life-world, quest for human flourishing, and decision to live a faithful life. The spiritual information is relevant because it enables the believer to make inferences about issues or situations in the sensible world.[129]

Before proceeding to the second way of *expanded sense*, that is, moving to how it-makes-spirit transforms itself into a surplus of it-makes-sense, let us tarry a bit at the site of intersection of it-makes-spirit and it-makes-sense. The sense of being able to declare it-makes-spirit would not come up if there were no surrounding it-makes-sense. What sense would it make in attributing the property of it-makes-spirit to a situation or decision if the person had not (never) known it-makes-sense? What would it be like to know that a given decision, action, or speech makes spirit and yet be unable to say something sensible about it? The plausibility of it-makes-spirit comes from having set it up as intending or attending senses, intelligibility. Take away all characterization of sense, sensibility, intention, and understanding from it-makes-spirit and it dissolves into nothing.[130] It-makes-spirit is nothing; rather, it is something that adds value to it-makes-sense, and lives its life in the phenomenal, historical realm as "fatted" sense.

Let us now turn to the second way it-makes-spirit is ultimately it-makes-sense: *expanded sense*. Next, imagine the inputting of the bit (byte) of spiritual information into decision-making as a process. The person starts with a real (phenomenal, hard, nonspiritual) sensible condition but

---

127. Weston, *Kierkegaard and Modern Continental Philosophy*, 172.
128. Weston, *Kierkegaard and Modern Continental Philosophy*, 171–72, inspired this thought.
129. Taylor, *Language Animal*, 21.
130. Taylor, *Language Animal*, 32.

needs the second-order spiritual information to reach a better decision. The information is graciously provided by God's Spirit (as generally assumed), and the person plugs this valued data into a decision model. What we have is something like this: $S \to \Delta S \to S^1$, where S = sensible formation, ΔS = spiritual information, and S^1 = more (increased) sensible information, *a growing sense*, bulging with surplus insight produced and fed back into the starting real nonspiritual information. The S^1 becomes S in another process (round), and the whole process starts all over again.

Based on the two ways (the working of inference and *expanded sense*) it-makes-spirit is transformed into it-makes-sense, we can venture a crude Saussurean proposition: in it-makes-spirit there are only differences in sense without positive spirit. This means that we cannot understand the spiritual bit of information as an alignment of the suprasensible and physical world; rather, we align differences in spirit (suprasensible) with differences in sense (signification).[131] In other words, it-makes-spirit gets "its meaning only in the field of its contrasts," the differences in its sense read against plain sense, the difference in its sense-added (expanded sense).[132]

These two ways of showing how it-makes-spirit bleeds into it-makes-sense should not be construed to mean that the two orientations to life, life-views, are equivalent. Discursive concepts, sense-certainty, assertions, or formulated notions can never fully translate or express "intuition" or spiritual insight. A great deal of the content of it-makes-spirit is an "immediate" and "pre-sensual" apprehension of the situation at hand.[133] Having said this, I do not want to leave you with the impression that the senses are merely there to express ideas, insight, information from the spiritual realm or whatever bit of data is passable through them. The senses themselves are shapers and guides of an individual's spiritual insight. No believer interprets or utters it-makes-spirit with absolute impartiality; she is always conditioned by her senses, which here include doctrines and all mental and physical activities.

---

131. Taylor, *Language Animal*, 20.

132. Taylor, *Language Animal*, 20.

133. I have put the two words in scare quotes to indicate that intuitions are not really immediate or pre-sensual as Charles Peirce taught us. I have made this point earlier; but here I am using them in the sense ordinary Pentecostals deemed spiritual insights to be operating in the lives of believers.

Conclusion
Unconcluding Provocations

OPENING PROVOCATIONS

THE PENTECOSTAL HYPOTHESIS IS in truth a complicated network of mode of inquiry, power of fantasy and imagination, openness to divine freedom, and ethos of discernment and decision-making, built with Christ as its chassis.[1] It is the *pharmakon* of the Pentecostal movement, thanks to its capability to convert the spirit-quenching epistemic resources of modernity into seeding strength of faith, to transform modernity's sources of death into capacity for healing Christian spirituality—thanks, indeed, to its dual ability to affirm (engender, regenerate) and transgress (profane, assault) the ethos of modernity in decision-making. In this dance of embrace and exclusion we catch a glimpse of what we may call Pentecostal rationality.

I suppose every religion knows its own truth in the form of a dominant hypothesis, the question it puts to the world to receive feedback that serves to critique and correct its praxis. We can only begin to grasp a religion's rationality when we comprehend the subtle operations of its dominant hypothesis. In this book, I have identified (arguably) the dominant hypothesis of Pentecostalism as it-does-not-make-sense-but-it-makes-spirit. My goal is to establish Pentecostal rationality, that is to say, the complex interplay of

---

1. It would be nice to do an ethnography of the full panoply of the Pentecostal personal decision-making strategy as it revolves around the formula of "it does not makes sense, but it does make spirit." That is to say, show how the permutations of this formula pan out in everday decision-making: (*a*) it does not make sense, but it makes spirit; (*b*) it does not make sense and it does not make spirit; (*c*) it makes sense and it makes spirit; (*d*) it makes sense, but does not make spirit; and (*e*) one cannot make an evaluation, a judgment either way. What if there is site above all the difference separating sense from spirit? Here I am thinking of such a site as the gap between sense and spirit. The gap is neither sense nor spirit. Or it is spirit inasmuch as it comes from sense; or it is sense insofar as it is the materiality of spirit.

sense and spirit, reason and faith in Pentecostals' interpretation of the world, personal decision-making, and social practices.[2] In this interplay, sense is transfigured into spirit; all that is solid (sense) melts into air (pneuma).[3]

From the sum of the knowledge we have gathered in this book, we can venture a proposition in terms of basic linguistic terminology: it-makes-sense is a noun and it-makes-spirit is a verb. It-does-not-make-sense-but-it-makes-spirit is the process of verbing a noun. Simply, it-makes-spirit verbs a noun. To verb a noun is to have a focused awareness of the "ideal image" of a situation, its "higher level" that is within its empirical traits or formal (phenomenological) condensations, and to set this other level as a challenge to attain. It is like deep listening to hear a voice from within the situation (noun), to hear the verb calling it to become what it must truly be. Pentecostals care to transfigure "sense" into spirit because of their quest for human flourishing, which is partly refracted through their deep inclination to the Pentecostal hypothesis and the Pentecostal principle—the capacity to constitute alternate ways of knowing and the capacity to begin, respectively.

To verb a noun is to cognize a state of affairs as a *statu nascendi*. This is to regard situations, objects, or determinates as not fixed but as always coming into being. "We can characterize them in terms of three features: (1) they are in motion; (2) still indeterminate [not finalized] and thus open to many further determinations; and (3) directed toward the future [human flourishing]. In other words, rather than 'appearances,' they are 'appearings.'"[4]

Thus, it-makes-spirit is an evaluative judgment on it-makes-sense that ascribes transfigured likeness to a certain situation (state of affairs) outside a person's control for the sake of the person's own flourishing (or goals and projects).[5] This judgment is constitutively connected to the Pentecostal hypothesis, a concrete way of engaging the world that is expressed in forms of alternate ways of knowing that are keyed to a certain "Christology."

The epistemological and social ethical issues relating to Pentecostal practices that we have analyzed are rooted in and organized by a particular understanding of what Jesus Christ means to Pentecostals in everyday practices. We examine these practices not as they relate to matters of church dogma, moral laws, and ontological debates about Jesus's divinity but how they should inform Christology. In everyday Pentecostal practices, theology, or more precisely Christology, is transformed into a decision-making

---

2. This way of putting across my notion of the Pentecostal hypothesis is indebted to Jameson, "Foreword," in Sartre, *Critique of Dialectical Reason*, 2:xii–xiii.

3. Pardon the allusion to Marx and Engels' *Communist Manifesto*.

4. Shotter, *Speaking, Actually*, 180.

5. This definition is an adaptation of Martha Nussbaum's description of the Greek Stoics' view on emotions. See Nussbaum, *Upheavals of Thought*, 22.

matrix or epistemological paradigm or converted into an ontology on the account of grounding decision-making or everyday prudence on the inescapable formal features of Jesus as Christ.

The development of the thesis and the supporting argumentation takes the following form. The first chapter is in the form of a sermon (or altar-speech), the most common rhetorical style for impacting knowledge and ideas in Pentecostal churches. The rest of the book is the unpacking of this sermon, which is itself philosophical for the academic community and for pastor-scholars. Starting our exposition from the sermonic delivery style is not the only way this book attempts to present its philosophical discussions in a Pentecostal style. In the chapters following the first, we hear many voices, many academic "tongues" speaking, with no clear goal of the author attempting to harmonize them into one totalizing authorial voice. Yet the polyphonic display of voices—as in Fyodor Dostoevsky's novels—do not hinder understanding. Different readers will understand each voice in her own mother's (academic, ecclesial, philosophical or theological, Pentecostal or non-Pentecostal) tongue.

Chapters 1 and 2 demonstrate that Jesus Christ is the one that founds and impels the middle space that is the living power of the Pentecostal hypothesis. Chapters 3 and 4 present an alternate epistemology as the principle of form-structuring power of the Pentecostal hypothesis, the vitality that animates the production of ways of knowing that resist cognitive injustice and imperialism. In these four chapters we see how Pentecostals imagine and anticipate not only a better world but also better levels of human flourishing. The Pentecostal hypothesis as a way of being and knowing hopes to better explain, predict, and control their worlds.

The descriptions, analyses, and theorizations of these four chapters primarily constitute a meditation on what Pentecostals mean by *It does not make sense, but it makes spirit*. But the *deep structure* of the chapters as a collectivity is a running commentary on the notion of the split Christ, and yet it repeatedly denies any monologic claim that the book is one on Christology. Ordinary Pentecostals bring some valent assumptions about Christ to the conversation between their spirituality and everyday decision-making or social existence. What I have tried to do in these forgoing chapters is to unconceal some of these assumptions. This act of unconcealment is very necessary if we want to understand the epistemically crucial points of Pentecostals' belief-system as informed by the religious experiences of *who Christ is*. Yes, this question (or declarative statement) of *who Christ is* was what was put to me by a New York Pentecostal congregation in November 2017. These were believers who already know and live by the Spirit of Christ, and yet they wanted me to explain him to them in ways that resonate with their everyday epistemic practices. These were Christians who could intuitively interpret Matthew 14:22–32 in terms of engaging Christ in or as the middle space, the gap of existence, as I explained in chapter 1. In the story, Jesus was walking on water; he was between the safety of the two shores of the Sea of Galilee. Peter decided to join him in walking on water; he left the safety of the boat and stepped on vastly deep seawater. In this courageous act, he was exposed to the in-between, engaging the watery depths between him and Jesus and situating himself in the crack between sense (reason) and spirit (foolishness). By faith, he left the *sensible* place of the hard boat and walked into the "foolish" place of soft water. Peter had the courage to step into a *tehomic* void, emblematic of the birth and rebirth of creation. Members of the New York congregation interpret themselves as a people willing to step into the void between sense and *no-sense*. The cracks and pressures of the "gapped and dialogical" of their daily realities or situations invite them into the *tehomic* depths of sense-spirit hermeneutics.[6] Søren Kierkegaard's wisdom in describing the life of Christians as a turbulent sea is germane to making sense of their Christocentric spirituality:

> The believer continually lies out on the deep, has 70,000 fathoms of water beneath him. However long he lies out there, this still does not mean that he will gradually end up lying and relaxing onshore. He can become more calm, more experienced, find a confidence that loves jest and a cheerful temperament—but until the very last he lies out on 70,000 fathoms of water.[7]

In another place, he writes that the life of a follower of Christ demands that the person give herself over to "the mortal danger of lying out on 70,000 fathoms of water, and only there finding God."[8]

Thus, we have to read this book at two levels: alternate epistemology and alternate (unorthodox, incipient) Christology at alternating levels of visibility. Whether viewed from an alternate-epistemology or split-Christ perspective, you are looking at one and the same phenomenon. It is like the famous, ambiguous duck-rabbit drawing by the American Gestalt psychologist Joseph Jastrow. From one point of view the text is about epistemic struggles; from another point of view it is a philosophy of split-Christ, which is not a Christology. It is just a shifting perspective on one and the same object. It is not two objects brought together in the form of a synthetic identity. The middle space of split-Christ is the embodiment of the dynamics of an alternate epistemology and the alternate epistemology is the

---

6. The words between quotation marks are from Boyarin, *Intertextuality*, 14, 17.
7. Kierkegaard, *Stages on Life's Way*, 444.
8. Kierkegaard, *Concluding Unscientific Postscript*, 232.

split-Christ in everyday processes of knowledge production. The object is not changed, but there are two different takes from two angles of vision. The epistemology and split-Christ are not parts that add up to a greater whole. It is one complex indivisible whole, with parts that overlap and cohere with one another, that can and must be looked at from multiple standpoints. We cannot get the richness of the subject matter or its theology (philosophy) from only a single standpoint. But it seems Pentecostal theologians (philosophers) of Christology or epistemology have rested contentedly focusing only on a single perspective.

This work as well as the majority of my writings on Pentecostalism give voice to the dimensions that the current crop of theologians and philosophers has been unable (or unwilling) to include in their analyses and narratives. To the extent that theology can be described as a map of faith, Pentecostal theologians (philosophers), in general, are adept at mapping the bright, lovely above-sea-level terrain of the Pentecostal Christian faith. I tend to map the ocean floors, those deep and dark places in the Pentecostal faith (movement) where the sunlight of logical and systematic thinking has not penetrated, yet they are filled with life, creativity, splits, and volcanic eruptions. Among other things, I try to capture the excess around which the life of everyday Pentecostalism turns. I theorize the excess that sticks out or cannot be integrated or incorporated into holistic theology (systematic or constructive). Is this not what makes Pentecostalism what it is? Is Pentecostalism not that form of Christianity that directly assumes/embodies the excess that makes Christianity a religion with a strange drive to enjoy (access) God in excess of "ordinary" religions? Or is Christ not a figure of an excess of life, fount of excess of redemptive blood, and bearer of the excess burden of the sin of humanity? I give voice to the excess (which may well be traumatic excess to uppity Pentecostal theologians) that disturbs the harmonious image of Pentecostal theology that some fine theologians and philosophers have been putting out for the upper-class guardians of mainstream "guild" theology. Mine is the theology of the excess that prevents Pentecostal theology or, for that matter, Christian theology from becoming a harmonious *All*. This is the theology or philosophy of split.[9] Its goals are to understand Pentecostalism as an internal disturbance, a prime mover, and a challenger within Christianity, besides comprehending Pentecostalism as the structural excess of Christianity.

Pentecostalism is that form of Christianity where the interiority and exteriority of Christianity overlaps. The overlap cannot be completed— there is always a remainder, the indivisible remainder. All of this is to say

---

9. Žižek, *On Belief*, 96, 103–5, inspired this passage.

that Pentecostalism emerged from (and is still situated in) the *order of Being* of Christianity and it is also a cut, an interruption in the same *order of Being*. Thus, it is properly a gap, an immanent antagonism within Christianity, a split between Christianity and that which is excluded/occluded from Christianity itself. This gap did not preexist Pentecostalism but is in a way retroactively posited by Pentecostalism itself. All this, perhaps, means that all scholarship that tries to penetrate the depths of Pentecostalism (or Pentecostal theology) to uncover the substance of (pure) Christianity (or Christian theology) within it should be rejected. The finding that Pentecostalism has not attained the reality of Christianity (Christian theology) in itself or that it has not fully understood Christianity (Christian theology)—the trumpeting of its incompleteness—misses the point. The very sign of Pentecostal incompleteness—the epistemological incompleteness—is the sign that Pentecostalism has touched the heart, the *Real* of Christianity (Christian theology). The epistemological incompleteness is a reflection of the "ontological" incompleteness of Christianity (Christian theology). Christianity (Christian theology) itself is *non-all*, not wholly consistent.[10]

Parting Provocations

Are the decisions flowing out of it-makes-spirit significantly different in outcome from those made by free and autonomous agents who are not Pentecostals but who are committed to a value system or moral responsibility beyond rational calculations? To address this, let us resort to rational choice language to reframe the discussion about "It does not make sense but makes spirit." To make sense is to choose an action that maximizes one's utility, that is, after careful survey of cost and benefit, the agent opts for the course of action that adds benefit to the balance of the two. Rationality (making sense) here is about choosing the maximum net benefit that fits what the agent, the person prefers. To make spirit is to follow a course of action that deviates from this rule, and thus it is technically to make an irrational choice.

Is the "choice" for (of) the spirit really irrational? Has the person not made a choice that fits best her preference? In the end we may conclude that she is rational to the extent that we can impute positive value to benefits from her spirituality or when we assess the impact of spirituality on her overall wellbeing. The moment the Pentecostal believer moves her rational-choice interlocutor to concede this point, she loses in another way. She begins to search for a clear criterion to distinguish decisions deriving from it-makes-spirit from any other altruistic or any quantifiable emotional

10. Žižek, *Incontinence of the Void*, 18–19, 21, 26–27, inspired this passage.

benefit. What if a person's love for the spotted owl or bald eagle leads him to act in ways that at first blush we consider irrational, but on further reflection, we concede that, in fact, he may have acted rationally (as we did for the Pentecostal)? What if such a man claims that it makes environmental spirit for him to go beyond the demands of the rigors of the rational choice framework? What if a revolutionary (terrorist?), choosing a seemingly irrational course of action, claims that his action makes revolutionary spirit? The Pentecostal, the environmentalist, and the revolutionary are all able to explain their actions or choices according to their own purposes and ideas. So if what grounds it-makes-spirit is only the performative declaration of the decider and not some communally acceptable standard for exchange of publicly accessible reasons, then we cannot really distinguish between the claims of these three agents without *a priori* showing preference for one private reason or the other. Outside a close circle of certain believers, this is not enough for public policy. Indeed, it-makes-spirit as a social ethics is not ready for prime time. But it works in the private sphere of life. And I believe in it. Others may not believe in it but claim that it works for them. This reminds me of Slavoj Žižek's anecdote about Neils Bohr, the famous quantum physicist:

> Surprised at seeing a horse-shoe above the door of Bohr's country house, a fellow scientist exclaimed that he did not share the superstitious belief that horse-shoes kept evil spirits away, to which Bohr snapped back, "I don't believe in it either. I have it there because I was told that it works even when one doesn't believe in it." This is indeed how ideology functions today: nobody takes democracy or justice seriously, we are all aware of their corrupted nature, but we participate in them, we display our belief in them, because we assume that they work even if we do not believe in them.[11]

Is this what is happening with many Pentecostals? Do you think it-makes-spirit functions as an ideology? Not exactly—there are many folk, especially the type I met in the New York congregation, who sincerely believe in it-makes-spirit and it works for them. It was the need to decipher their common saying, made popular by their leader Pastor Elsie Obed, that set up the philosophical journey we have all embarked on in this book.

This route of the journey took a high road around both modernist and regnant Pentecostal theories of epistemology and Christology to illuminate a Pentecostal theory of decision.[12] This book is ultimately about practical

---

11. Žižek, *First as Tragedy*, 51.
12. The metaphor of the high road around academic disciplines or faddish

wisdom and the ways in which Pentecostal practical wisdom imagines, sees, or orders everyday decisions and the world. Before now there was no scholarly account of a Pentecostal theory of decision, no clear account of the decision process of everyday Pentecostals. This book has filled that gap, with its focus on excellence in deliberation at the point of tension between Reason and Spirit. It presents practical wisdom as an important constituent of the Pentecostal account of human good living. All this is not to deny that many scholars and non-Pentecostals consider Pentecostal practical wisdom as putting too huge a strain on deliberative rationality.[13]

---

philosophies comes from Neville, *The Highroad around Modernism*.

13. Nussbaum, *Fragility of Goodness*, 51–82, inspired this paragraph

Bibliography

Abram, David. *The Spell of the Sensuous: Perception and Language in a More-than-Human World*. New York: Pantheon, 1996.
Acolatse, Esther. *Powers, Principalities and the Spirit: Biblical Realism in Africa and the West*. Grand Rapids: Eerdmans, 2018.
Agamben, Giorgio. *The Coming Community*. Translated by Michael Hardt. Theory out of Bounds 1. Minneapolis: University of Minnesota, 1993.
———. *The Time That Remains: A Commentary on the Letter to the Romans*. Translated by Patricia Dailey. Stanford: Stanford University Press, 2005.
Alfaro, Sammy. *Divino Compañero: Toward a Hispanic Pentecostal Christology*. Eugene, OR: Pickwick, 2010.
An-Na'im, Abdullahi Ahmed. *Islam and the Secular State: Negotiating the Future of Shari'a*. Cambridge: Harvard University Press, 2008.
Arendt, Hannah. *Between Past and Future: Eight Exercises in Political Thought*. New York: Penguin, 1954.
———. *The Human Condition*. Chicago: University of Chicago Press, 1958.
———. *The Life of the Mind*. 2 vols. New York: Harcourt Brace Jovanovich, 1977–78.
———. "Martin Heidegger at Eighty." In *Heidegger and Modern Philosophy: Critical Essays*, edited by Michael Murray, 293–303. New Haven: Yale University Press, 1978.
———. *The Origins of Totalitarianism*. New York: Schocken, 2004.
Aristotle. *Nichomachean Ethics*. Translated by Robert C. Bartlett and Susan D. Collins. Chicago: University of Chicago Press, 2011.
Attridge, Derek. "Innovation, Literature, Ethics: Relating to the Other." *PMLA* 114 (1999) 20–32.
Badiou, Alain. *Saint Paul: The Foundation of Universalism*. Translated by Ray Brassier. Stanford: Stanford University Press, 2003.
———. *Theory of the Subject*. Translated by Bruno Bosteels. New York: Continuum, 2009.
Bakhtin, Mikhail. *The Dialogical Imagination: Four Essays*. Edited by Michael Holquist. Translated by Caryl Emerson and Michael Holquist. Austin: University of Texas Press, 1981.
———. *Problems of Dostoevsky's Poetics*. Edited and translated by Caryl Emerson. Minneapolis: University of Minnesota Press, 1984.
———. *Rabelais and His World*. Translated by Helene Iswolsky. Bloomington: Indiana University Press, 1984.

———. *Speech Genres and Other Late Essays*. Edited by Caryl Emerson and Michael Holquist. Translated by Vern W. McGee. Austin: University of Texas Press, 1986.

Bantum, Brian. *Redeeming Mulatto: A Theology of Race and Christian Hybridity*. Waco: Baylor University Press, 2010.

Barth, Karl. *Church Dogmatics. 1/1: The Doctrine of the Word of God*. Translated by G. W. Bromiley. Edinburgh: T&T Clark, 1975.

Birmingham, Peg. *Hannah Arendt and Human Rights: The Predicament of Common Responsibility*. Bloomington: Indiana University Press, 2006.

Boyarin, Daniel. *Intertextuality and the Reading of Midrash*. Bloomington: Indiana University Press, 1994.

Brown, Wendy. "American Nightmare: Neoliberalism, Neoconservatism, and De-democratization." *Political Theory* 34 (2006) 690–714.

Butler, Judith. *Giving an Account of Ourselves*. New York: Fordham University Press, 2005.

Caputo, John D. "How to Avoid Speaking of God: The Violence of Natural Theology." In *Prospects for Natural Theology*, edited by Eugene Thomas Long, 128–50. Washington, DC: Catholic University of America Press, 1992.

———. "Is Continental Philosophy of Religion Dead?" In *The Future of Continental Philosophy of Religion*, edited by Clayton Crockett, B. Keith Putt, and Jeffrey W. Robbins, 21–33. Bloomington: Indiana University Press, 2014.

———. *The Weakness of God: A Theology of the Event*. Bloomington: Indiana University Press, 2006.

Caruth, Cathy. *Unclaimed Experience: Trauma, Narrative, and History*. 20th anniv. ed. Baltimore: Johns Hopkins University Press, 2016.

Castelo, Daniel. *Pentecostalism as a Christian Mystical Tradition*. Grand Rapids: Eerdmans, 2017.

Certeau, Michel de. *The Mystic Fable, Vol. 1: The Sixteen and Seventeenth Centuries*. Translated by Michael B. Smith. Chicago: University of Chicago Press, 1992.

———. *The Mystic Fable, Vol. 2: The Sixteen and Seventeenth Centuries*. Text established and presented by Luce Giard. Translated by Michael B. Smith. Chicago: University of Chicago Press, 2015.

Chesterton, G. K. "A Defence of Detective Stories." In *The Art of the Mystery Story*, edited by H. Haycraft, 3–6. New York: Universal Library, 1946.

———. *Orthodoxy*. 1908. Reprint, New York: Snowball Classics, 2015.

Clark, J. P. "Ibadan." In *A Collection of Poems, 1958–1988: J.P. Clark-Bekederemo*. Washington, DC: Howard University Press, 1991.

Clark, Katerina, and Michael Holquist. *Mikhail Bakhtin*. Cambridge: Belknap Press of Harvard University Press, 1984.

Contino, Paul J., and Susan M. Felch. "Introduction: A Feeling for Faith." In *Bakhtin and Religion: A Feeling for Faith*, edited by Susan M. Felch and Paul J. Contino, 1–24. Evanston: Northwestern University Press, 2001.

Cone, James H. *The Spirituals and the Blues: An Interpretation*. Maryknoll, NY: Orbis, 1992.

Crane, Tim. *The Meaning of Belief: Religion from an Atheist's Point of View*. Cambridge: Harvard University Press, 2017.

Crawley, Ashon. "Black. Queer. Born Again." *Aeon*, July 2, 2018. https://aeon.co/essays/black-queer-born-again-a-life-in-and-out-of-the-church.

Crockett, Clayton, B. Keith Putt, and Jeffrey W. Robbins, eds. *The Future of Continental Philosophy of Religion*. Bloomington: Indiana University Press, 2014.
Crosby, Donald A. *The Extraordinary in the Ordinary: Seven Types of Everyday Miracle*. Albany: SUNY Press, 2017.
Depoortere, Frederiek. *Christ in Postmodern Philosophy: Gianni Vattimo, René Girard and Slavoj Žižek*. New York: T&T Clark, 2008.
Dolar, Mladen. *A Voice and Nothing More*. Cambridge: MIT Press, 2006.
Drucker, Peter. "The Theory of the Business." *Harvard Business Review*, September-October 1994, 95–104.
Eisenstein, Paul, and Todd McGowan. *Rupture: On the Emergence of the Political*. Evanston: Northwestern University Press, 2012.
Farneth, Molly. "Hegel's Sacramental Politics: Confession, Forgiveness and Absolute Spirit." *The Journal of Religion* 95 (2015) 183–97.
———. *Hegel's Social Ethics: Religion, Conflict, and Rituals of Reconciliation*. Princeton: Princeton University Press, 2017.
Fenn, Richard K. *Liturgies and Trials: The Secularization of Religious Language*. Oxford: Blackwell, 1982.
Feyerabend, Paul. *Against Method*. 4th ed. New York: Verso, 2010.
Girard, Rene. *The Scapegoat*. Baltimore: John Hopkins University Press, 1989.
———. *Violence and the Sacred*. Baltimore: John Hopkins University Press, 1977.
Grant, Ruth W. *Strings Attached: Untangling the Ethics of Incentives*. Princeton: Princeton University Press, 2012.
Gribetz, Sarit Kattan. "Jewish Response to the Spring 2017 McGinley Lecture." Response to "Judging Justly: Judgment in Jewish, Christian and Muslim Traditions," delivered by Patrick J. Ryan, March 28–29, 2017, Fordham University, New York.
Habermas, Jürgen. "Learning from Catastrophe? A Look Back at the Short Twentieth Century." In *The Postnational Constellation: Politcal Essays*, translated and edited by Max Pensky, 38–57. Cambridge: MIT Press, 2001.
Harris-Perry, Melissa V. *Sister Citizen: Shame, Stereotypes, and Black Women in America*. New Haven: Yale University Press, 2011.
Hauerwas, Stanley. *A Community of Character: Toward a Constructive Christian Social Ethics*. Notre Dame: University of Notre Dame Press, 1981.
Hector, Kevin. *Theology without Metaphysics: God, Language, and the Spirit of Recognition*. Cambridge: Cambridge University Press, 2011.
Hegel, Georg Wilhelm Friedrich. *Phenomenology of Spirit*. Translated by A. V. Miller. Oxford: Oxford University Press, 1977.
Heidegger, Martin. "Time and Being." In *On Time and Being*, translated by Joan Stambaugh, 1–24. New York: Harper & Row, 1972.
———. *What Is a Thing?* Translated by W. B. Barton Jr. and Vera Deutsch. Chicago: Regnery, 1968.
Horton, Robin. *Patterns of Thought in Africa and the West: Essays on Magic, Religion, and Science*. New York: Cambridge University Press, 1993.
Jacobsen, Douglas. *Thinking in the Spirit: Theologies of the Early Pentecostal Movement*. Bloomington: Indiana University Press, 2003.
Jameson, Fredric. Foreword to *Critique of Dialectical Reason, Vol. II (Unfinished)*, by Jean-Paul Sartre, ix–xxiii. Edited by Arlette Elkaïm-Sartre. Translated by Quintin Hoare. London: Verso, 2006.

Janz, Paul D. *God, the Mind's Desire: Reference, Reason and Christian Thinking.* Cambridge: Cambridge University Press, 2004.

Kärkkäinen, Veli-Matti. *Christology: A Global Introduction.* Grand Rapids: Baker Academic, 2016.

Kaufman, Eleanor. "The Saturday of Messianic Time: Agamben and Badiou on the Apostle Paul." In *Paul and the Philosophers*, edited by Ward Blanton and Hent de Vries, 297–309. New York: Fordham University Press, 2013.

Kearney, Richard. *The God Who May Be: A Hermeneutics of Religion.* Bloomington: Indiana University Press, 2001.

Keller, Catherine, Michael Nausner, and Mayra Rivera. *Postcolonial Theologies: Divinity and Empire.* St. Louis: Chalice, 2004.

Kierkegaard, Søren. *Concluding Unscientific Postscript.* Translated by Howard V. Hong and Edna H. Hong. Princeton: Princeton University Press, 1992.

———. *Either/Or.* Edited and translated by Howard V. Hong and Edna H. Hong. 2 vols. Princeton: Princeton University Press, 1990.

———. *Stages on Life's Way.* Translated by Howard V. Hong and Edna H. Hong. Princeton: Princeton University Press, 1988.

———. *Works of Love.* Edited and translated by Howard V. Hong and Edna H. Hong. New York: HarperCollins, 2009.

Kiess, John. *Hannah Arendt and Theology.* London: Bloomsbury T&T Clark, 2016.

Levinas, Emmanuel. *Totality and Infinity: An Essay on Exteriority.* Translated by Alphonso Lingus. Pittsburgh: Duquesne University Press, 1969.

Lock, Charles. "Bakhtin and the Tropes of Orthodoxy." In *Bakhtin and Religion*, edited by Paul J. Contino and Susan M. Felch, 97–119. Evanston: Northwestern University Press, 2001.

Lodahl, Michael E. *Shekinah Spirit: Divine Presence in Jewish and Christian Religion.* New York: Paulist, 1992.

Loder, James E. *The Logic of the Spirit: Human Development in Theological Perspective.* San Francisco: Jossey-Bass, 1998.

———. *The Transforming Moment.* 2nd ed. Colorado Springs: Helmers & Howard, 1989.

Lipton, Bruce H. *The Biology of Belief: Unleashing the Power of Consciousness, Matter and Miracles.* Carlsbad, CA: Hay House, 2015.

Luhrmann, T. M. *When God Talks Back: Understanding the American Evangelical Relationship with God.* New York: Knopf, 2012.

MacGaffey, Wyatt. "Dagbon, Oyo, Kongo: Critical and Comparative Reflections on Sacrifice." In *Ifá Divination, Knowledge, Power, and Performance*, edited by Jacob K. Olupona and Rowland O. Abiodun, 141–57. Bloomington: Indiana University Press, 2016.

Macherey, Pierre. *Hegel or Spinoza.* Translated by Susan M. Ruddick. Minneapolis: University of Minnesota Press, 2011.

MacIntyre, Alasdair. *After Virtue: A Study in Moral Theology.* 2nd ed. Notre Dame: University of Notre Dame Press, 1984.

———. *Ethics in the Conflicts of Modernity: An Essay on Desire, Practical Reasoning, and Narrative.* Cambridge: Cambridge University Press, 2016.

McGowan, Todd. *Capitalism and Desire: The Psychic Cost of Free Markets.* New York: Columbia University Press, 2016.

McGrayne, Sharon Bertsch. *The Theory That Would Not Die*. New Haven: Yale University Press, 2011.
Meditz, Robert E. *The Dialectic of the Holy: Paul Tillich's Idea of Judaism within the History of Religion*. Berlin: de Gruyter, 2016.
Mihailovic, Alexandar. *Corporeal Words: Mikhail Bakhtin's Theology of Discourse*. Evanston: Northwestern University Press, 1997.
Milbank, John. "Paul against Biopolitics." In *Paul's New Moment: Continental Philosophy and the Future of Christian Theology*, edited by Slavoj Žižek and Creston Davis, 21–73. Grand Rapids: Brazos, 2010.
———. *Theology and Social Theory: Beyond Secular Reason*. Malden, MA: Blackwell, 1990.
Moltmann, Jürgen. *The Trinity and the Kingdom: The Doctrine of God*. Translated by Margaret Kohl. Minneapolis: Fortress, 1993.
Nancy, Jean-Luc. *Dis-Enclosure: The Deconstruction of Christianity*. Translated by Bettina Bergo, Gabriel Malenfant, and Michael B. Smith. New York: Fordham University Press, 2008.
———. *The Inoperative Community*. Translated by Peter Connor et al. Minneapolis: University of Minnesota Press, 1991.
———. *The Sense of the World*. Translated and with a foreword by Jeffrey S. Librett. Minneapolis: University of Minnesota Press, 1997.
Niebuhr, H. Richard. *The Meaning of Revelation*. New York: Macmillan, 1941.
Neville, Robert C. *Defining Religion: Essays in Philosophy of Religion*. Albany: SUNY Press, 2015.
———. *Eternity and Time's Flow*. Albany: SUNY Press, 1993.
———. *The God Who Beckons: Theology in the Form of Sermons*. Nashville: Abingdon, 1999.
———. *The Highroad around Modernism*. Albany: SUNY Press, 1992.
———. *The Truth of Broken Symbols*. Albany: SUNY Press, 1996.
———. *Ultimates*. Philosophical Theology 1. Albany: SUNY Press, 1994.
Norton, Anne. "Pentecost: Democratic Sovereignty in Carl Schmitt." *Constellations* 18 (2011) 389–402.
Nussbaum, Martha C. *Creating Capabilities: The Human Development Approach*. Cambridge: Belknap Press of Harvard University Press, 2011.
———. *The Fragility of Goodness: Luck and Ethics in Greek Tragedy and Philosophy*. Cambridge: Cambridge University Press, 1986.
———. *Poetic Justice: The Literary Imagination and Public Life*. Boston: Beacon, 1995.
———. *Upheavals of Thought: The Intelligence of Emotions*. Cambridge: Cambridge University Press, 2001.
Obadare, Ebenezer. *Pentecostal Republic: Religion and the Struggle for State Power in Nigeria*. London: Zed, 2018.
Oliverio, Bill. *Theological Hermeneutics in the Classical Pentecostal Tradition: A Typological Account*. Netherlands: Brill, 2012.
Pinkard, Terry. "What Is a 'Shape of Spirit'?" In *Hegel's Phenomenology of Spirit: A Critical Guide*, edited by Dean Moyar and Michael Quante, 112–29. Cambridge: Cambridge University Press, 2008.
Poole, Randall A. "The Apophatic Bakhtin." In *Bakhtin and Religion: A Feeling for Faith*, edited by Susan M. Felch and Paul J. Contino, 151–75. Evanston: Northwestern University Press, 2001.

Pui-lan, Kwok. *Postcolonial Imagination and Feminist Theology*. 1st ed. Louisville: Westminster John Knox, 2005.

Rae, Murray. *Kierkegaard and Theology*. London: T&T Clark, 2010.

Rambo, Shelly. *Resurrecting Wounds: Living in the Afterlife of Trauma*. Waco: Baylor University Press, 2017.

Reinhard, Kenneth. "Paul and the Political Theology of the Neighbor." In *Paul and the Philosophers*, edited by Ward Blanton and Hent de Vries, 449–65. New York: Fordham University Press, 2013.

Richter, Gerhard. "Critique and the Thing: Benjamin and Heidegger." In *Sparks Will Fly: Benjamin and Heidegger*, edited by Andrew Benjamin and Dimitris Vardoulaskis, 27–63. Albany: SUNY Press, 2015.

Sacks, Jonathan. *To Heal a Fractured World: The Ethics of Responsibility*. New York: Schocken, 2005.

Santos, Boaventura de Sousa. *Epistemologies of the South: Justice against Epistemicide*. London: Routledge, 2014.

Sartre, Jean-Paul. *Being and Nothingness*. Translated and introduced by Hazel E. Barnes. New York: Washington Square, 1956.

Schiller, Friedrich. *On the Aesthetic Education of Man and Letters to Prince Frederick Christian von Augustenburg*. Translated by Keith Tribe. New York: Penguin, 2016.

Shotter, John. *Conversational Realities Revisited: Life, Language, Body and World*. Chagrin Falls, OH: Taos Institute, 2008.

———. *Getting It: Withness-Thinking and the Dialogical in Practice*. New York: Hampton, 2011.

———. *Speaking, Actually: Towards a New "Fluid" Common-Sense Understanding of Relational Becomings*. Farnhill, UK: Everything Is Connected, 2016.

Smith, James K. A. *Thinking in Tongues: Pentecostal Contributions to Christian Philosophy*. Grand Rapids: Eerdmans, 2010.

Spivak, Gayatri Chakravorty. *A Critique of Postcolonial Reason: Toward a History of the Vanishing Present*. Cambridge: Harvard University Press, 1999.

Suurmond, Jean-Jacques. *Word and Spirit at Play: Towards a Charismatic Theology*. Translated by John Bowden. Grand Rapids: Eerdmans, 1994.

Steinby, Liisa. "Concepts of Novelistic Polyphony: Person-Related and Compositional-Thematic." In *Bakhtin and His Others: (Inter)subjectivity, Chronotype, Dialogism*, edited by Liisa Steinby and Tintti Klapuri, 37–54. London: Anthem, 2014.

Stiltner, Brian. *Toward Thriving Communities: Virtue Ethics as Social Ethics*. Terrace Heights, MN: Anselm Academic, 2016.

Stout, Jeffrey. *Democracy and Tradition*. Princeton: Princeton University Press, 2004.

Suna-Koro, Kristine. *In Counterpoint: Diaspora, Postcoloniality, and Sacramental Theology*. Eugene, OR: Pickwick, 2017.

Taylor, Charles. *Dilemmas and Connections*. Cambridge: Harvard University Press, 2002.

———. *The Language Animal: The Full Shape of the Human Linguistic Capacity*. Cambridge: Harvard University Press, 2016.

———. *A Secular Age*. Cambridge: Belknap Press of Harvard University Press, 2007.

———. *Sources of the Self: The Making of the Modern Identity*. Cambridge: Harvard University Press, 2002.

Tillich, Paul. *Christianity and the Encounter with World Religions*. Chicago: University of Chicago Press, 1963.

———. *Dynamics of Faith*. New York: Harper, 1958.
———. *The Socialist Decision*. Translated by Franklin Sherman. New York: Harper & Row, 1977.
———. *Systematic Theology*. Vol. 3, *Life and the Spirit; History and the Kingdom of God*. Chicago: University of Chicago Press, 1963.
Wariboko, Nimi. *The Charismatic City and the Public Resurgence of Religion: A Pentecostal Social Ethics of Cosmopolitan Urban Life*. New York: Palgrave Macmillan, 2014.
———. *Economics in Spirit and Truth: A Moral Philosophy of Finance*. London: Palgrave Macmillan, 2014.
———. *Ethics and Time: Ethos of Temporal Orientation in Politics and Religion of the Niger Delta*. Lanham, MD: Lexington, 2010.
———. *Nigerian Pentecostalism*. Rochester: University of Rochester Press, 2014.
———. *Patterns of Institutions in the Niger Delta: Economic and Ethological Interpretations of History and Culture*. Port Harcourt, Nigeria: Onyoma Research, 2007.
———. *The Pentecostal Principle: Ethical Methodology in New Spirit*. Grand Rapids: Eerdmans, 2012.
———. *The Split God: Pentecostalism and Critical Theory*. Albany: SUNY Press, 2018.
West, Cornel. *The Cornel West Reader*. New York: Basic Civitas, 1999.
Weston, Michael. *Kierkegaard and Modern Continental Philosophy: An Introduction*. London: Routledge, 1994.
Whitehead, Alfred North. *Science and the Modern World*. New York: Free Press, 1967.
Williams, Rowan. *Dostoevsky: Language, Faith, and Fiction*. Waco: Baylor University Press, 2008.
Wittgenstein, Ludwig. *Lectures and Conversations on Aesthetics, Psychology and Religious Belief*. Edited by C. Barrett. Oxford, Blackwell, 1966.
Yong, Amos. *Spirit, Word, Community: Theological Hermeneutics in Trinitarian Perspectives*. 2002. Reprint, Eugene, OR: Wipf and Stock, 2006.
Žižek, Slavoj. *Event: A Philosophical Journey through a Concept*. London: Penguin, 2014.
———. *First as Tragedy, Then as Farce*. New York: Verso, 2009.
———. *Incontinence of the Void: Economico-Philosophical Spandrels*. Cambridge: MIT Press, 2017.
———. *The Indivisible Remainder: On Schelling and Related Matters*. London: Verso, 1996.
———. *Less Than Nothing: Hegel and the Shadow of Dialectical Materialism*. London: Verso, 2012.
———. *On Belief*. London: Routledge, 2001.
———. "Paul and the Truth Event." In *Paul's New Moment: Continental Philosophy and the Future of Christian Theology*, edited by John Milbank, Slavoj Žižek, and Creston Davis, 74–99. Grand Rapids: Brazos, 2010.
———. *The Puppet and the Dwarf: The Perverse Core of Christianity*. Cambridge: MIT Press, 2003.
Žižek, Slavoj, and F. W. J. Schelling. *Abyss of Freedom; Ages of the World (Second Draft, 1813)*. Translated by Judith Norman. Ann Arbor: University of Michigan Press, 1997.
Zizioulas, John. *Being as Communion: Studies in Personhood and the Church*. Translated by John Meyendorff. Crestwood, NY: St. Vladimir's Seminary Press, 1997.
Zupančič, Alenka. *The Odd One In: On Comedy*. Cambridge: MIT Press, 2008.
———. *What Is Sex?* Cambridge: MIT Press, 2017.

Index

Abraham
　deciding to sacrifice his son, 49
　"forced" into the space where nothing made sense, 53, 57
　obedience of, 50
　story of, 47–48
absences, 112, 113
absolute spirit, 10, 10n23, 116–17, 120
abstract divine knowledge, 73
abstract reason (Enlightenment matter), 119
"abstractness," of it-makes-spirit, 153
abyss, 69, 69n15, 70
Acolatse, Esther, 19
actions, 112, 161
activities, basic to a study of Pentecostalism, 150
aesthetics, 14, 124, 125
affiliations, important for a person's wellbeing, 126
African Pentecostalism(s), 44, 45
Against Method (Feyerabend), xvii
Agamben, Giorgio, 78, 93
Alfaro, Sammy, 106
alibi, absence of, 125
alternate (unorthodox, incipient) Christology, 158
alternate epistemology, 158
ambiguity, versions of, xvi
answer-word, anticipation of Christ's, 150
appearance, giving the illusion of an ideal form, 147
"appearings," 156

Arendt, Hannah
　on absences, 112
　on freedom, 70
　on the gap, 112
　linking Kafka's parable to Nietzsche and Heidegger, 110–11
　putting "thinking ego" and actor into the gap, 113
　on (real) time occurring, 111
　on stepping into the continuum of time, 109
　on the time gap as constituted time, 110
　on "the tyranny of logicality," 135
argumentation, contrasting Pentecostal knowing with straightforward academic, 33
arguments, style of presentation of, 20–24
Aristotle, 125–26
as not (*hos me*), standpoint of the Pauline, 93
as-if-not stance, of Paul, 82
assumptions, defining what a community considers meaningful, 1–2
a-theos, reason seen as, 143
Attridge, Derek, 61–62
Augustine, 109
"authenticating," it-makes-spirit, 123n22

Babel, circumventing the logic of, xv
bad, meanings of, xiii
Badiou, Alain, xvi, 147

Bakhtin, Mikhail
  on dialogism in Dostoevsky's novels, 21, 22
  on interaction with nonpresent interlocutors, 148
  on the unity of ethics and aesthetics, 125
Bantum, Brian, 73, 99, 100
baptism into Christ Jesus, as baptism into his split, 85
Bayes' rule, inverse of, 137
being and rupture, coexisting in the same person, 11
being-in-their-epistemology, 43n25
belief
  for Abraham, 51
  in Christ undergirding you, 60
  with content, accepting Christ with, 53
  enabling a person to prepare, 59
  structuring relating to reality, 95
  taking a leap into what does not make sense, 49
"believe to pretend," 71
believer(s). *See also* Pentecostal believer
  dealing with God and the other, 152
  encountering multiple different realities, 66
  enduring perpetual movement toward the object of desire, 146
  as herself a gap, 67
  mass of, known as the body of Christ, 149
  seeking infinite wisdom to rest finite "wisdoms," 128
Benjamin, Walter, 78
Bentham, Jeremy, 71
biblical realism, social practice of, 19
biblical worldview, it-makes-spirit drawing meaning from, 19
binding, of higher to lower, 99
Birmingham, Peg, 112
black women in America, living in a crooked room, 102–3
Bloch, Ernst, 78

bodies, perichoretic dance of Christ's three, 149
bodies of his followers, Christ talking through, 148
bodily engaged Christ, 149, 150
Bohr, Neils, 161
books, as points of view on the world, 20
born-again believers, navigating the crack between spirit and sense, 65
born-again subjectivity, xiv
bread, dual nature of, 101
Butler, Judith, 30, 30n13

Capitalism and Desire (McGowan), 145
Caputo, John, 39
categories, special embodiment of, 92
cause and effect, world operating by, 51
certainty, of statements, 131
chains of reason and reasoning, as networks, 139–40
Chalcedonian Christology, hybridity and, 42
Chalcedonian Creed, doctrinal language of, 35
chapters, outline of, 16–20
character formation, it-makes-spirit as an instrument for, 138
Chesterton, G. K., 81–82, 83, 144
choices, explaining, 161
Christ. *See also* Jesus Christ
  accepting in pure belief, without content, 53
  connecting sense and spirit, 16
  in a crack between sense and spirit, 90
  dealt with at the ontic level, 85
  enabling his followers, xvii–xviii
  encountering as an event of knowledge, 46–62
  as the focus of "It does not make sense, but it makes spirit," 32
  as a frame for understanding epistemology, 86

as the gap separating and connecting sense and spirit, 11
informing Pentecostal epistemology, 32
internalizing the normative spirit of, 117
as the living embodied split between reality and the Real, 94
meeting in that space where there is no sense or immediate meaning, 52
as the missing element in the world, 52
not making sense to our contemporary world, 56
as the order of being and the contingency of rupture, 11
representing the dissolution of all holding human beings captive, 93
representing the split between reality and its inner depth, 93
as the sense of the spirit and spirit of the sense, 5
in that space where everything does not make sense, 53–54
two-natures-being of, 13
undergirding knowledge (decision), 42
Christ speaks, through the bodies of his believers, 148
Christ talks, meaning of, 148
Christian discourse. *See* religious discourse
Christian theologians, turning to philosophy for language, 35
Christianity, 89, 160
Christ-ness of Jesus, discerning, 107–8
Christ-obliged epistemology, 16–17
christological dialectic, activating, 8
Christologies, 103, 104
Christology
 as an attitude toward reality, 95
 as the belief in Christ, 95
 carrying into epistemology, 14
 connection between epistemology and, 13, 17
 as a decision-making matrix or epistemological paradigm, 156–57
 entering the sense/spirit that Christ himself is, 6
 epistemological and existential consequences, 35
 epistemology and, 97, 98–108
 as experienced in everyday spirituality, 86
 framed as an epistemological concern, 5
 making potentialities understandable, 24
 meshing with social reality, 32n17
 as a movement between the world as it is and the wished-for world, 93
 moving the power of from paper, ink, and bytes, 96
 Pentecostal epistemology located within, xi
 of Pentecostalism, 88
Christopraxis, of Christopathy, 31
church leaders, cannot abide with or in an empty space, 53
churches, claiming that they have Christ, 53
"civic" reason. *See* public reason
"civic reason," for Muslims, 26n5–27n5
cognition, of a subject, 150n120
cognitive injustice, social theories on, 68
color frequency, of each human being's identity, 108
The Coming Community (Agamben), 78
commitment to Christ, providing good perception, 14
the common, ix, x
common sense, 27, 93
communal relationships, driving quests for it-makes-spirit, 126
communal standards, for justifying a believer's claim to "hearing from God," 124
communism, as a utopia, 136

Index

community
  assumable truth of, 1
  it-makes-spirit addressing, 116
  scapegoating someone to bring peace, 106
  standards for justification, 124
  transforming [their] collection of norms and norm-generating practices, 119
conceptual Christ, translating into decision criterion, 63
conceptual proximity, of Pentecostal ideas (practices), 37
configuration of dispute, conceiving reality as a, 94
conformity to Christ, 118
conservative theology, presenting Christology as Truth, 89
"constitutive good," epistemology as, 75
"contact" with God, frequency of, 137
contemporary society, it-makes-spirit entangled in, 116
contents
  reaching out to Christ through other people's, 53
  of this world, 52
"context of mutual relevance," 18n42
continental philosophy, 30, 31–41. See also philosophy
continental thought, Pentecostal theology and, 25–45
contradictions, positing of, 8
co-promising option or position, 38
cracks, God in the midst of, 61
creative nothingness, 65
creativity, 76
"critique," as Martin Heidegger used it, 29–30
crooked room, living in, 102–3
Crosby, Donald A., 134–35
crucifixion of the flesh, 146
cultural materials, incorporated by innovative artists or scientists, 62
cut, interrupting human knowledge systems, 88

data (facts), manipulating, 120

Davis, Miles, xviii
death and life, making sense, 55
death of knowledge ("epistemicide"), 68
decision(s)
  affirming without fear of being contradicted by Enlightenment rationalism, 44
  arising from it-makes-spirit as effectuation, 122
  conforming to "spirit" and not merely to sense, 2
  in the form of Christ, 43
  making in correlation to faith, 130
  making under extreme uncertainty, 138
  transforming (sense) data into noumenal data (spiritual insights), 18
decision-act, 118
decision-maker, 66, 67
decision-making
  of conservative Christians, 25
  forming three modes in, xixn21
  formula for, ix
  grasping for "moral identity" of sense, xixn21
  model shaped by Christ's two-natures-being, 13
  Pentecostal hypothesis about, 1
  searching for a first and indubitable principle of, 3n6
  ultimate goal of Pentecostal, xvi
deed, 124, 125
deep structure, as a collectivity, 157
deliberative rationality, 162
democratic process, of Pentecostal citizens, 18
dense sense, reflexive appearance of, 134
dependence on Christ, primal awareness of total, 107
dependency, on the fruitfulness of the abyss, 69n15
depth of reality, described, 93–94
descendants of Abraham, multiplying, 48

Index | 175

destiny, it-makes-spirit discovering and disclosing unique, 135
detective in a police romance, as the agent of social justice, 83
determinates, always coming into being, 156
dialectic interdependence, between reason (sense) and its transgression, 83
dialogical act, decision-act as always, 118
dialogical imagination, in Pentecostal thought, 115–54
dialogue, 21
dichotomies, of the Sermon on the Mount, 99
direct belief in reason, tension versus belief in reason-through-distance, 81
discernment, as a process of give and take, 5
distorted logic, exposing, 103
divine, asserting itself without giving meaning, 51–52
"divine miracle," it-makes-spirit as a synonym for, 143
divine presence, 91
divine reality, not understood in rational terms, 9
divine speeches (words), guiding everyday decisions made in response to, 4
divine wisdom, 72
divine word, becoming clothed in flesh, 124
division, of it-makes-spirit from itself, 145
Dolar, Mladen, 15
dominant hypothesis, of every religion, 155
Dostoevsky, Fyodor, 21, 22
doubleness, 93
Du Bois, W. E. B., xii
duck-rabbit drawing, 158
duo-logical Christ, 92

economic ethics, trilogy relating to, 85n51

effects, as causeless, 143
Einstein, Albert, on Niels Bohr, 150–51
Elijah, hearing "a still small voice," 134
"embedded truth," 8
empirical facts, subject's desire distorting the field of, 146
emptied-out reason, 143
empty space, 52, 56
enchantic fury, of theology unbound, 38
enframing, Christology as a mode of, 95
Enlightenment rationality, 23, 69, 82
environmental information, modifying the "readout" of rationality-encoding logic, 80
epigenetics, meaning "control over the genetics," 80
epilogic mechanism, of the dynamic belief system, 80
episteme-Christology, 103, 104, 105
epistemic density, of a situation, 149
epistemic identity, of Pentecostal believers in Jesus, 45
epistemicide, causing, 68
the epistemological, defined, x
epistemological imaginations, of Pentecostals, 105
epistemological incompleteness, 160
Epistemologies of the South (Santos), 68
epistemology. *See also* Pentecostal epistemology
  being one with, 43
  bending back on Christ, 67
  "christological" view of in everyday Pentecostalism, 95–96
  Christology and, 98–108
  as decision-making or interpretation of reality, 14
  defined, xiv
  described, 5
  everyday, 17
  as existence, 143
  as the form of Christology, 97
  interpreting christologically, 74

epistemology *(continued)*
  intersecting with everyday Pentecostals' belief, 28
  of Pentecostals, x
  to Pentecostals as the voice of Christ, 12
  philosophical literature on not exhaustively engaged, 20
  as "the power of a historical reality, grasped in" christological frames, 24
  as a predicate within a particular community of Christ, 98
  as a strategy of managing risks pertaining to reality, 127
  taking place in decision, 30
  writing as the Christological turn, 88–114
ethical ideal, 73
ethical life, 124
ethicality, of epistemology, 75
ethics, 30n13, 124, 152
event
  of knowledge, 46–62
  as an open-ended promise, 139
  seeming to appear from nowhere, xvi
  as tragic, 128
evental site, jumping into, 57
events, dissolving circumstances, xvii
everyday epistemology, 17
everyday folk, on Christology lived by people on the ground, 89
everyday Pentecostal practices, 156
ex-, signifying what is outside, 79
excellence, Jesus Christ as a model of, 12
excess, 83, 104–5, 159
expanded sense, surplus over sense becoming, 153–54
ex-position, relation of, 78–79

faith
  of Abraham, 50–51
  being the substance of things hoped for, 60
  described, 65
  making into a space, 96
  modern Western rationality defining, 142
  as a personal act of commitment, 5
  "personhood" of, 96
  as a response to grace, 94
  "in-spite-of element" of, 130
  as a subjective disposition, 65
  as trust in Jesus Christ, 109
faith tradition, interacting with everyday human activities, 2
Farneth, Molly, 117, 119
fear of God, as the beginning of wisdom, 17
feeling (sense), for philosophy toward a higher and ultimate value, 9
fetish and symptom, functioning together, 132
fetishism, 131
Feyerabend, Paul, xvii
field of vision, becoming present in, 146
finite being, moving closer to the infinite, 146
flesh, subjecting to the Spirit, 13
folk theology, of Christ, 90
foolishness of God, as wiser than human wisdom, 50, 65
force of action, transforming existence, 113
form-structuring power, of the Pentecostal hypothesis, 157
foundation, the space having no, 58
"foundational certainty," about information received from the supernatural realm, 25
frame, characterized by incompleteness, 9
framework
  of knowing, 99
  to reimagine the possibilities of sense data and rational decision-making theory, 151
"free activity," 27
freedom, 70
functions, understanding things or people by, 47
future
  concealing itself, 111

humans creating, 109
  as a potentiality, 111n62
  promise of a better, 145

gain in utility, 71
gap(s)
  becoming the foundation for miracles, 134
  believer as herself a, 67
  Christ appearing to spring out of, 61
  Christ as the original, 85
  as an effect of presumed duality, 70
  hope as the disposition or existential attitude toward, 94
  inner voice interpretation of, 135
  in knowledge, reality, and God, 134
  naming the place of be-ing, 113
  between the original and the translated meaning, 72
  presence of humans in as the (real) time, 111
  presence of the decision-maker in, 67
  producing a rupture extending into, 110
  producing in a moment of deflection, 112
  in reality, 62
  between sense and reason, 84
  between sense and spirit, xviii, 5, 11, 92, 150, 155n1
  of time, 67, 109
  transposing Christ into, 114
genes and epigenetics (environmental signals), analogy to, 79–81
Girard, René, 106
Global Pentecostalism, 44, 45
goal, of Pentecostal decision-making, xvi
God
  calling things which do not exist as though they did, 60
  defined as incapable of direct observation, 148
  "economic nature" of the Christian Trinitarian, 85
  encountering where it doesn't make sense, 54
  knowledge as metaphysics of the presence of, xiv
  as life has conquered nonbeing, vanquished death, 144
  meeting in the in-between, 54
  promises of, xv
  reaching the believer's mind, 122
  as Spirit, 128, 129
  telling Abraham to sacrifice his son, 48
  in that nothing that is between the something of the world, 58
  as the ultimate sovereign ruler of political systems, 12
God the Father, 85, 86, 133
gods and spirits, invisibility of or the direct inaudibility of, 148
good, meanings of, xiii
grace
  available to all human beings everywhere, 95
  interrupting the chain of cause and effect, 66
  perishable quality of as amissible, 66
  referring to the quality of an event or encounter with reality, 94
grasping by faith, 133
a growing sense, bulging with surplus insight, 154

habits, of Pentecostal epistemology, 12
habitude, Christology as, 97
Hagar, 60–61
Harris-Perry, Melissa, 102–3
the "He," parable of, 110
"hearing ear," developing, 3
heavenly Christ, 149
Hegel, 71
Hegelian absolute spirit, 10, 120
Heidegger, Martin, 29–30, 110–12
here and the there, Jesus as somewhere between, 54
hermeneutic-ized Jesus, deciphering, 90
"hidden dialogicality," 148–49

historical Jesus the Christ, 92
historical practices, of Pentecostals with regard to God's Spirit, 91
historical-critical method, of biblical interpretation, xii
holistic theology, theorizing on the excess, 159
Holy Spirit. *See also* the Spirit; Spirit of Christ; Spirit of God
   always full of gigantic joy, 144
   as a common blessing to all, 22
   in the context of a search for a methodology for social ethics, 86
   Jesus giving to the disciples, 102
   not locating the believer in a spirit-matrix of decision-making or knowing, 141
   not predictable, 137
   in Pentecostal theology, 105
   regarded as a symbol of God, xvi
   relating to any celebration of it-makes-spirit, 19
"holy" subjectivity, xiv
hope, 59, 60, 94
horse-shoe, above the door of Bohr's country house, 161
Horton, Robin, 93, 148
how of knowing, 31, 43, 44
"how" of relationality, 42
human beings
   in the battle between the past and future, 110
   becoming time, 111, 111n62
   between the infinite past and the infinite future, 109
   not liking a space where there is nothing, 52–53
human flourishing
   exploring possibilities for, 40
   holding reason or sense to the demands of, 140
   it-makes-spirit promoting, 126
   promise of, 144–45
   quest for, 156
human frailties, "repressing" the role of, 131
human life, suspended within the flow of Jesus's hyphen, 74
human limits, region transcending, 146
human promise, plagued by uncertainty, slipperiness, and ambiguity, xv
human sacrifices, God does not accept, 50
human sense, xv, xvi
human violent behavior, Jesus's death changing the kernel of, 106
human word, 123, 124
humanity, interacting with divinity, 1
humility, of it-makes-spirit, 130
hybrid epistemology, 100
hybrid space, inhabiting between flesh and spirit, 73
hybridity, of Jesus Christ, 31, 41–45
hyphenated Jesus-Christ, 74
"hypotenuse," in a right triangle, 32n17
hypotheses, about God's behavior, 138
hypothesis. *See also* Pentecostal hypothesis
   "as an actual or potential habit for thought and action," xix
   defined, 1
   engaging decision-making with deliberation, 4
   as a principle for thought and action, 2
   shaped by symbols and vulnerable to correction, 3
   as a theory about spirituality and dynamic things, 2
hypothetical inquiry, 3n6

the ideal form, positing the ontological priority of, 147
ideology, 15, 16, 161
imagination
   connecting the objective (social reality) and subjective (trust in Christ) dimensions of faith, 33n17
   dialogical, 115–54
   epistemological, 105
   lending to objective reality, 149
   modernist, ix

spiritual, 30
the impossible, 146–47
in him all things consist, 59
in-between
    Peter exposed to, 158
    as a space, 27–28, 149
incompleteness, 9, 68, 160
infinite responsibility, call to, 152
inner form, of it-makes-spirit, 124
inner treasure (*agalma*), of Reason, 82
inner voice, interpretation of, 135
innovation, 76
insertion of humans, producing a
    rupture, 110
intellect, contemplating a thing,
    150n120
intellectual issues, transfer of religious
    energy to, 34
intelligence, 96
"inter" character, of Christ's transgressive identity, 99
interiority and exteriority, of Christianity overlapping, 159–60
interpretation, it-makes-spirit as
    always an, 133
intersection, of it-makes-spirit and
    it-makes-sense, 153
intuition, 6
intuitions, as not really immediate or
    pre-sensual, 154n133
"is" and the "ought," grasping of a
    unity of, 7
Isaac, 47, 48, 49
Ishmael, 61
it does not make sense, but it makes
    spirit, 4
    as the dominant hypothesis of
        Pentecostalism, 155
    explaining theologically (philosophically), 26
    friends interpretation of, 54
    handling the claim of, xvii
    multiple interpretations of, xviii
    negotiated in interactions, 18
    overthrowing the power of sense,
        18
    suspending legitimate doubts, xv
    testing every day, 2

understanding, 46, 60
it-does-not-make-sense, xv, xixn21
iterability, repetition of, 112
it-makes-sense
    always coming too late, 152
    becoming it-makes-spirit, 119
    captured in religious human subjectivity, 121
    described, xiii
    forming a preexisting coherent
        framework, 22
    inclining people to accomplished
        facts, 27
    moving to it-makes-spirit, 7–8
    moving to spiritual consciousness
        or "true knowledge," 6
    as a necessary obstacle to it-makes-spirit, 147
    as a noun, 156
    recognizing as a symbol, 129
    referring to evidence of sense perception, 138
    referring to the secular conception
        and practices of knowledge, xiv
    setting it-makes-spirit in motion,
        16
    translating into "it does not make
        sense, but it makes spirit," 63
    truth for, 120
it-makes-spirit
    adding value to it-makes-sense, 153
    "addressing" believers and nonbelievers, 116
    as an apprehension of the situation,
        154
    as a binding of assertion and refusal
        of it-makes-sense, 100
    as both morality and ethics, 152
    bringing Pentecostals to the borders of secular justification of
        arguments, 18
    cannot be devoid of reason, 126
    carrying no straightforward, single
        meaning, 115
    common understanding of, 6
    conserving the stability of a spirit-pleasure-oriented life, 83–84
    contradicting rational thought, 9

it-makes-spirit *(continued)*
   defining an action, behavior, or decision as good, xiii
   distinguishing decisions deriving from, 160–61
   embodying a type of dissatisfaction with sense-data, 145
   enacting a dialogical sense of empirical data, 23
   as an event of knowledge, 66
   examining, 6
   as a form of justification, 116
   as a form of social ethics, 80
   forms of, 124
   as a gesture of critique, 80–81
   going beyond sense perception or reason, 129
   as a good principle for decision-making, 136–37
   as internally split, 147
   interpreting social reality or senses, 19
   investigating in private deliberation, 125
   invigorating the experience of the Holy Spirit, 138
   key findings concerning, 151–54
   manifestation of, not common to all, 22
   meaning of, xvi
   meant to be universally applied to all decisions, 4
   multiple, independent consciousnesses of, 22
   as the mystical mind refracting the "light" of reason, 108
   not an immediate presence of divine information, 123
   not meaning utter foolishness, 57
   organized on the basis of carnival, 124
   orienting to the transfiguring power of Christ, 27
   as part of virtue ethics, 126–27
   performing sense (rationality) into a new way of being in the world, 101
   plausibility of, 153
   pointing to the "existence and repression of desires," 145
   as a principle of thematic composition, 132
   as the process of the rising and passing away of all particular reasons, 122
   questioning, 140–44
   as rationality made contextual, 151
   reactions to, 84
   reducing uncertainty in decision-making, 137
   referring to knowledge not available to everyone, xiv
   referring to the inner contemplative self, 134
   as a response to the question or press of decision or deliberation, 153
   as the revelation of the Holy Spirit, 5
   as right over and against it-makes-sense, 75
   as sense cutting into sense, 141
   as sense in ecstasy, 129
   separating from the object of it-makes-sense, 130
   signaling something beyond human-divine relationship, 145
   signifying the unshakable promise of God, xv
   as social ethics, 117–28
   as a social structure, 118
   spirituality of, 128–40
   as subjectivity making itself into its own sense, 143
   supplementing or complementing sense-certainty, 84
   as a testament of resistance against Enlightenment rationality, 22
   transformed into it-makes-sense, 154
   transforming the present, 5
   translating into nonmetaphysical norms, practices, and laws, 119
   truth for, 120
   as ultimately it-makes-sense, 153
   unifying sense and subject, 120

unifying the objective and subjective sides of knowing, 127
utilizing both objective and nonobjective types of information for decision-making, 137
uttering, 22
verbing a noun, 156
as a way of limiting risks, 127
"it-makes-spirit and not sense," 77, 126

Jastrow, Joseph, 158
Jesus
  becoming the man/woman in the gap, 114
  becoming the space in which high and low are present, 99
  as both recognizable and unrecognizable in his resurrected form, 101
  ob-jected his body against himself, 101
  as a personal savior "transcending" human sensory capacity, xiv
  putting into the center of Pentecostal imaginary, 31
  as simultaneously a divine person and a point of view, 90
  walking on water, 158
  as the way, the truth, and life of knowing, 74–75
Jesus Christ. See also Christ
  approaching through Abraham, 47
  being faithful to, 11
  being truly committed to, ix
  in the crack between spirit and hard reality, 91
  as everything in the world, 59
  finding the world's contents as unimportant, 52
  founding and impelling the middle space, 157
  in the garden of Gethsemane, 97
  as hybridity, 41–45
  as the middle space, 43
  as a middle space, 61
  as the middle space, 73
  name of operating in Pentecostal circles in four ways, 12
  as the Pentecostal symbol of epistemology, 13
  place in the religion of the Father, 89
  running to places to find, 54
  as the same yesterday, today, and forever, 144
  symbolizing a medium between sense and spirit, 74
  uninterrupted unity with, xvi
  walked through the space called resurrection, 55
  as the wisdom of the world, 96
  as the word of God, 58
Jesus-hyphen-Christ, as the middle space, 73–74
Jesus-in-the-world, 90
justification
  community standards for, 116, 124, 141
  distinctions of, xiii
  it-makes-spirit and, 18
  of religious discourse, 151
  of revelational reason, x–xi, 151
  of "secular" philosophy, 8

Kafka, 110
Kant, 13n33
Kantian ethical subject, 71
kenosis, of reason, 143
Kierkegaard, Søren, 97, 141, 152, 158
kingdom (kin-dom) of God, 99, 107
knowing
  denying the importance of secular ways of, 143
  framework of, 99
  how of, 31, 43, 44
  Pentecostal, 127
  Pentecostal way ("how") of, 33
  as a relationship, 98
  way of, 62
knowing and not-knowing, intersecting language and experience, 44
knowing Christ, 49, 58

knowledge
- disposition toward production of, 68
- "higher," 7
- Pentecostals' conception of, xiv
- recognition of other forms of, 68
- sources of, 4
- as a spirit floating above dense materiality, xiv

knowledge systems, Christ's presence ruptures preexisting, 65

knowledge-commodity, produced in the secular sphere, 73

Lacan, Jacques, 146
Lady Wisdom, Word and Spirit as articulated by, 105
language
- of parole and langue, 78
- of a Pentecostal preacher, 23

langue, 78, 79
laughter, 15, 16
leadership, fetishist view of, 131–32
letting-be, as to make spirit, 20
Levinas, Immanuel, 152
liberal elite, pluralism of the current, 12
liberal theology, on Christology as a symbol of meaning, 89
licensing inference, 153
life, linking spiritual principles to, 125
life-in-spirit, testing faithfulness to, 3
life-view, 97
light, Jesus as, 108
light and darkness, dividing light into, 108
limit concept, that Pentecostals encounter, 145–46
lived Christology, of everyday Pentecostals, 106
locus epistemologicus, Pentecostal life as, 43
Loder, James, 19
logic, 33, 95
logical core, exposing reality's, 93
logicality [or spirituality], self-coercive force of, 135
logics, of Pentecostal worlds, 1–24

logocentrism, 151
"logy," of Christology displaced by intuition, 98
love, 94
love of power, 140
Luhrmann, Tanya M., 3, 25–26

"makes-sense," 118
"makes-spirit," 123n22
making spirit, 11
man, in the interval between past and future, 110
man/woman, becoming time itself, 113
Marx, Karl, 73, 136
material and physical facts (knowledge), turning into pure discarnate spiritual knowledge, 16
material substance, betting on subjective belief, 137
McGowan, Todd, 145
meaning
- emerging from it-makes-spirit, 142
- finding in the world, 51
- of a situation, 149
- suspended for Abraham, 49

meaning-making, not available to or exercised by Abraham, 51
memberships, important for a person's wellbeing, 126
message, of a Pentecostal preacher, 33
Messiah, advent of, 78
metaphor of Christ, as the middle space, 66–75
middle, Abraham caught in, 49
middle space
- characterization of Jesus Christ as, 61
- conceptions of time and temporality undergirding, 109
- difficulties involved in interpreting Christ as, 63
- as elusive as the real itself, 41
- Jesus Christ as, 43, 61, 157
- metaphor of Christ as, 66–75
- of not knowing, 49
- parables of Christ as, 75–81
- Pentecostal "functioning" of Christ as, 35

between the present and the to-come, 74
of split-Christ, 158–59
theological theorization of Jesus Christ as, 63
time and temporality undegirding, 113
Mihailovic, Alexandar, 125
Milbank, John, 96
mind of God, communicating to ordinary folk, 132
ministers, deception of young by old prophets, 56–57
miracles, Paul not interested in, 55
missing space, stepping into to meet God, 51
modern world, has forgotten spirit or deracinated sense from spirit, xixn21
modernist imagination, challenging, ix
modernity, living in the crooked room of, 103
monotheism, relocating conflict from "out there" to "in there," 133n61
moral identity, of a sense different for a Pentecostal observer, xixn21
Moralität, overcoming, 127
morality, as a binding constraint on the believer, 152
mortal danger, 158
multiphilosophic argument, of this book, 34
mutual relevance, context of, 18
mysticism, 82
mystics, experiencing God, 108

Nancy, Jean-Luc, 78
natality, event of, 67
neither/nor hybridity, displaying, 100
Neville, Robert Cummings
  on the aesthetic dimension, 14
  on hypothesis, 2
  on style relating to philosophical arguments, 3–4
  on truth, xiii, 15, 120–21
Niebuhr, H. Richard, 127–28
Nietzsche, parable of the "now" (*Augenblick*), 110

Nigerian Pentecostalism (Wariboko), 118, 134
Noah, 59
noetic knowledge, 25
noncorporeal Christ body, relating to other bodies, 148
normative judgment, Pentecostal process of, 119
normativity, truth of it-makes-spirit as, 6
norms, 7, 97, 152
nothingness, 58
noun, verbing, 156
Nussbaum, Martha, 126

Obadare, Ebenezer Babatunde, 31n14
Obed, Elsie Nene, xvii, xviii, xix, 46, 46n1, 60, 161
object of knowledge, perceiving and cognizing as a thing, 150n120
objective data, modified by subjective belief, 137
objective reality, 3n6, 77
objects, always coming into being, 156
observable objects (bodies), behaviors of, 148
ontology, 127
opening provocations, 155–60
oral literature, of a Pentecostal preacher, 33–34
Oral Roberts University, xii
order of Being, of Christianity, 160
"organs" or "mouths" of God, leaders as always, 131
orthodox Chalcedonian vision of Christ, 35
the other, 61, 71
other-being, creating, 91
outer from, of it-makes-spirit, 124

parable(s)
  about the kingdom of the Messiah, 78
  of Christ as middle space, 75–81
  of genes and epigenetics, 79–81
  of langue and parole, 78–79
  of silence, 76–78

184 | Index

paradigm of the Spirit, formula for, ix
parole (it-makes-sense), 78, 79
participative act, Christ as, 43
particularity, of personal religious experience, 120
parting provocations, 160–62
passage, between it-makes-sense and it-makes-spirit, 8
Passover bread, as Christ's physical body, 101
past, 111, 111n62
past and future, as antagonists, 110
path
    of sense, 65–66
    of spirit, 66
    of split Christ, 66
    of the world, 56
paths, of life, 65–66
Paul
    on Abraham, 55
    on faith, 59
    on the foolishness of God, 65
    interested only in the resurrection, 54–55
    on the low and weak and despised, 139
    not mentioning one miracle of Jesus Christ, 54
Peirce, Charles Sanders, xix, 2, 154n133
Pentecostal academy, "correctness" of the dominant, 40
Pentecostal activity, taking as basic, 150
Pentecostal believer. *See also* believer(s)
    evaluating the significance of her own life, 152
    mimicking Christ, who is the "original" gap, 85
    minding the gap between sense and spirit, xviii
    relationship to [Reason] as subjection, 82
    relinquishing self-certainty (self-sufficient knowledge), 120
Pentecostal Christology
    described, 89
    as the directional principle of epistemology, 24
    epistemological dimensions of everyday, 43
    as an event of communion, 107
Pentecostal conception, of Jesus Christ, 61
Pentecostal construct, on spirit, 119
Pentecostal decision model, 3
Pentecostal discourse, 9
Pentecostal epistemological praxis, 105
Pentecostal epistemology. *See also* epistemology
    appreciating the truth of, 34
    articulated within the spaces, 100
    captured in processes of *Christformation*, 12
    christological energy driving, 11–12
    christological enframing of, 17
    "Christology" informing or undergirding, 24
    as confirmation of a worldly knowledge system, 143
    disclosing Christology, 13
    impact of Jesus's life on the deep structure of, 106
    on knowing, 98
    organized by the interplay of word and spirit, 105
    responding to the voice of Christ, xiii
    "secret" of, 81–82
    as a social ethic, 43
    this book as a site of, 34
    translating the life of Christ into a framework, 97
    understanding, ix–x
Pentecostal ethics, as aesthetics, 124
Pentecostal excesses, disturbing regnant interpretations of Christianity, 104
Pentecostal habitus, 97
Pentecostal hypotenuse, 32n17
Pentecostal hypothesis. *See also* hypothesis
    about decision-making, 1

cannot be stated directly, 32–33
constituting alternate ways of
    knowing, 67
covering the two ends of Christol-
    ogy and social reality, 32n17
dealing with the ontical, 85
deformative effects of, ixn1
described, ix, 2
engaging the world in forms of
    alternate ways of knowing, 156
formed in response to Christ's
    word, 150
as a mode or way of inhabiting the
    world, 68
not a property of Pentecostals
    alone, 68
offering only in shape-shifting,
    fleeting, transfinite profiles, 33
as one type of unappreciated episte-
    mology, 69
as *pharmakon* of the Pentecostal
    movement, 155
as a stance within the gap of
    decision-making, 67
thriving in dialogical interaction of
    a bodily engaged Christ, 149
Pentecostal incompleteness, 160
Pentecostal knowing, 127
Pentecostal life, 37, 116
Pentecostal mindset, 94
Pentecostal philosophy. *See also*
    philosophy
    engendering a new, 8
    forming, 9
    pointing to an emerging non-
        isolationist, 10
    as too close to continental philoso-
        phy, 41
Pentecostal phronesis, 4. *See also*
    practical wisdom (*phronesis*)
Pentecostal practices, 10, 36, 156
Pentecostal principle, 23, 86, 136
*The Pentecostal Principle: Ethical
    Methodology in New Spirit*, 86
Pentecostal rationality, establishing,
    155
Pentecostal reason, 28, 29
Pentecostal spirituality, 13, 135

Pentecostal split, based on Protestant
    theory, 65
Pentecostal style, 34, 157
Pentecostal subject, fueled by a sense
    of duty, 71
Pentecostal theologians
    approaching continental philoso-
        phy of religion, 39–40
    mapping Pentecostal Christian
        faith, 159
    on Pentecostal discourse and con-
        tinental philosophy existing in
        stark opposition, 37
    slow in appreciating the helpfulness
        of philosophy, 35
Pentecostal theology. *See also*
    theology
    attuning to, 41
    continental thought and, 25–45
    Holy Spirit in, 105
    methods of revealing, 29
    as shocking to the academic mind,
        28
    as a study of cracks, 39
Pentecostal theory of decision, 162
Pentecostal thinking, exploring the
    depths of, 63–87
Pentecostal thought, dialogical imagi-
    nation in, 115–54
Pentecostal tradition, path of meaning
    and reason within, 30
Pentecostal worldview, 36
Pentecostalism
    driven by the search for truth, 13
    foregrounding phenomenological
        analysis with continental phi-
        losophy, 35
    incompleteness of, 160
    not forcing those who study it into
        narrow straits of scholarship, 38
    seeing Christ in a different way, 90
    working with a radical Christology,
        88
Pentecostality, 41
Pentecostals
    on academic, university philosophy,
        10

186 | Index

Pentecostals *(continued)*
    appealing to self-sufficient communal standards of justification, 141
    on Christ as a hermeneutic of existence, 90
    on Christology as a radically subjective position, 94
    conceiving Christ as the crack in the world, 69
    conceiving reality as a configuration of dispute, 94
    counting on God to deliver the goods in the future, 144
    decision process of everyday, 162
    decision-making "models," 137–38
    defined by stereotypes, xii
    domesticating the universality of Calvary, 95
    engaging ultimate dimensions of life, 123
    epistemology of, 97, 100
    fashioning an image of Jesus-in-the-world, 90
    on gaps in knowledge, reality, and God, 134
    gathering together "sense" and "spirit" to forge a framework of knowing, 99
    grasping the world through language or discursive practices, 18–19
    imposing a system by driving toward the middle, 92
    on the impossible, 146
    lending imagination to objective reality, 149
    lived messiness of, 39
    making decisions, 2
    on needing invocation of breath, 102
    not considering reason evil, 128
    projecting their sense of self onto the external reality, 133
    realizing the truth of a statement, 3
    rejecting the universal work of Jesus Christ, 95
    roles in presidential campaigns in the United States, x
    seeing a ghost under every rock, 146
    seeing God against the background of the void of desires, 89
    shaming and aggressive humiliation of ordinary, xi
    shaping lives to conform to the name of Jesus, 12
    struggling to know what really counts, 17
    transcending strict limitations of logic and recalcitrant existence, 91
    transfiguring "sense" into spirit, 156
    transposing Christ into the gap, 114
    understanding conservative, x
    understanding not as objects but as subjects, 150
    wanting to be dependent on the Holy Spirit, 136
perception, as difficult to attain, 14
performative speech, exuding the power of, xviii
personal decision-making, ix, 26, 155n1
personal decisions, linking to Jesus Christ, 43
"personhood," of faith, 96
Peter, 142, 158
pharmakon, of the Pentecostal movement, 155
phenomenal reality, 91
Phenomenology of Spirit (Hegel), 117
philosophers, 35, 36
philosophical academy, fierce guardians of, 10
philosophical analysis, of the reasoning process of Pentecostals, 26n5
philosophical approach of this book, 37
philosophy, 8, 10, 37. *See also* continental philosophy; Pentecostal philosophy
pistis (faith, trust), hypostasis of, 96
Plato, on ideal forms, 147
playfulness, 27, 28
plurality of consciousnesses, in Dostoevsky's novels, 22

pneumasation, 70, 145
pneumatology, 86
police romance, on morality, 83
the political, relation to the epistemological, x
political governance, model of, 12
polyphonic presentation, of arguments or viewpoints, 21–22
polyphony, as a style of philosophic argumentation, 22
positive value, imputing to benefits from spirituality, 160
possibilities, 40, 66
possibility-to-be, life creating, 27
post-Enlightenment rationality, 81, 82
power
　of Christ, 94
　of God, 59
　love of, 140
　of spirit, 140
　used to change people's behavior, 19–20
practical consciousness, 133
practical reason, 97, 126
practical wisdom (*phronesis*). *See also* Pentecostal phronesis
　described, 4
　as an important constituent of the Pentecostal account of human good living, 162
　producing, 5
　as a virtue, 125–26
　without reason, 125
praxis, 6, 105, 125
presence of humans in the gap, as the (real) time, 111
present
　as always already past, 5
　as the place of "actuality of time," 111n62
　in the sense of presence, 111
　split Christ primarily speaking to, 109
"pretend to believe," 71
Princeton Theological Seminary, xi–xii
principle, for belief and action, 1

prism of Pentecostal faith, light going through, 108
productivity, losing by taking away the obstacle, 136
promise of a better future, of it-makes-spirit, 144
provocations, unconcluding, 155–62
public reason. *See also* reason
　giving in the public square, 26n5
　it-makes-spirit as a nascent path to, 18
　it-makes-spirit as a path to, 115, 116n3
"public reason character," 28
Pui-lan, Kwok, 41–42
pure event, 64
pure knowability, 72
pure signifier, *this* as, 142
Pythagorean theorem, 32n17

question of decision, for applying sense-certainty, 152

Rambo, Shelly, 102
rational choice language, 160
rational coding system, 80
rational system, 118
rationalist epistemology (sense), philosophical coordinates of, 15
rationality
　as the condition of possibility of it-makes-spirit, 136
　deliberative, 162
　Enlightenment, 23, 69, 82
　making fluid, 151
　of modernity, 83
　Pentecostal, 155
　post-Enlightenment, 81, 82
　shaming, belittling and humiliating Pentecostals, 40
rationality (making-sense), choosing the maximum net benefit, 160
rationalization, by followers of super-anointed Pentecostal pastors, 132
rational-logic system, responses to the belief system, 80
the Real, 11

reality
- act of cutting, 89
- acting according to the dictates of, 120
- cuts in the fabric of, 109
- dimensions of, 133
- distinguished from depth of reality, 93
- distorted in a crooked room, 103
- endowing with spirit, 122
- gap between sense and spirit inherent to, 92
- grounding of, xvi
- hyphen in the texture of, 74
- as internally unstable, 16
- not coinciding with itself, 94
- as only one of many possible realities, 23
- that leaders are flawed beings and not angels, 131
- traditional cosmological vision of, 121

reason. *See also* public reason
- as the absolute excess, 83
- abstract, 119
- emptied-out, 143
- escaping the "metaphysics" of modern, 140
- holding at a distance, 82
- instilled and provoked by the sensorial field, 76–77
- not sufficient unto itself, 76
- Pentecostal, 28, 29
- practical, 97, 126
- rejecting as an a ahistorical universal, 127
- remaining overtly dependent upon spirit, 77
- revelational, xi, 151–52
- transformation into spirit, 7
- use of inadequate, 129
- wanting nothing of a dream or deeper meaning, 121

reason (sense), as an internal condition of spirit, 15
reasoning mind, Pentecostalism not a war against, 28, 50n2
reasoning process, of Pentecostals, 44

"reasons," espousing for one's actions, 115
receptive knowing, 143
re-enfleshed word, resurrection power of, 123
religious discourse
- character of, 39
- characterizing from the point of salvation, 64
- justification of, x–xi, 151

religious epistemology ("spirit"), philosophical coordinates of, 15
religious symbols, truth of, 14n37
repetition, it-makes-spirit resting on, 143–44
resources, for analyses of Pentecostal issues, 39
restraining force, it-makes-spirit as, 138
resurrected figure, inhabiting the space between spectrality and materiality, 102
resurrection, 54, 55, 56, 101
retroactive causation, 79
revelation, 5, 128
revelational reason, xi, 151–52
risk in faith, taking, 27
ritual and spiritual practices, name of Jesus relating to, 12
rupture, grace as a, 94

"sacramental" character, of reason or sense, 129
sacred canopy of it-makes-spirit, "repairing," 151
Sadean subject, of the unreserved will to jouissance, 71
salvation, wrought by Jesus, 95
Santos, Boaventura de Sousa, 68–69, 87
Sarah, 61
Sartre, 43n25
scapegoat mechanism, 106
Schelling, F. W. J., 79
scholars, 36
scholarship, 160
Scholem, Gershom, 78

sciences, as a monologic form of knowledge, 150n120
"scientific America," questioning being Pentecostal, xi
second-order spiritual information, 154
"secular" philosophy, justification and refutation of, 8
self on the self, techniques of, xiv
self-division, of it-makes-spirit, 145
self-emptying, process of, 120
self-sufficient communal standards, 10
self-surrender, sacrifice, of free deciders, xvi
sense
  (re)construction of, 133
  containable possibilities harbored in every, 139
  dream of doing away with, 136
  implying human word/promise, xv
  "inner greatness" of, 134
  interacting with spirit, 1
  interpreted as inertia for ordinary Pentecostals, 17–18
  as the limit, or outside of spirit, 88
  moving into a different spacing, 139
  not emptied of spirit, 77
  not sufficient unto itself, 76
  power of, 18
  as the presupposition of spirit, 129
  shifting to spirit (it-makes-spirit), 78
  soliciting out of its thrownness, 139
  standing for positive ontological order, 11
  structured as spirit, 5
sense and non-sense (un-sense), 65
sense and no-sense, 158
sense and spirit
  brought to the same place, 130
  interpretations of the dialectics of, xv
  middle space between, 113
  relationship of, 5
  as sources of knowledge, 4
sense data
  movement to spiritual data, x
  reimagining the posssibilities of, 151
  serving as inputs to spiritual knowledge, xiii
  turning into spiritual data, 16
  unifying divine purpose behind, 151
sense system of the world, coming out from to know Christ, 55–56
sense-certainty, 118, 130
sense-knowledge, Pentecostals risking, 30
senses, 59, 154
sense-spirit, 42, 76, 77
sense-spirit hermeneutics, tehomic depths of, 62, 158
sensible formation, spiritual information increasing, 154
sensible place, left by Peter to walk into the "foolish" place, 158
Sermon on the Mount, 99
"shape of consciousness," 7
"shape of spirit," 7
"shape of world," 7
shit (excrement) and hidden treasure, as parts of the same thing, 82–83
signification, of it-makes-sense, 143
silence, parable of, 76–78
Simon the sorcerer, 71
situation, 40, 77, 156
situational facts, Pentecostals discerning, 27
Smith, James K. A., 19
social dimensions of Pentecostal Christology, 5
social ethics
  connecting with epistemology to Christology, xv, 43
  following the grammars and scripts of ordinary people, 86–87
  it-makes-spirit as, 117–28
social groups, possessing alternative ways of knowing, 68
social imaginary, surplus emerging from the splitting of, 104

social level, in the shaping of dialogue between the believer and her reality (situation), 124
social realities, 32n17–33n17, 94, 125
social scientists, not studying Pentecostal philosophy as a way of life, 37
social terms, defining revelation in, 128
social violence, exposing, 106
social-ethical analyses, of Pentecostals, 37
soft information, derived from mere subjective believability, 137
Son of God, Savior and Lord, personal name of, 12
space
  between absolute sense and absolute foolishness, 49–50
  created by a community to experience God's presence, 65
  in existence, 54
  finding in between the somethings of the world, 61
  of grace, 66
  of nothingness, 61
  of promise, 66
  that has no foundation, 58
  where we are totally dependent on the foolishness of God's wisdom, 61
"space of appearing," 135–36
space-time, where reality makes spirit, 91
spatial mapping, of epistemology, 31
speaking from sense, 131
speaking tongues (uninterpretable tongue-speech), as an excess on human language, 104–5
spirification, 123
the Spirit, 34, 86. See also Holy Spirit
spirit, 4–5
  aligning differences in with differences in sense (signification), 154
  as breath needed to animate reason, 76
  connoting God's word/promise, xv
  constituting the limit, or outside of sense, 88
  as context for temporal modes of sense, xixn21
  double meaning: of Hegelian or Pentecostal, 119
  as the existence and renewal of possibility itself, 27
  as fulfillment of sense, 129
  happening through sense, 77
  manufacturing from sense, 134
  as nonbeing, 11
  not hiding shortcomings of sense, 141
  restraining the "lawlessness" of senses, 138
  as a seized sense splitting reality, 77
  as sense "in becoming," 84
  as ultimately knowable through the senses, 121
spirit and sense, bound together like langue and parole, 78
"spirit of adultery," casting out of, 63–64
Spirit of Christ, 106, 117–18, 134. See also Holy Spirit
Spirit of God, 19n44, 54, 58. See also Holy Spirit
Spirit-Christology (or wisdom-Christology), framework of, 105
spirit-content, of the talking Christ, 148
spirit-filled life, trying to achieve, 75
Spirit-filled social life, characteristics of, 119
spirits, 19, 148
spiritual data, movement from sense data to, x
spiritual form or an ideal form, seeing behind mere appearance, 147
spiritual formation, relatedness of mind and world resulting in, 7
spiritual imagination, 30
spiritual information, relevance of, 153
spiritual knowledge, xiii, 73
spiritual life, not functioning outside the flesh, 136

spiritual maturity, disparity in levels of, 122
spiritual understanding, redirecting back to the empirical use of the senses, 152
spiritual word of knowledge, becoming "flesh," 123
spirituality
  of it-makes-spirit, 128–40
  Pentecostal, 13, 122, 135
spiritualization, of ignorance, 138
Spirit-Word-Community, triad of, 19
split
  between Christianity and that which is excluded/occluded, 160
  conceiving existence as, 62
  at the core of it-makes-spirit, 135
  deployment of the theme or theory of, 85
  between it-makes-sense and it-makes-spirit, 8
  remaining an intrinsic duality of One, 70
  theology or philosophy of, 159
split Christ
  capturing the reality of divine presence, 91
  epistemological character of "neither/nor-but," 100
  everyday Pentecostal notion and practice of, 94
  expressing and formalizing a consciousness, 92
  kind of faith required, 65
  naming an epistemic space, 95
  as a new epistemic framing, 89
  as the Pentecostal spatialization of faith, 96
  philosophy of, 158
  temporality of, 108–14
  theory of, 91–98
split God, idea of, 133
The Split God (Wariboko), 118
split nature, of Christ, 101
split reality, 70, 91
standards of Christ, alignment to, 117–18

statu nascendi, cognizing a state of affairs as, 156
style, 4
subject
  cannot be perceived and studied as a thing, 150n120
  desire of disrupting her field of vision, 146
  Pentecostal, 71
  punching a hole in historicization, 113
subjective dimension, of knowledge, 69
subjective dispositions, for Pentecostals, 65–66
subjective nature, of it-makes-spirit, 122
subjectivity, making transition from the sense to the spirit possible, 121
substance, 59, 60, 119
sun, rising every morning, 144
Suna-Koro, Kristine, 42
superconscious mind, as mediator, 108
Suurmond, Jean-Jacques, 105
symbol(s)
  Holy Spirit as, xvi
  hypothesis shaped by, 3
  of the "is" and the "ought," 73
  it-makes-sense as, 129
  Jesus Christ as, 13, 74
  liberal theology presenting Christology as meaning of, 89
  of "middle space," 35
  theology as, 89
  truth of religious, 14n37
symptom, 131
system of death, Jesus's resurrection and, 56
system of separation, cracks in the fabric of, 131

tacit knowledge, 44
talking Christ, response to, xiii, 12
tehomic void, Peter stepping into, 158
temporal gap (the middle space), 67
temporal modes, of any sense, xixn21

temporal orientation, ways of thinking about, 113
temporal structure, implied by the notion of the split Christ, 108–14
tensions, 37, 73, 81
thatness, of the noumenal, 142
the theological, understanding of, 40
theology. *See also* Pentecostal theology
   conservative presenting Christology as truth, 89
   of the excess, 159
   as experienced in everyday spirituality, 86
   exploring unbound, 38
   folk, 90
   holistic, 159
   liberal presenting Christology as a symbol of meaning, 89
theorization, of Jesus Christ, ix
thesis of this book, development of, 157
"thing-in-itself," 13n33
things, as both material and immaterial, 92
thinking, 5, 63–87
the Third Space
   continental philosophy as, 36
   Jesus Christ as a kind of spiritual, 41
   Pentecostal way of knowing on, 42
   postcolonial theoretic notion of, 42n21
   utilization of Pentecostal philosophy as, 37
the *this*, the it-makes-spirit, happening today, 142
this is that communal standard, 141–42
thisness, of the phenomenal realm, 142
Thomas, 101, 102
thought, dialogic quality of, 21, 115–54
Tillich, Paul, xvin12, 128
time, 110, 113
"Time and Being" (Heidegger), 111
time gaps, 67, 109

to-come, the order of, 140
to-make-spirit, xiv–xv, xixn21
tradition, 2, 30, 112–13
tragedy born out of religion, 133
transcendent, human attempts to encounter, 141
transfigured likeness, 156
transformation of impossibilities into possibilities, 64
translation, problems with the metaphor of, 72
trilogy, relating to persons of the trinity, 85n51
trope, of gap (split), 62
true life-in-the-spirit, 94
trust, 69
truth
   as carryover of value from the object, 121
   described, xiii
   of the hyphen exceeding knowledge, 74
   irrupting as an event, xviii
   meanings of, xiii
   movement of being-toward, 6
   stuck in aborted movement, 9
   ways of conceptualizing, 120
twoness, forms of, 120
typos (location and motor) of time, man as, 113
tyranny, of logicality, 135

uncertainty
   human promise plagued by, xv
   managing worlds of, 138
   reducing, 137
   religious struggle to understand in the face of, 141
unconcealment, of Pentecostal assumptions, 157
universal singularity, subject of faith as, 64
universal work of Christ, 95
universality, 120, 153
unknowability, of God as not an obstacle, 85
Upper Room, as a meeting of past and present, 102

"use values," leaving out of the translation exercise, 72
utility, 71, 160
utterance, bringing its own truth into being, xviii

values, in the life of Christ carried into epistemology, 14–15
violence, imitating Christ in eschewing, 106
virtue ethics, 127
voice of God, hearing in the inner self, 135
voiceless thing, in opposition to the subject, 150n120
voices, polyphonic display of, 157
void, 69, 70–71

"want-to-know," transforming into "want-to-know-something," 66
way of knowing, 62
weakness of God, as stronger than human strength, 65
Wendy Brown, xviii
West, Cornel, xvii
What Is a Thing (Heidegger), 29
"what is" of existence, 73
When God Talks Back (Luhrmann), 3, 25
white light, composed of all of frequencies, 108
Whitehead, Alfred North, 141
who Christ is
    as the conceptualization of Christology, 67
    explaining, 157–58
    opening a crack in being, 89
    Pentecostals interpreting, 84–85
    summary statement of, 46–47
Who Christ is sermon, 46

"whos," distinctiveness of our individual, 112
wisdom, 27, 96, 128
Wittgenstein, Ludwig, 150
word from the Holy Spirit, human word becoming, 123
word of God, worlds framed by, 58
work of the Spirit, as the work of Jesus the Christ, 106
work of tradition (*nomos*), 112–13
world
    arose from nothing, 58
    cannot come to an understanding of its true identity, 52
    Christ as the excluded part of regnant systems of knowledge of, 52
    ensuring that believers do not come to that space where things do not make sense, 57
    looking where things appear to be cracking, 61
    making sense via cause and effect, 51
worldly systems, resurrection as a subtraction from, 56
worldly wisdom, portraying knowing as a relationship, 98
worldview
    biblical, 19
    Christology becoming, 97
    Pentecostal, 36, 89
    providing, 105
wrong, invoked in a fallen world, 94

Yong, Amos, 19, 31n15

Žižek, Slavoj, 71–72, 136, 142, 161
Zizioulas, John, 107
Zupančič, Alenka, 84

www.ingramcontent.com/pod-product-compliance
Lightning Source LLC
Chambersburg PA
CBHW021726220426
43662CB00008B/725